COLLECTION EDITOR: **JENNIFER GRÜNWALD**
ASSISTANT EDITORS: **ALEX STARBUCK & NELSON RIBEIRO**
EDITOR, SPECIAL PROJECTS: **MARK D. BEAZLEY**
SENIOR EDITOR, SPECIAL PROJECTS: **JEFF YOUNGQUIST**
SVP OF PRINT & DIGITAL PUBLISHING SALES: **DAVID GABRIEL**
BOOK DESIGNER: **RODOLFO MURAGUCHI**

EDITOR IN CHIEF: **AXEL ALONSO**
CHIEF CREATIVE OFFICER: **JOE QUESADA**
PUBLISHER: **DAN BUCKLEY**
EXECUTIVE PRODUCER: **ALAN FINE**

OF THE QUEEN. First printing 2013. ISBN# 978-0-7851-8393-8. Published by MARVEL WORLDWIDE, INC., a subsidiary of MARVEL ENTERTAINMENT, LLC. OFFICE OF PUBLICATI 10020. Once Upon a Time © ABC Studios. All Rights Reserved. All characters featured in this issue and the distinctive names and likenesses thereof, and all related indicia are trad ween any of the names, characters, persons, and/or institutions in this magazine with those of any living or dead person or institution is intended, and any such similarity which m d its logos are TM & © Marvel Characters, Inc. **Printed in the U.S.A.** ALAN FINE, EVP - Office of the President, Marvel Worldwide, Inc. and EVP & CMO Marvel Characters B.V.; DAN B imation & Digital Divisions; JOE QUESADA, Chief Creative Officer; TOM BREVOORT, SVP of Publishing; DAVID BOGART, SVP of Operations & Procurement, Publishing; C.B. CE pment; DAVID GABRIEL, SVP of Print & Digital Publishing Sales; JIM O'KEEFE, VP of Operations & Logistics; DAN CARR, Executive Director of Publishing Technology; SUSAN EX MORALES, Publishing Operations Manager; STAN LEE, Chairman Emeritus. For information regarding advertising in Marvel Comics or on Marvel.com, please contact Ni ndisla@marvel.com. For Marvel subscription inquiries, please call 800-217-9158. **Manufactured between 6/21/2013 and 7/29/2013 by R.R. DONNELLEY, INC., SALEM, V**

ONCE UPON A TIME

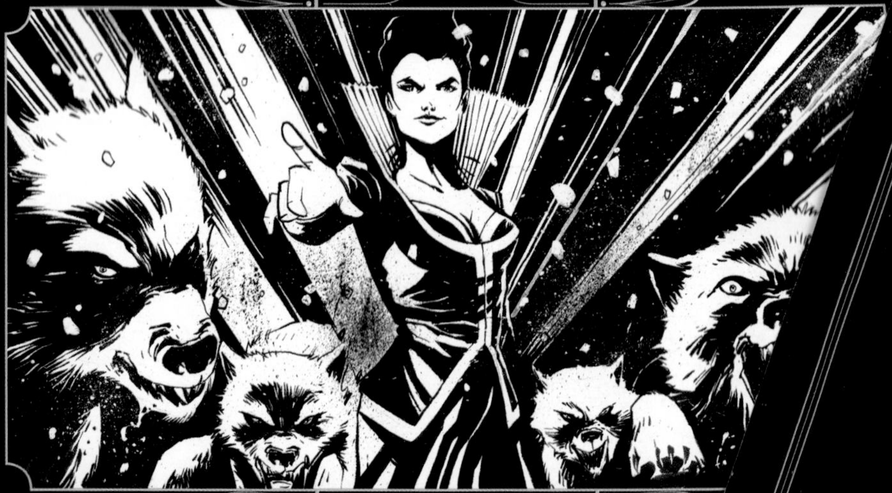

SHADOW OF THE QUEE

ONCE UPON A TIME: SHADO
West 50th Street, New York, NY
of ABC Studios. No similarity be
is purely coincidental. Marvel an
Publisher & President - Print, An
SVP of Creator & Content Develo
Editorial Operations Manager; AL
Director of Marvel Partnerships, a

10 9 8 7 6 5 4 3 2 1

ONCE UPON A TIME

SHADOW OF THE QUEEN

Based on the television series *Once Upon a Time*
created by Edward Kitsis & Adam Horowitz

DANIEL T. THOMSEN
PLOT

CORINNA BECHKO
SCRIPT

CHAPTER 1
MICHAEL DEL MUNDO
ART & COLORS

CHAPTER 2
VASILIS LOLOS
ART & COLORS

CHAPTER 3
MIKE HENDERSON
ART

JOHN RAUCH
COLORS

CHAPTER 4
MICHAEL KALUTA
PENCILS

MIKE HENDERSON & SCOTT HANNA
WITH **MICHAEL KALUTA**
INKS

CHRISTOPHER SOTOMAYOR
COLORS

VC'S CORY PETIT
LETTERS

EMILY SHAW
ASSISTANT EDITOR

MARK PANICCIA
SENIOR EDITOR

When you see this: AR, open up the MARVEL AR APP (available on applicable Apple ® iOS or Android TM devices) and use your camera-enabled device to unlock extra-special exclusive features!

Hey folks!

We're thrilled you decided to pick up our first **ONCE UPON A TIME** graphic novel for Marvel. As most of you know, we've spent the past few years bringing fairy tales to Sunday nights on ABC, and in that time we've spun together dozens of stories and characters from Snow White and Rumplestiltskin all the way to Dr. Frankenstein and Robin Hood.

As our mythology grew, we realized we had more stories to tell than episodes of television to tell them with, and one of our favorite characters from the first season is someone we wanted to see a lot more of -- the Huntsman. Our timeline in Fairy Tale Land is full of untold stories that take place from the time the Evil Queen stole the Huntsman's heart to the day the Queen's Curse swept the kingdom away to Storybrooke. And, yeah, the Huntsman was forced into Regina's servitude, but did that mean all of his inherent honor and goodness went away? Would he still find ways to be a hero? Or even to be a positive influence on Regina? That's what we're here to find out!

Marvel generously hooked us up with a terrific writer and some of their most talented artists, and this book is the result of our first collaboration. If you're a fan of the show, we hope it fills in some of the blanks in the complicated relationship you've already seen between Regina and the Huntsman. And if you haven't seen the show yet and this story is your cup of tea... well, good news -- you've got a lot of episodes to catch up on!

Sincerely,

Eddy Kitsis
& Adam Horowitz

Creators, **ONCE UPON A TIME**

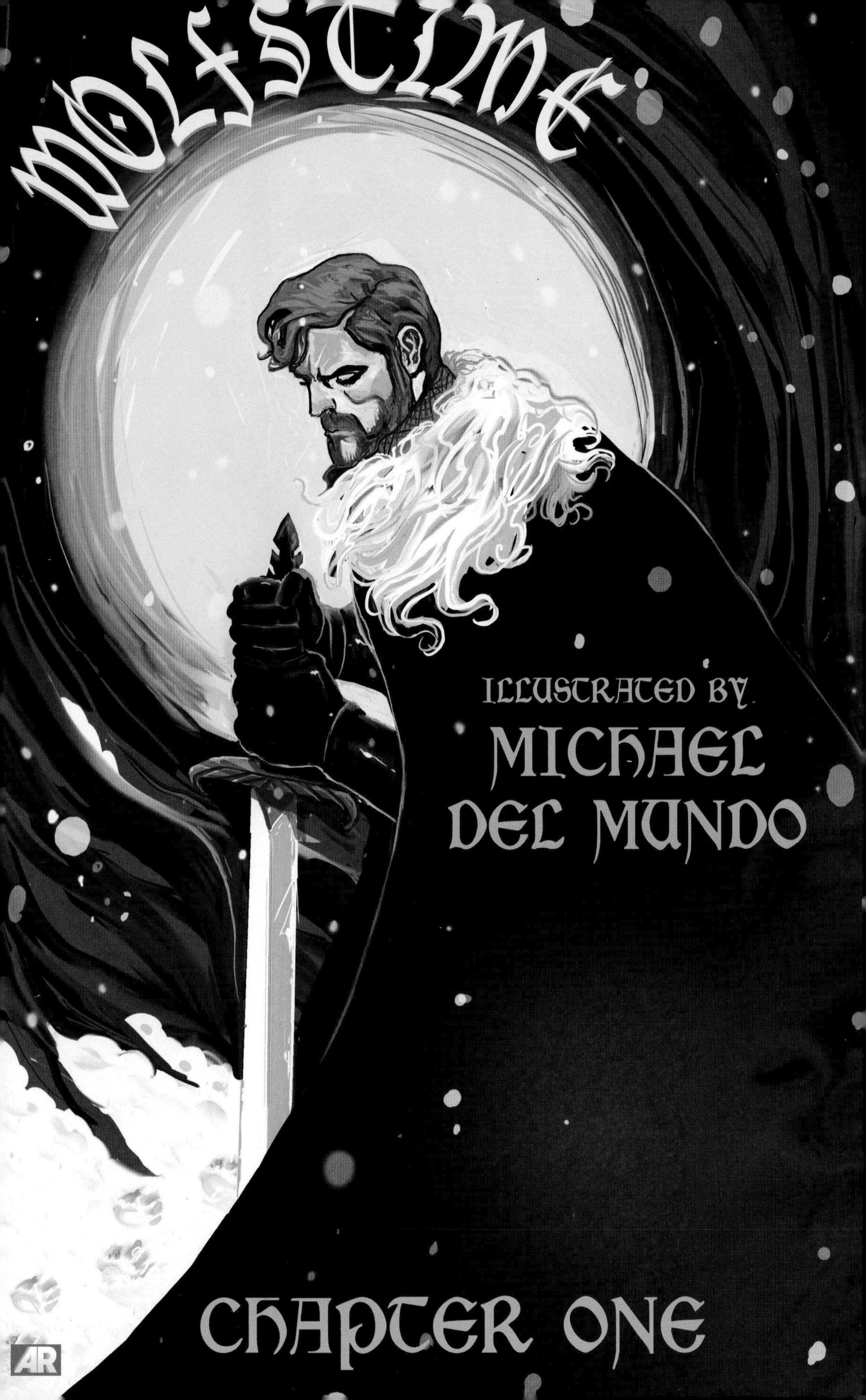
WOLFSTIME
ILLUSTRATED BY
MICHAEL DEL MUNDO
CHAPTER ONE

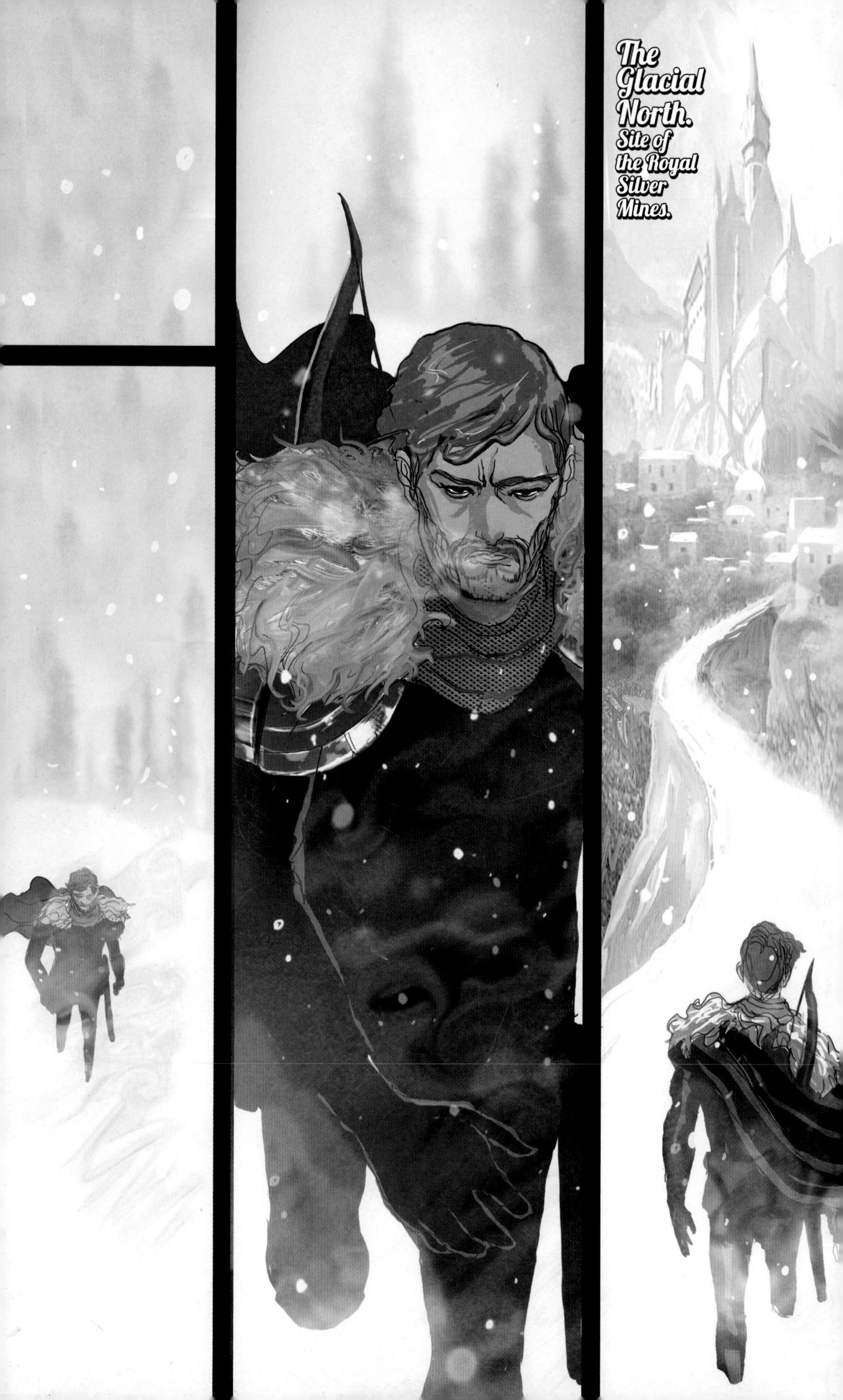
The Glacial North. Site of the Royal Silver Mines.

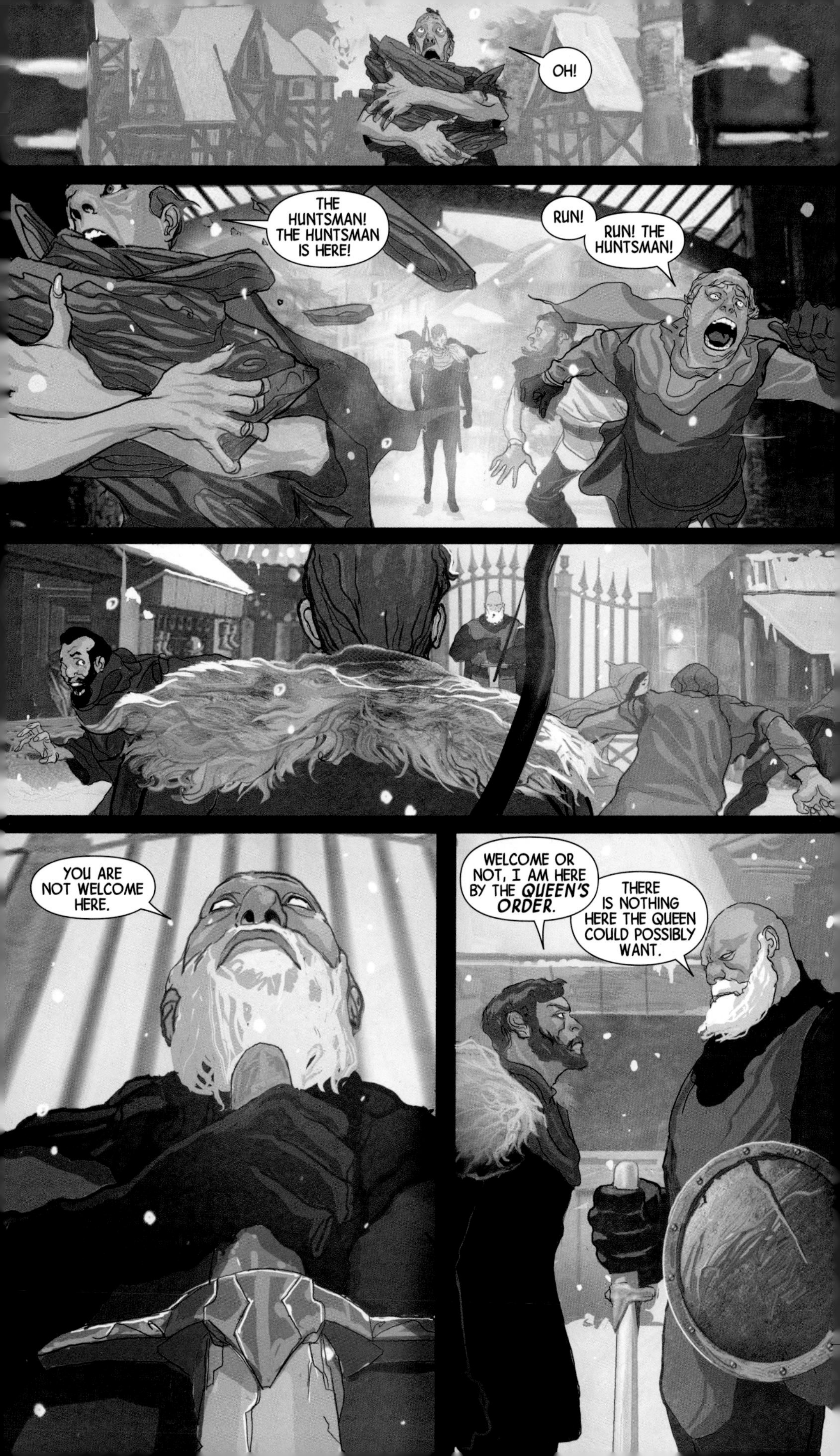
OH!
THE HUNTSMAN! THE HUNTSMAN IS HERE!
RUN!
RUN! THE HUNTSMAN!
YOU ARE NOT WELCOME HERE.
WELCOME OR NOT, I AM HERE BY THE *QUEEN'S ORDER*.
THERE IS NOTHING HERE THE QUEEN COULD POSSIBLY WANT.

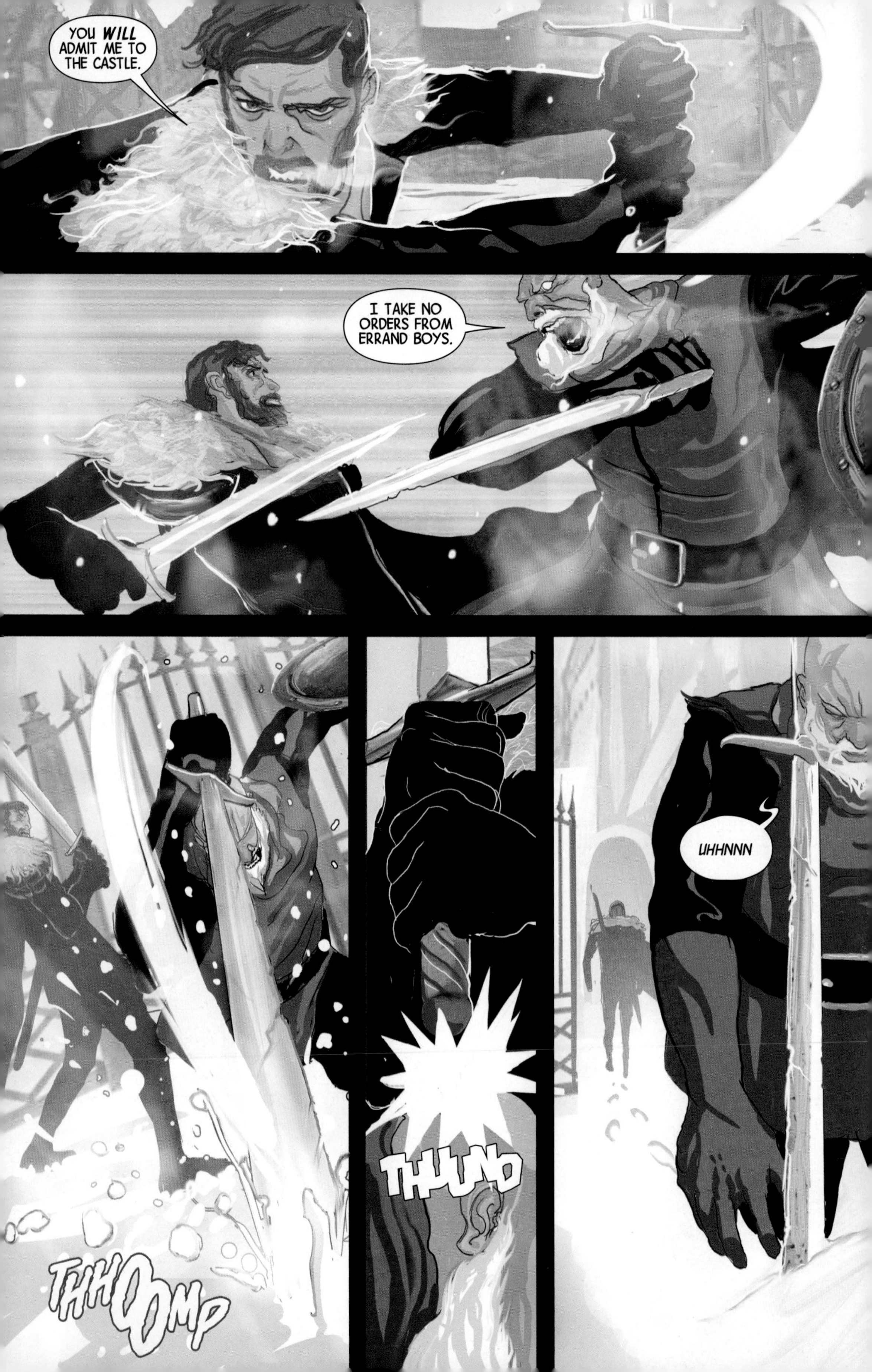
YOU WILL ADMIT ME TO THE CASTLE.
I TAKE NO ORDERS FROM ERRAND BOYS.
THHOOMP
THUUND
UHHNNN

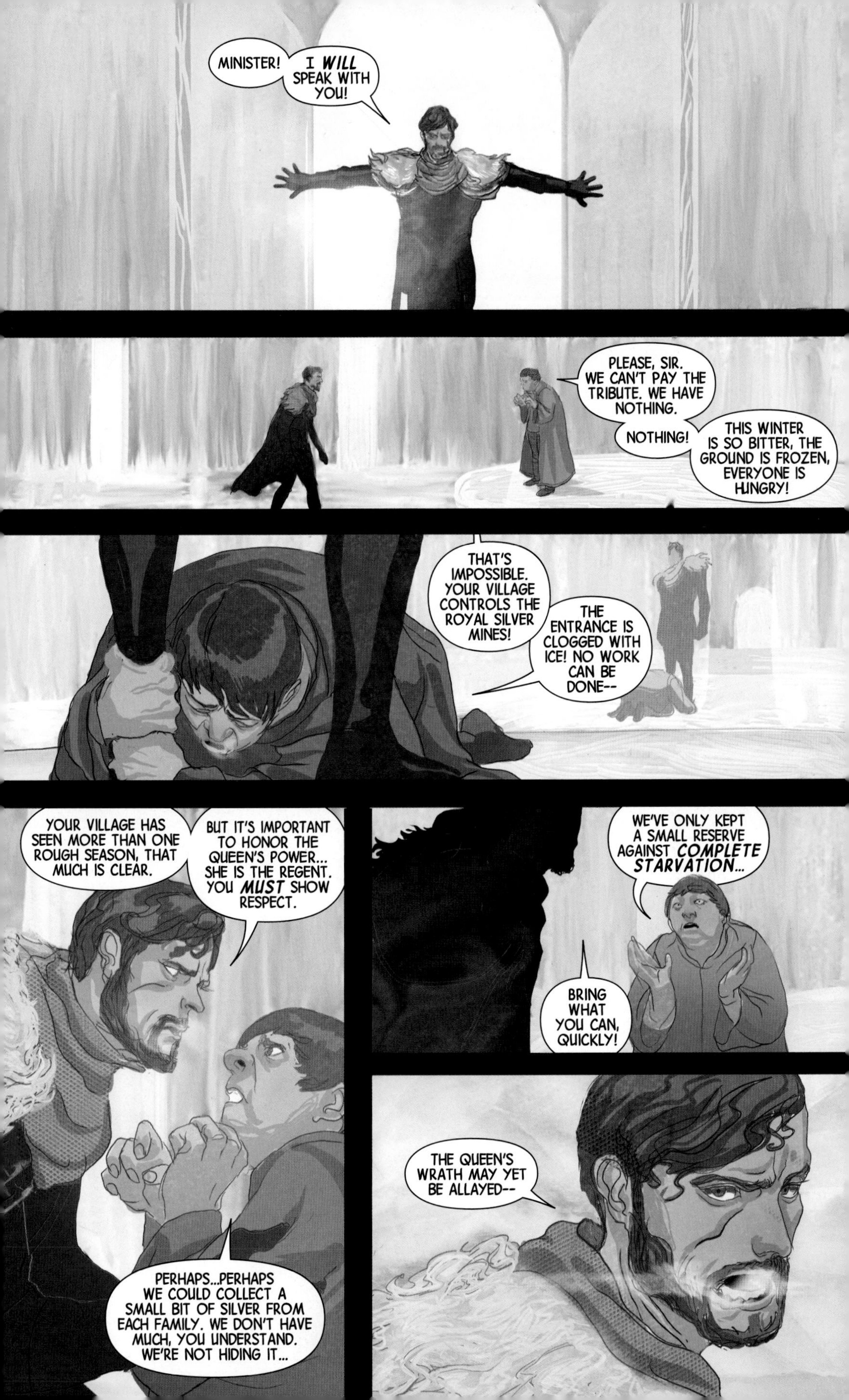
MINISTER!
I WILL SPEAK WITH YOU!
PLEASE, SIR. WE CAN'T PAY THE TRIBUTE. WE HAVE NOTHING.
NOTHING!
THIS WINTER IS SO BITTER, THE GROUND IS FROZEN, EVERYONE IS HUNGRY!
THAT'S IMPOSSIBLE. YOUR VILLAGE CONTROLS THE ROYAL SILVER MINES!
THE ENTRANCE IS CLOGGED WITH ICE! NO WORK CAN BE DONE--
YOUR VILLAGE HAS SEEN MORE THAN ONE ROUGH SEASON, THAT MUCH IS CLEAR.
BUT IT'S IMPORTANT TO HONOR THE QUEEN'S POWER... SHE IS THE REGENT. YOU MUST SHOW RESPECT.
PERHAPS...PERHAPS WE COULD COLLECT A SMALL BIT OF SILVER FROM EACH FAMILY. WE DON'T HAVE MUCH, YOU UNDERSTAND. WE'RE NOT HIDING IT...
WE'VE ONLY KEPT A SMALL RESERVE AGAINST COMPLETE STARVATION...
BRING WHAT YOU CAN, QUICKLY!
THE QUEEN'S WRATH MAY YET BE ALLAYED--

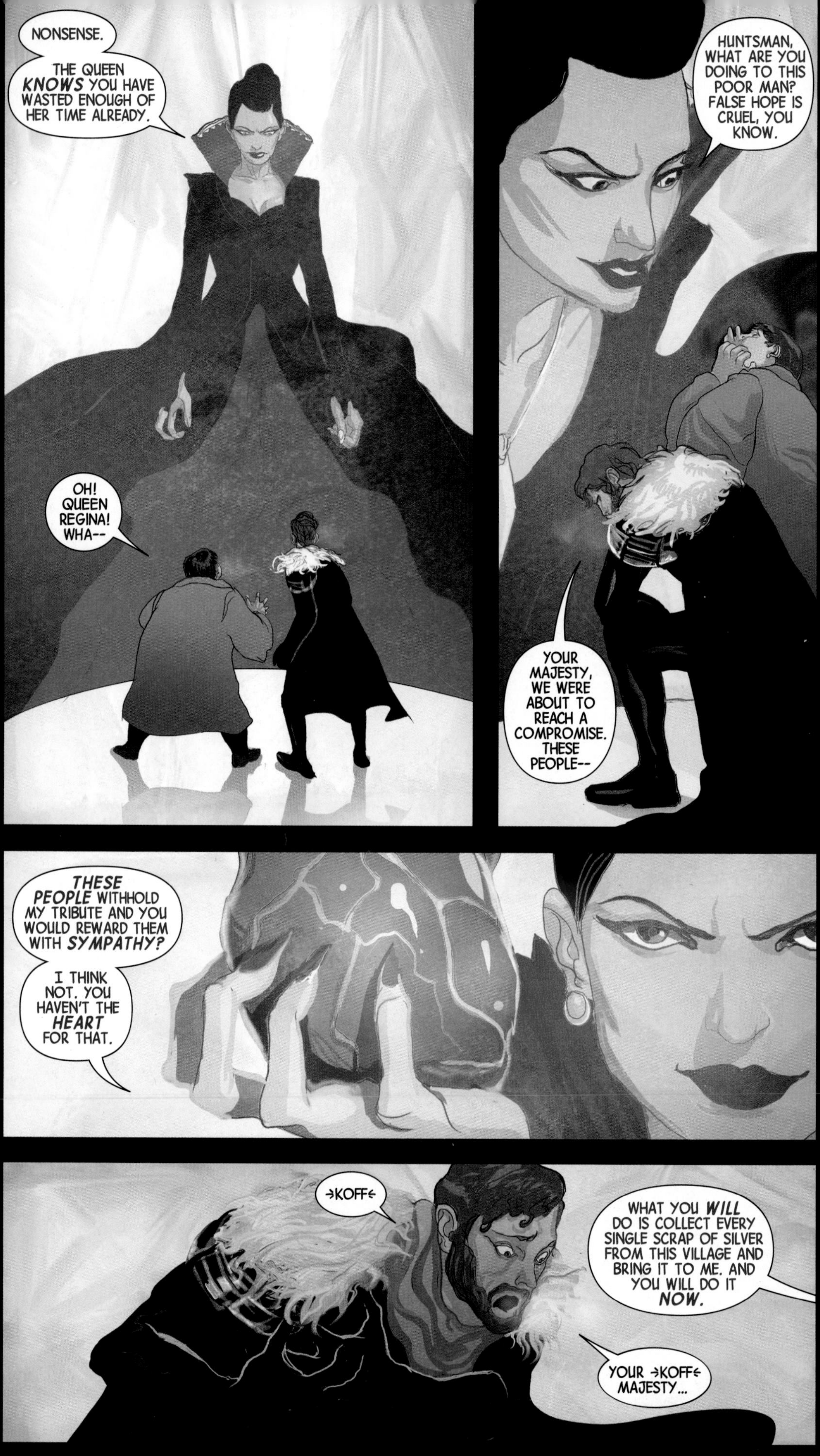
NONSENSE.
THE QUEEN KNOWS YOU HAVE WASTED ENOUGH OF HER TIME ALREADY.
OH! QUEEN REGINA! WHA--
HUNTSMAN, WHAT ARE YOU DOING TO THIS POOR MAN? FALSE HOPE IS CRUEL, YOU KNOW.
YOUR MAJESTY, WE WERE ABOUT TO REACH A COMPROMISE. THESE PEOPLE--
THESE PEOPLE WITHHOLD MY TRIBUTE AND YOU WOULD REWARD THEM WITH SYMPATHY?
I THINK NOT. YOU HAVEN'T THE HEART FOR THAT.
›KOFF‹
WHAT YOU WILL DO IS COLLECT EVERY SINGLE SCRAP OF SILVER FROM THIS VILLAGE AND BRING IT TO ME. AND YOU WILL DO IT NOW.
YOUR ›KOFF‹ MAJESTY...

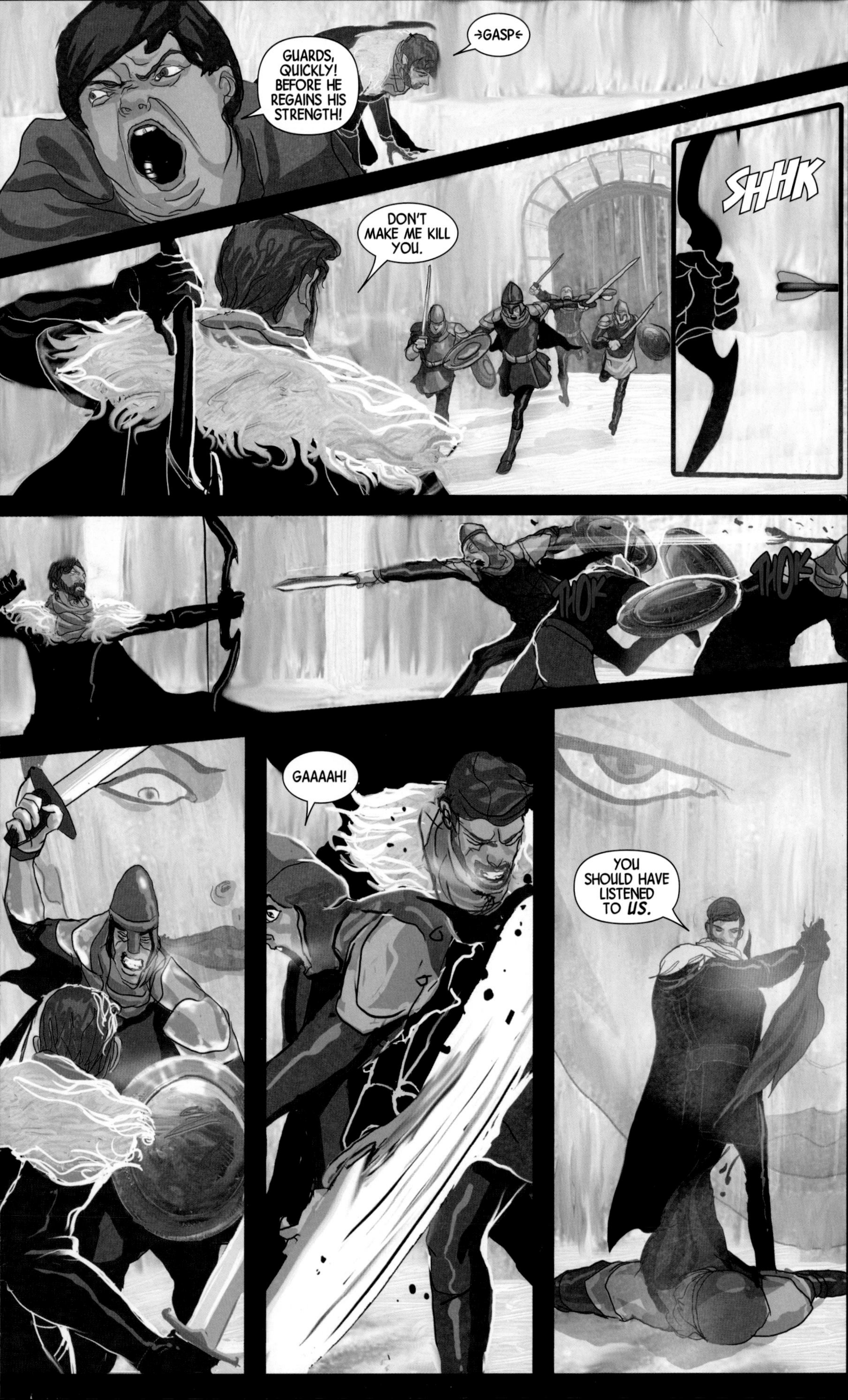
GUARDS, QUICKLY! BEFORE HE REGAINS HIS STRENGTH!
GASP
DON'T MAKE ME KILL YOU.
SHHK
THOK
THOK
GAAAAH!
YOU SHOULD HAVE LISTENED TO US.

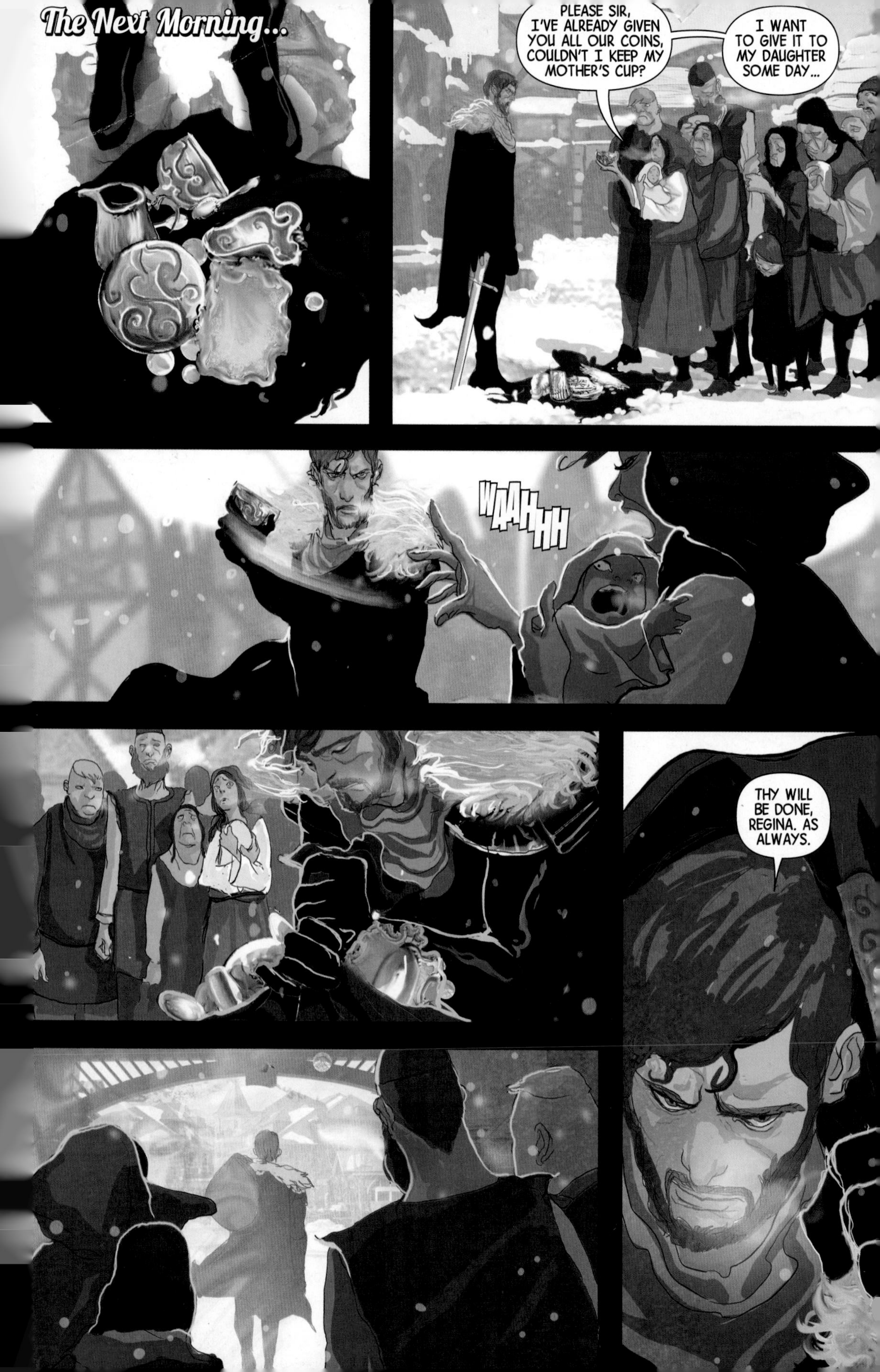
The Next Morning...
PLEASE SIR, I'VE ALREADY GIVEN YOU ALL OUR COINS, COULDN'T I KEEP MY MOTHER'S CUP?
I WANT TO GIVE IT TO MY DAUGHTER SOME DAY...
WAAHHH
THY WILL BE DONE, REGINA. AS ALWAYS.

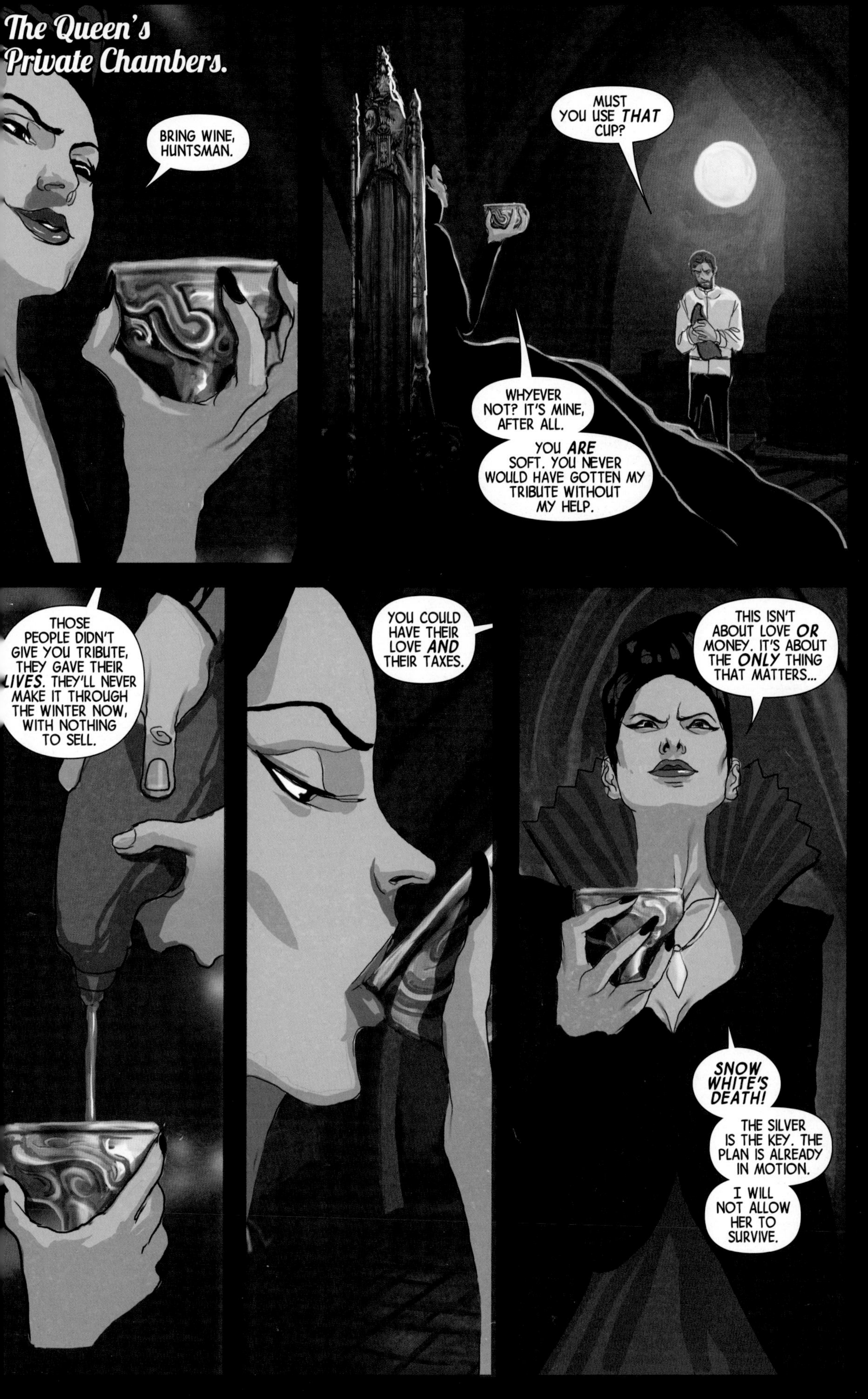
The Queen's Private Chambers.
BRING WINE, HUNTSMAN.
MUST YOU USE THAT CUP?
WHYEVER NOT? IT'S MINE, AFTER ALL.
YOU ARE SOFT. YOU NEVER WOULD HAVE GOTTEN MY TRIBUTE WITHOUT MY HELP.
THOSE PEOPLE DIDN'T GIVE YOU TRIBUTE, THEY GAVE THEIR LIVES. THEY'LL NEVER MAKE IT THROUGH THE WINTER NOW, WITH NOTHING TO SELL.
YOU COULD HAVE THEIR LOVE AND THEIR TAXES.
THIS ISN'T ABOUT LOVE OR MONEY. IT'S ABOUT THE ONLY THING THAT MATTERS...
SNOW WHITE'S DEATH!
THE SILVER IS THE KEY. THE PLAN IS ALREADY IN MOTION.
I WILL NOT ALLOW HER TO SURVIVE.

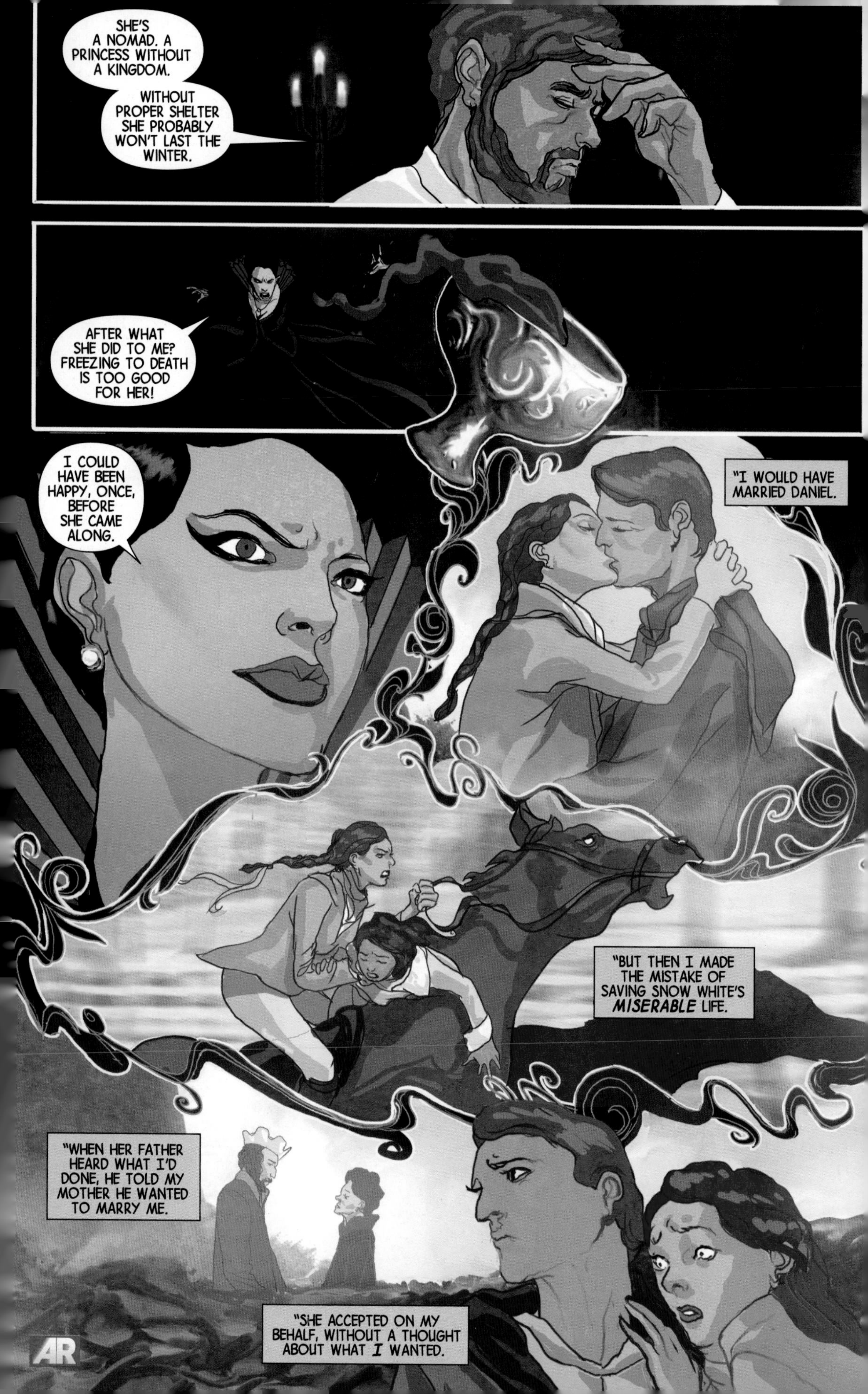

SHE'S A NOMAD. A PRINCESS WITHOUT A KINGDOM.
WITHOUT PROPER SHELTER SHE PROBABLY WON'T LAST THE WINTER.
AFTER WHAT SHE DID TO ME? FREEZING TO DEATH IS TOO GOOD FOR HER!
I COULD HAVE BEEN HAPPY, ONCE, BEFORE SHE CAME ALONG.
"I WOULD HAVE MARRIED DANIEL.
"BUT THEN I MADE THE MISTAKE OF SAVING SNOW WHITE'S *MISERABLE* LIFE.
"WHEN HER FATHER HEARD WHAT I'D DONE, HE TOLD MY MOTHER HE WANTED TO MARRY ME.
"SHE ACCEPTED ON MY BEHALF, WITHOUT A THOUGHT ABOUT WHAT *I* WANTED.
AR

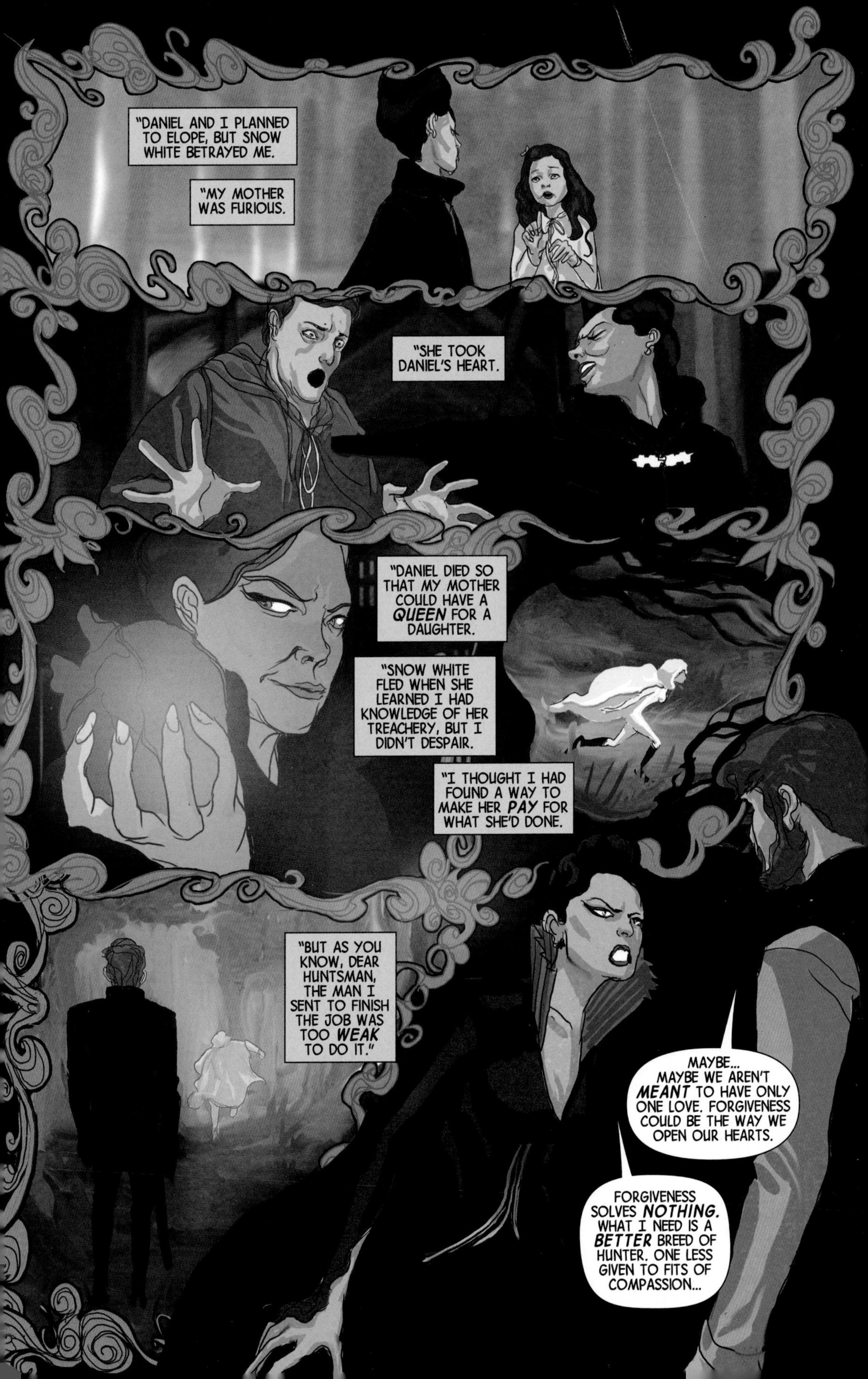

"DANIEL AND I PLANNED TO ELOPE, BUT SNOW WHITE BETRAYED ME.
"MY MOTHER WAS FURIOUS.
"SHE TOOK DANIEL'S HEART.
"DANIEL DIED SO THAT MY MOTHER COULD HAVE A QUEEN FOR A DAUGHTER.
"SNOW WHITE FLED WHEN SHE LEARNED I HAD KNOWLEDGE OF HER TREACHERY, BUT I DIDN'T DESPAIR.
"I THOUGHT I HAD FOUND A WAY TO MAKE HER PAY FOR WHAT SHE'D DONE.
"BUT AS YOU KNOW, DEAR HUNTSMAN, THE MAN I SENT TO FINISH THE JOB WAS TOO WEAK TO DO IT."
MAYBE... MAYBE WE AREN'T MEANT TO HAVE ONLY ONE LOVE. FORGIVENESS COULD BE THE WAY WE OPEN OUR HEARTS.
FORGIVENESS SOLVES NOTHING. WHAT I NEED IS A BETTER BREED OF HUNTER. ONE LESS GIVEN TO FITS OF COMPASSION...

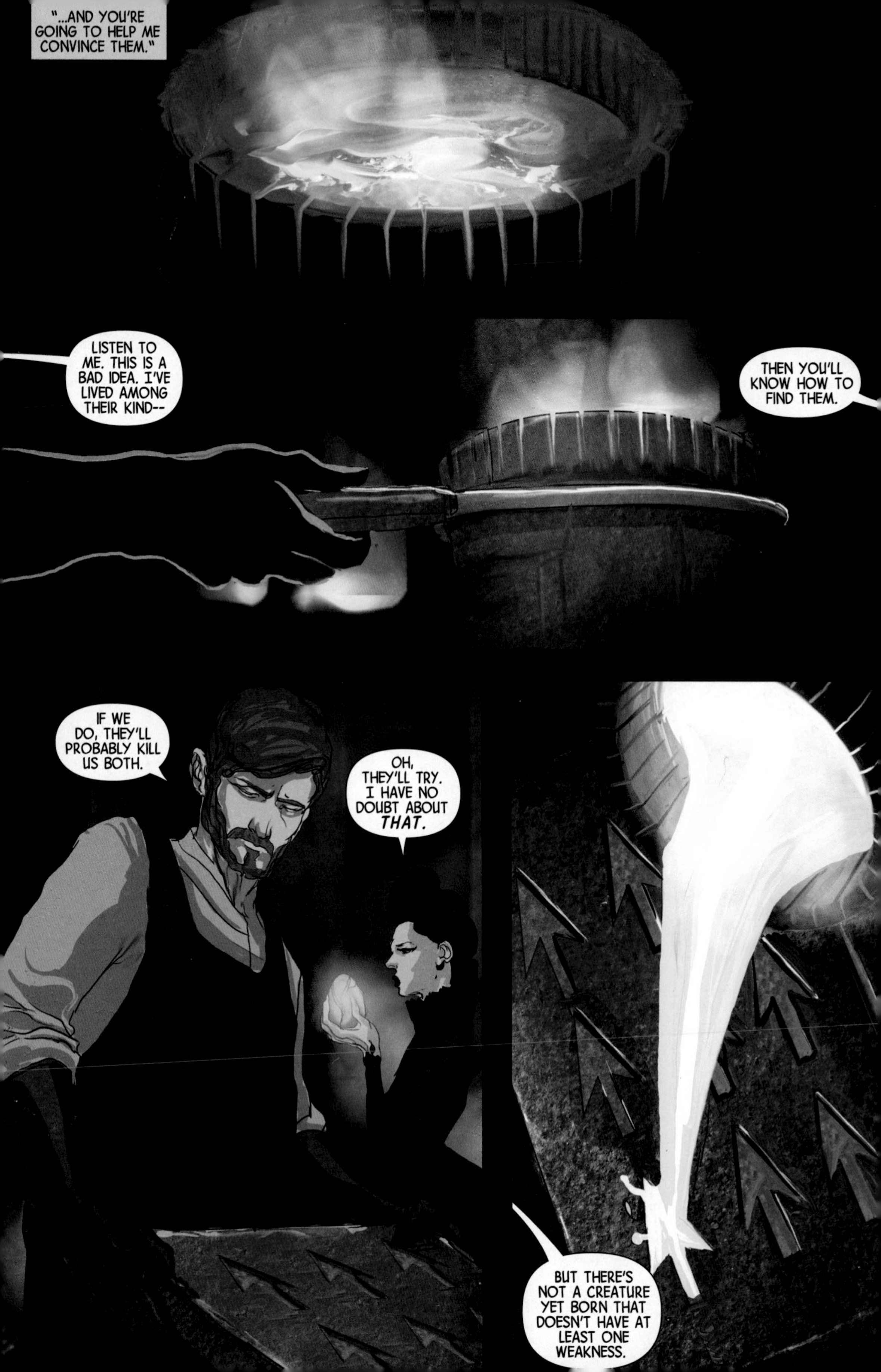
"...AND YOU'RE GOING TO HELP ME CONVINCE THEM."
LISTEN TO ME. THIS IS A BAD IDEA. I'VE LIVED AMONG THEIR KIND--
THEN YOU'LL KNOW HOW TO FIND THEM.
IF WE DO, THEY'LL PROBABLY KILL US BOTH.
OH, THEY'LL TRY. I HAVE NO DOUBT ABOUT *THAT*.
BUT THERE'S NOT A CREATURE YET BORN THAT DOESN'T HAVE AT LEAST ONE WEAKNESS.

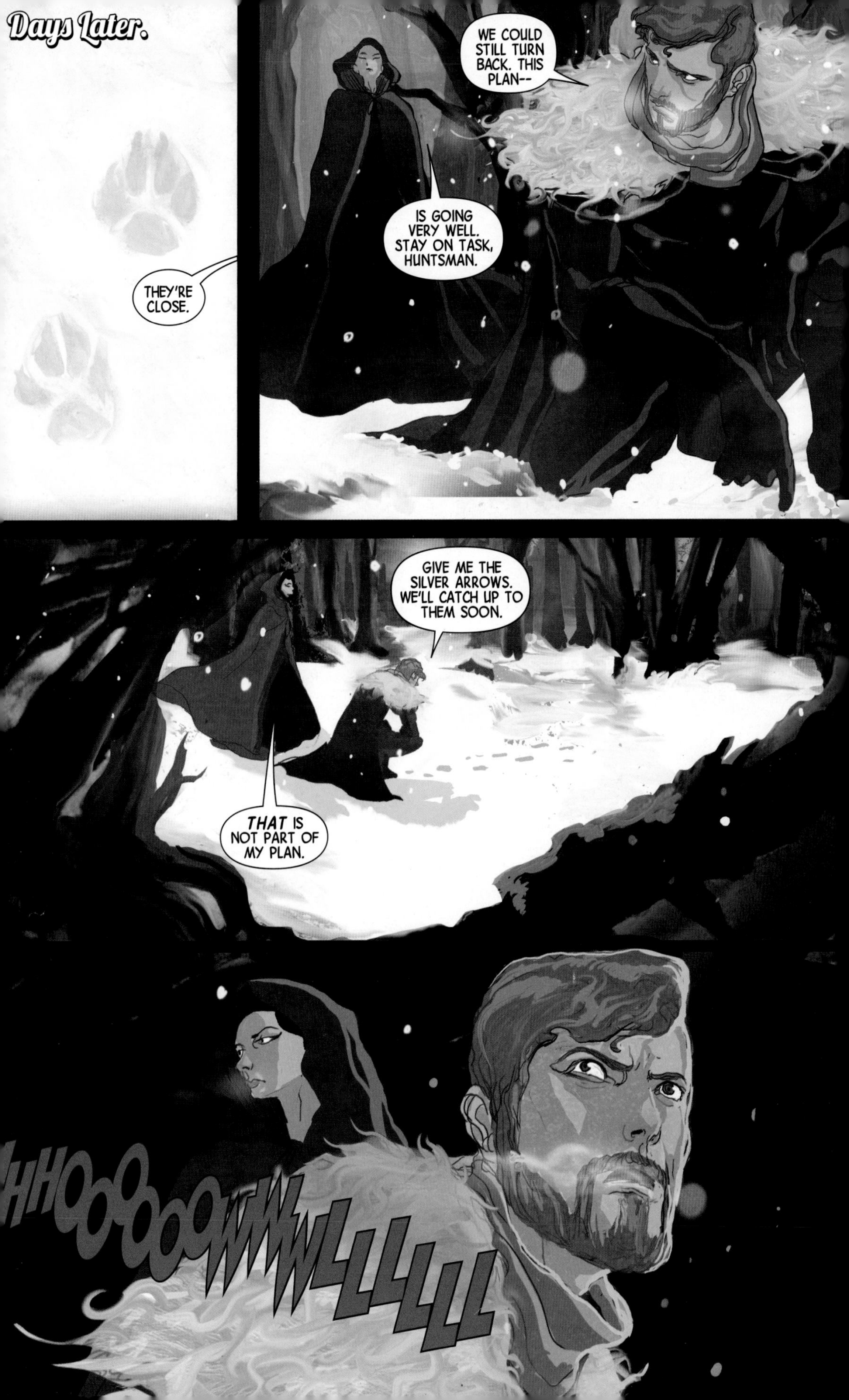
Days Later.
WE COULD STILL TURN BACK. THIS PLAN--
IS GOING VERY WELL. STAY ON TASK, HUNTSMAN.
THEY'RE CLOSE.
GIVE ME THE SILVER ARROWS. WE'LL CATCH UP TO THEM SOON.
THAT IS NOT PART OF MY PLAN.
HHOOOOOOWWLLLLLLL

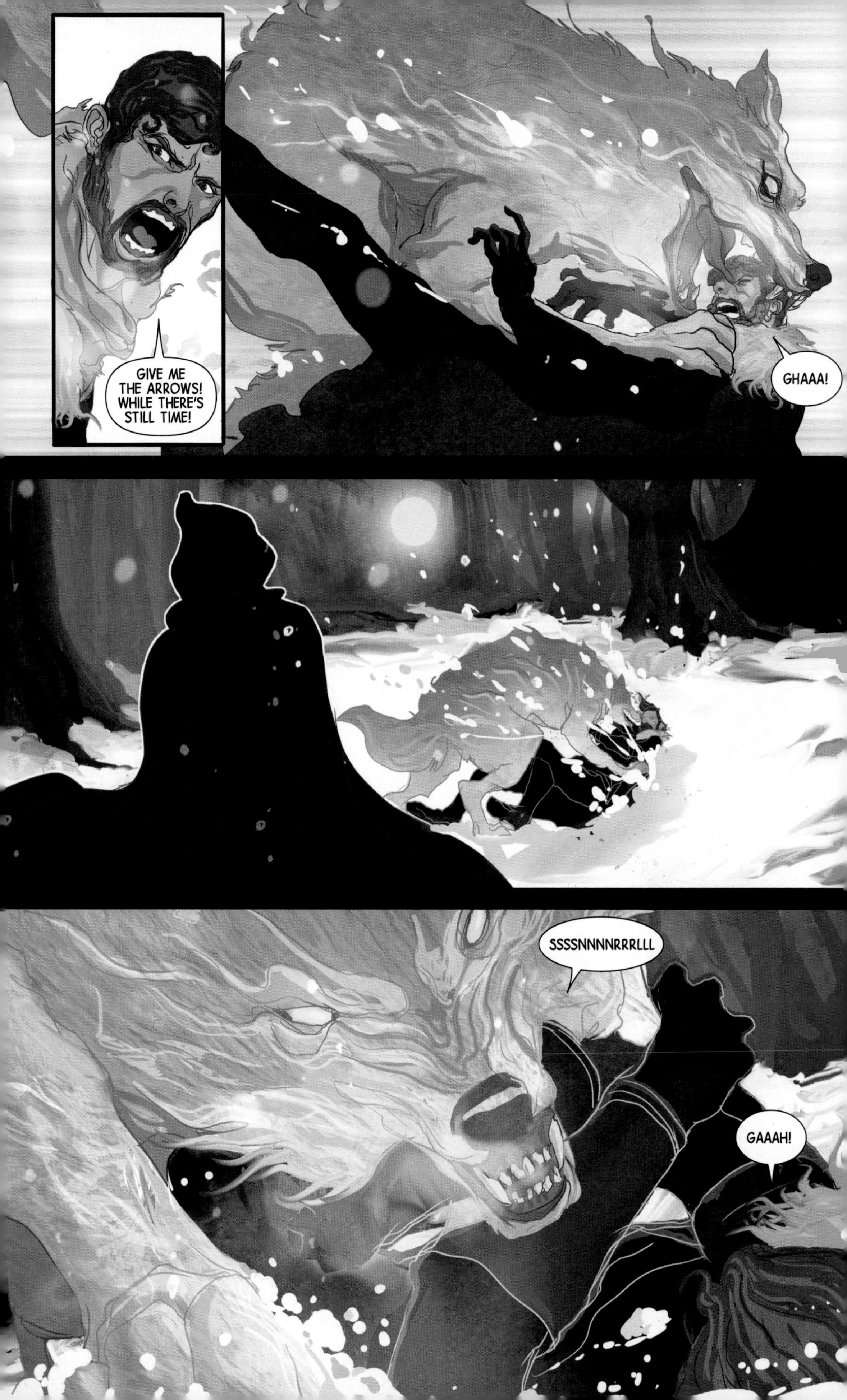
GIVE ME THE ARROWS! WHILE THERE'S STILL TIME!
GHAAA!
SSSSNNNNRRRLLL
GAAAH!

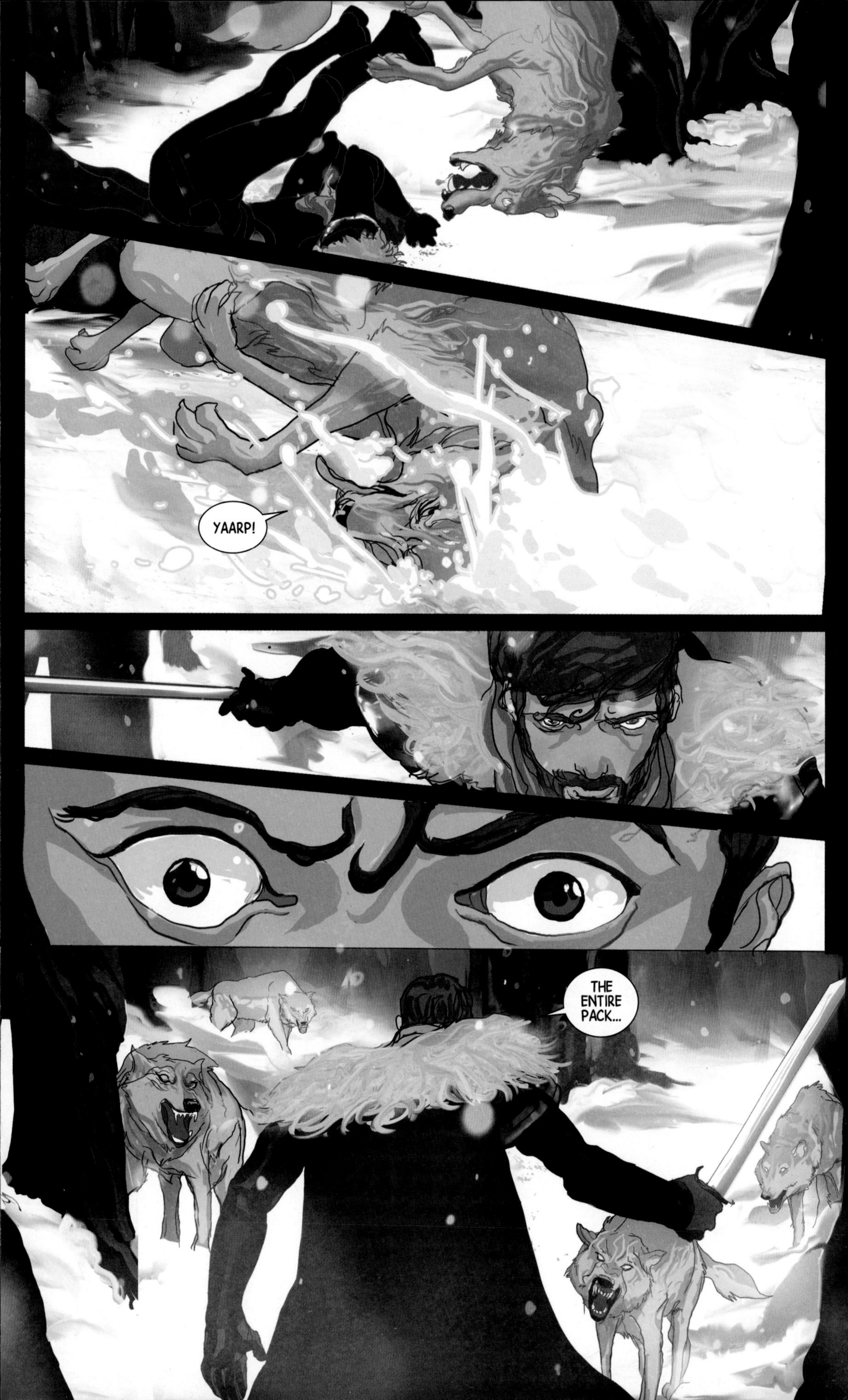
YAARP!
THE ENTIRE PACK...

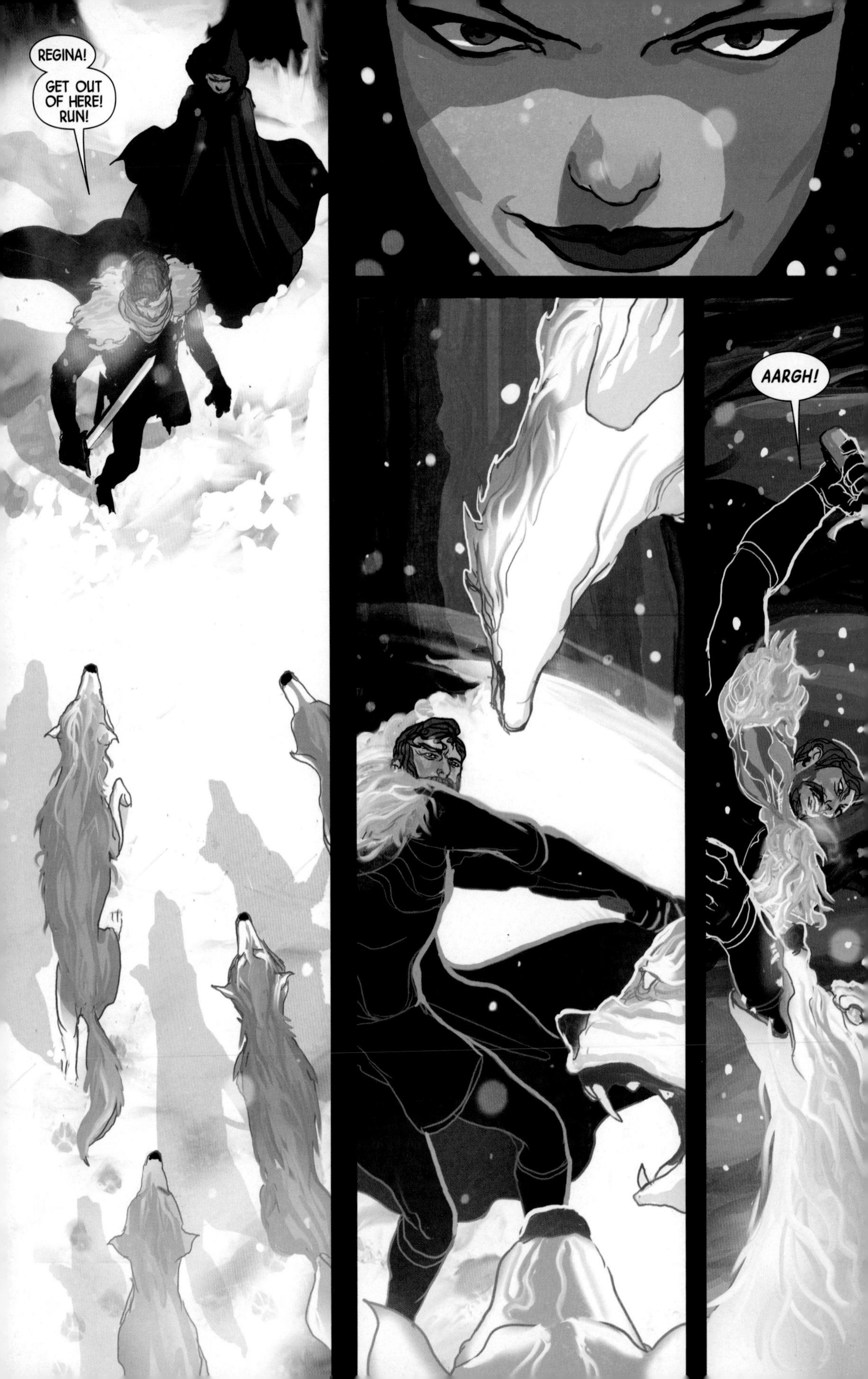
REGINA!
GET OUT OF HERE! RUN!
AARGH!

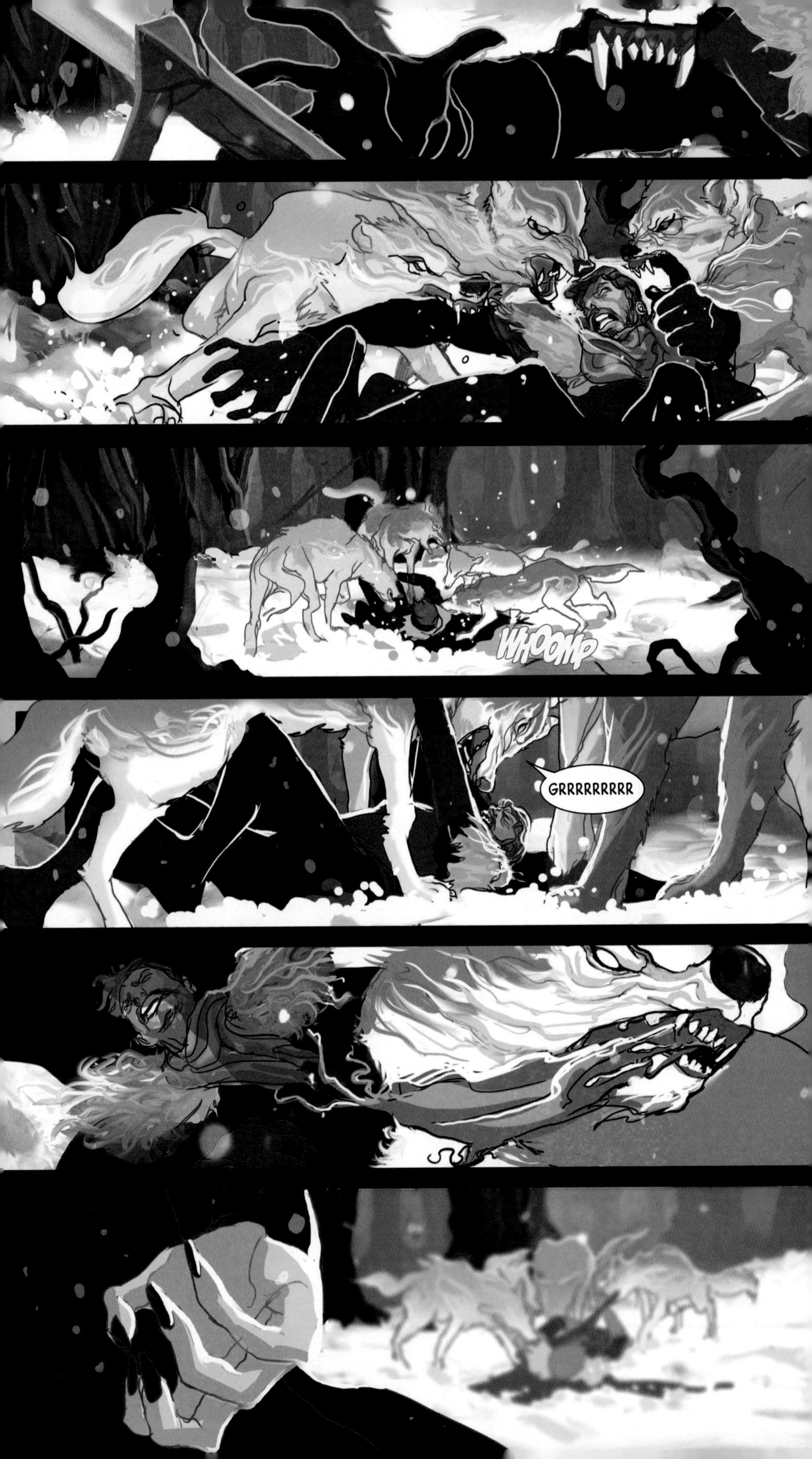
WHOOMP
GRRRRRRRRR

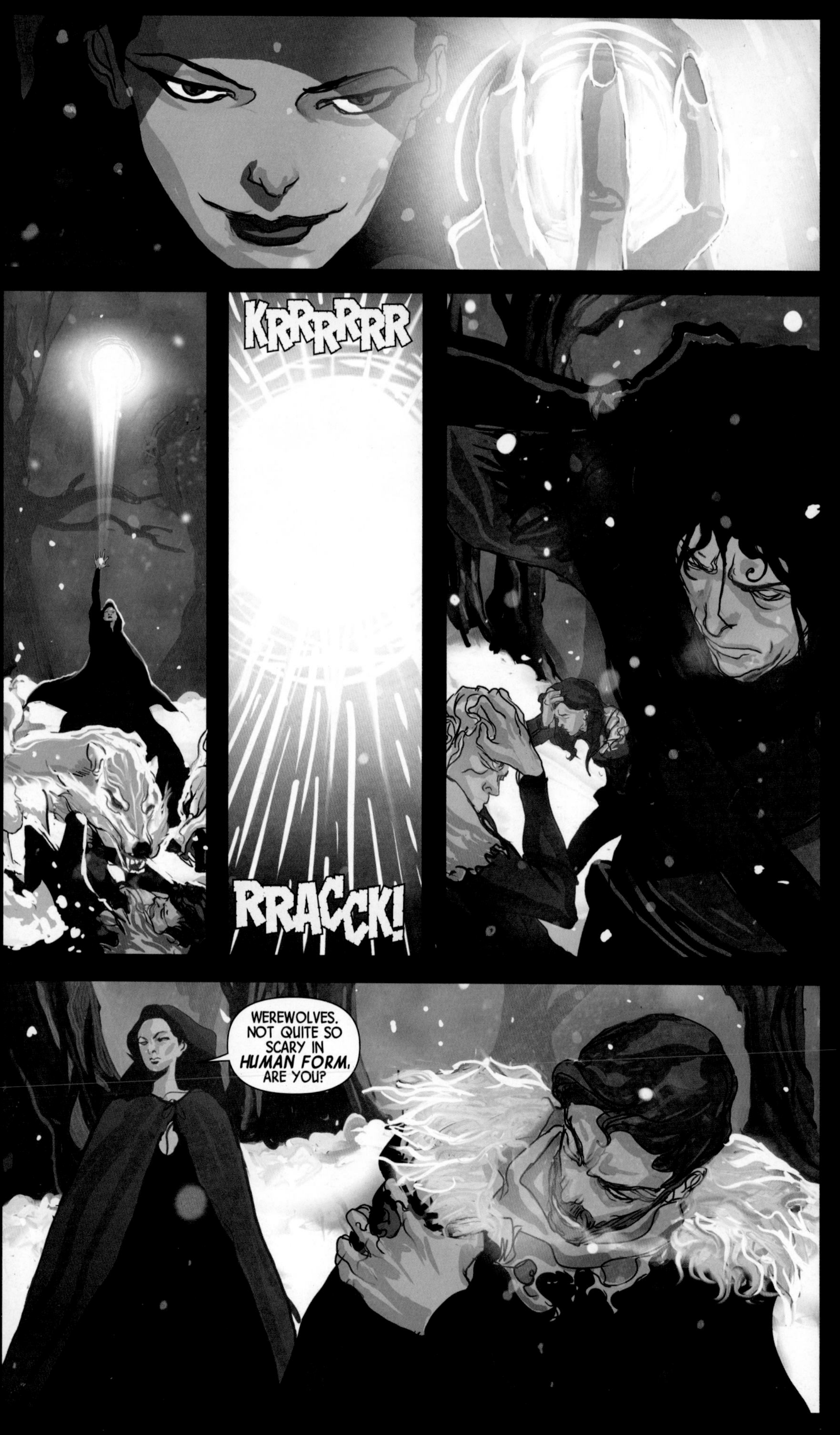
KRRRRRRR
RRACCK!
WEREWOLVES. NOT QUITE SO SCARY IN HUMAN FORM, ARE YOU?

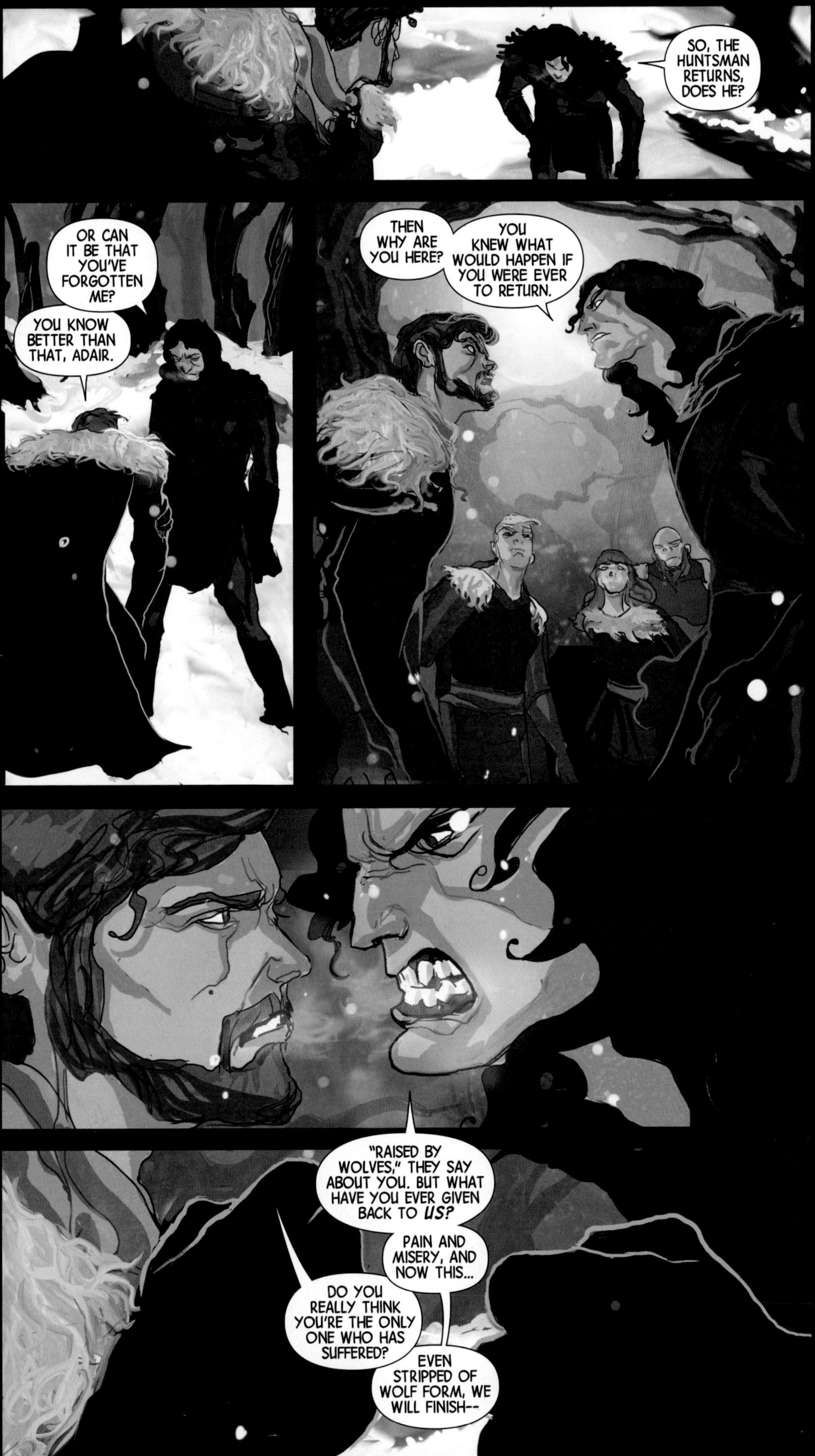
SO, THE HUNTSMAN RETURNS, DOES HE?
OR CAN IT BE THAT YOU'VE FORGOTTEN ME?
YOU KNOW BETTER THAN THAT, ADAIR.
THEN WHY ARE YOU HERE?
YOU KNEW WHAT WOULD HAPPEN IF YOU WERE EVER TO RETURN.
"RAISED BY WOLVES," THEY SAY ABOUT YOU. BUT WHAT HAVE YOU EVER GIVEN BACK TO US?
PAIN AND MISERY, AND NOW THIS...
DO YOU REALLY THINK YOU'RE THE ONLY ONE WHO HAS SUFFERED?
EVEN STRIPPED OF WOLF FORM, WE WILL FINISH--

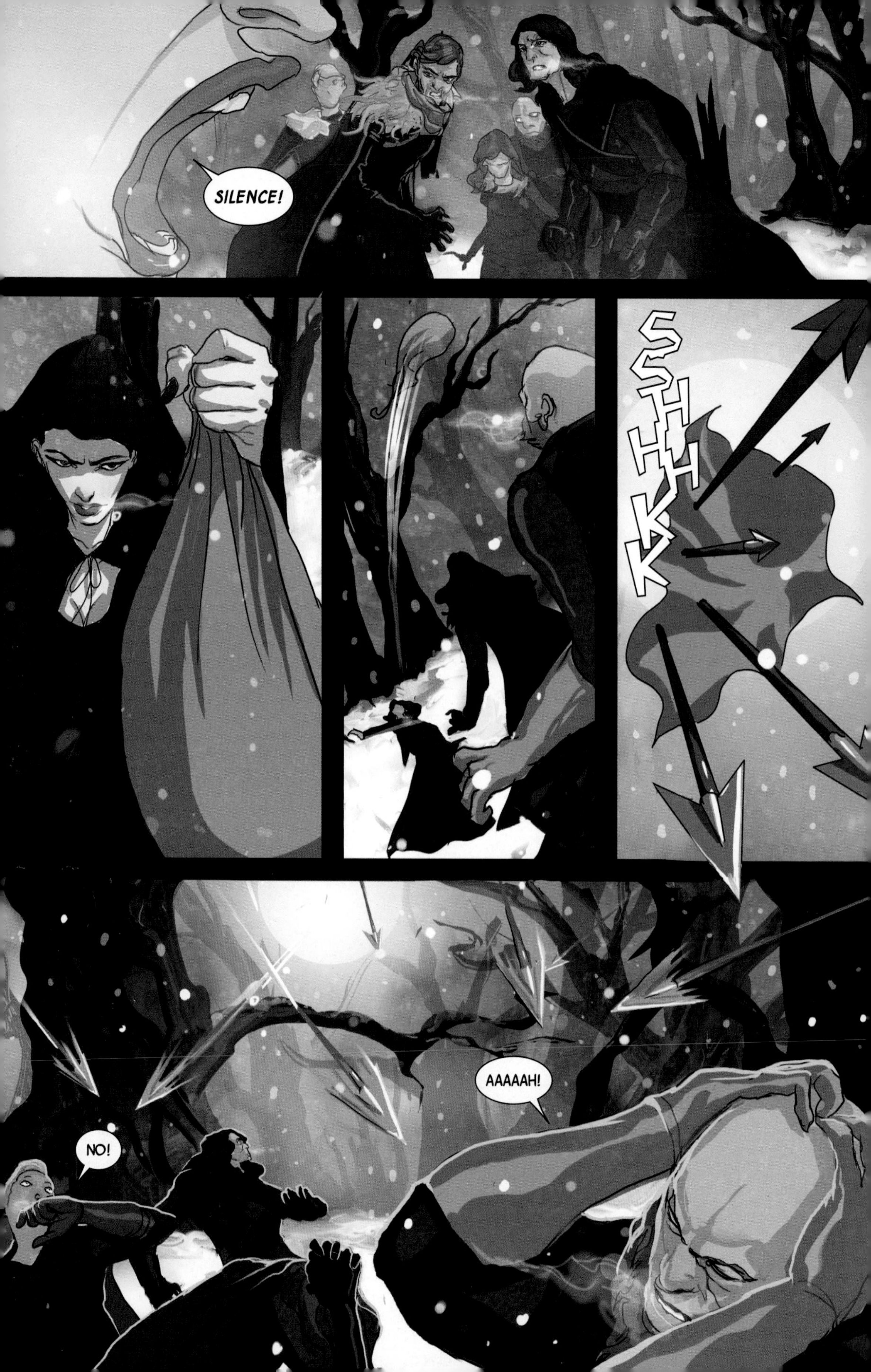
SILENCE!
SSHHHHKKK
AAAAAH!
NO!

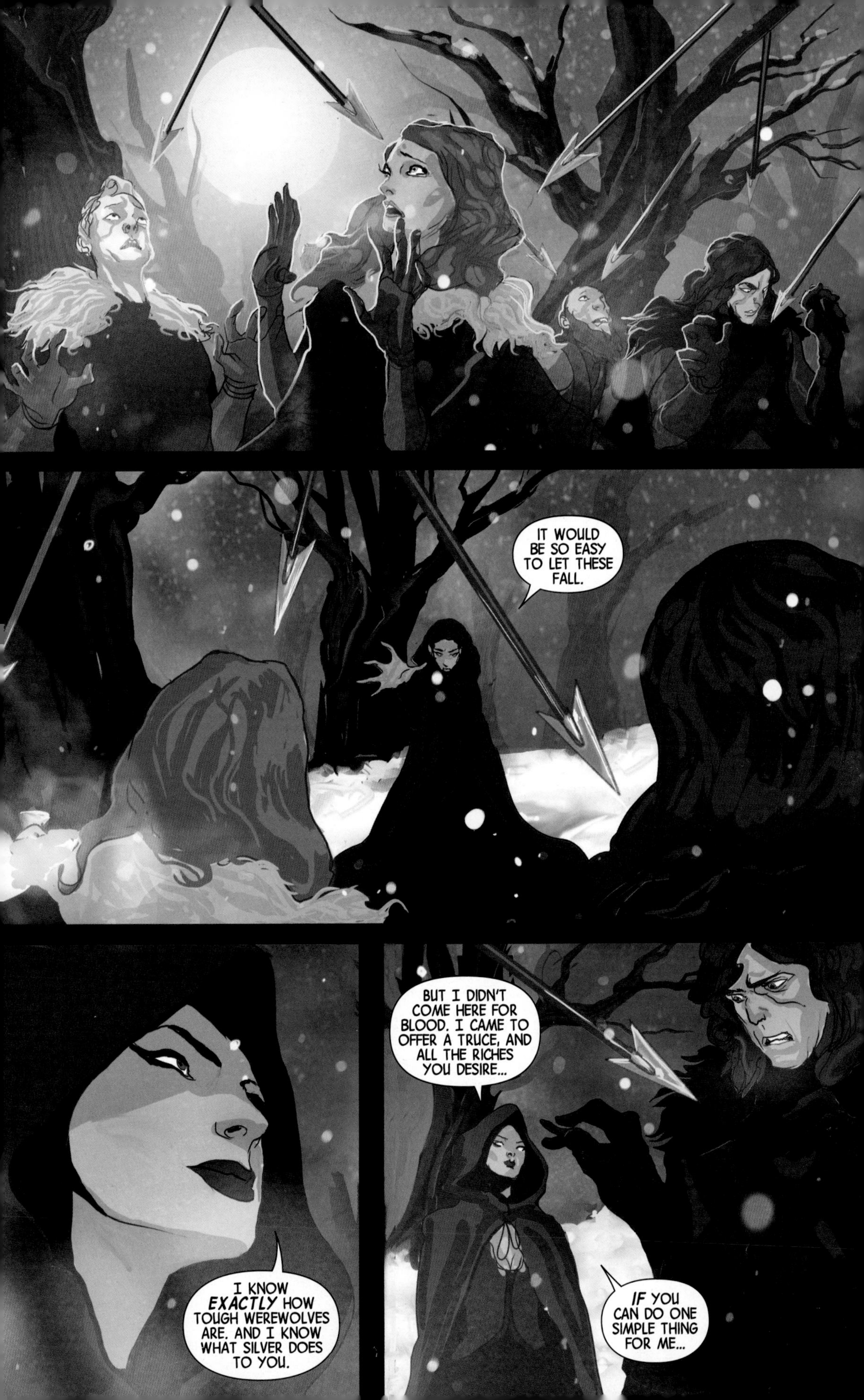
IT WOULD BE SO EASY TO LET THESE FALL.
I KNOW EXACTLY HOW TOUGH WEREWOLVES ARE. AND I KNOW WHAT SILVER DOES TO YOU.
BUT I DIDN'T COME HERE FOR BLOOD. I CAME TO OFFER A TRUCE, AND ALL THE RICHES YOU DESIRE...
IF YOU CAN DO ONE SIMPLE THING FOR ME...

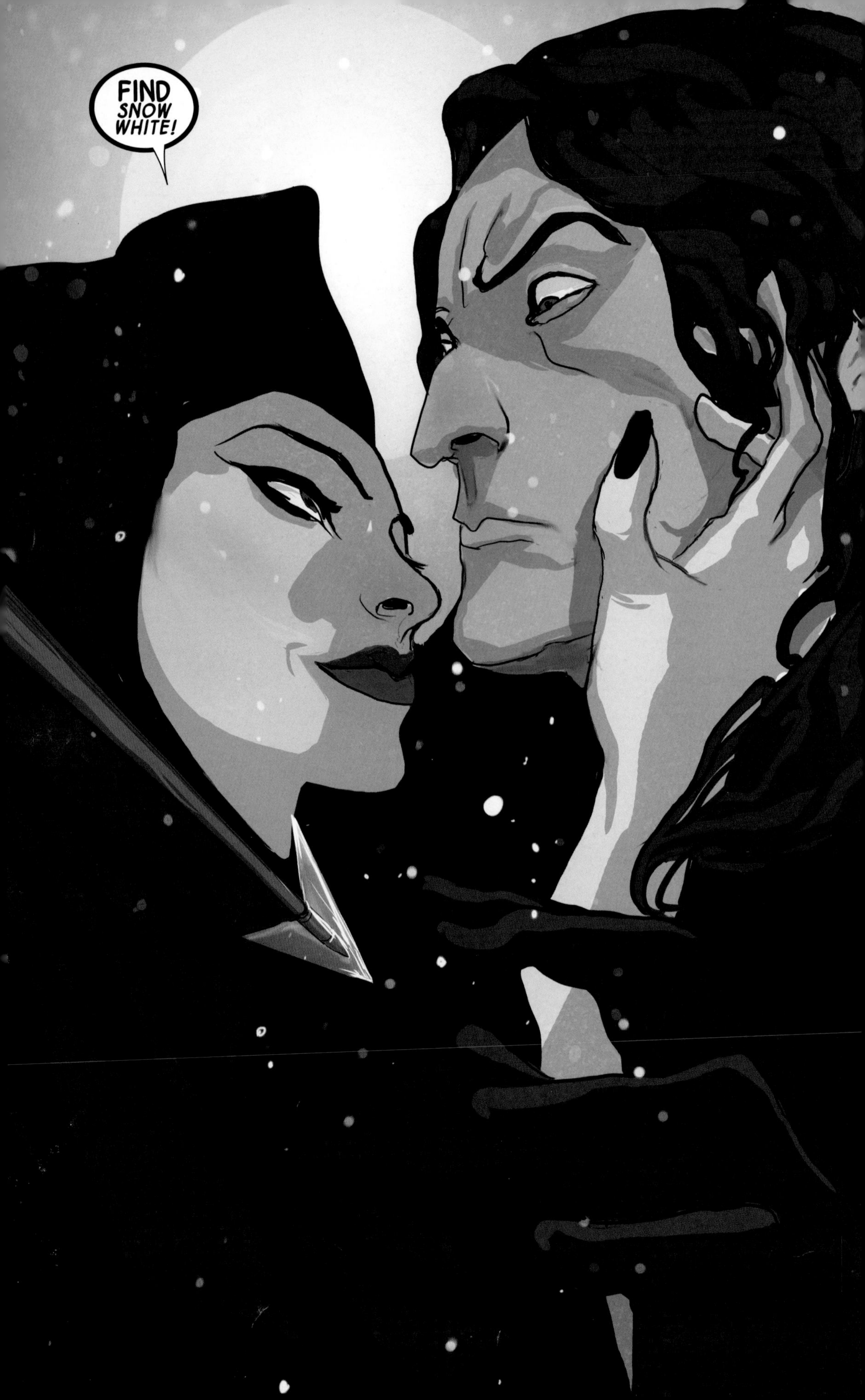
FIND SNOW WHITE!

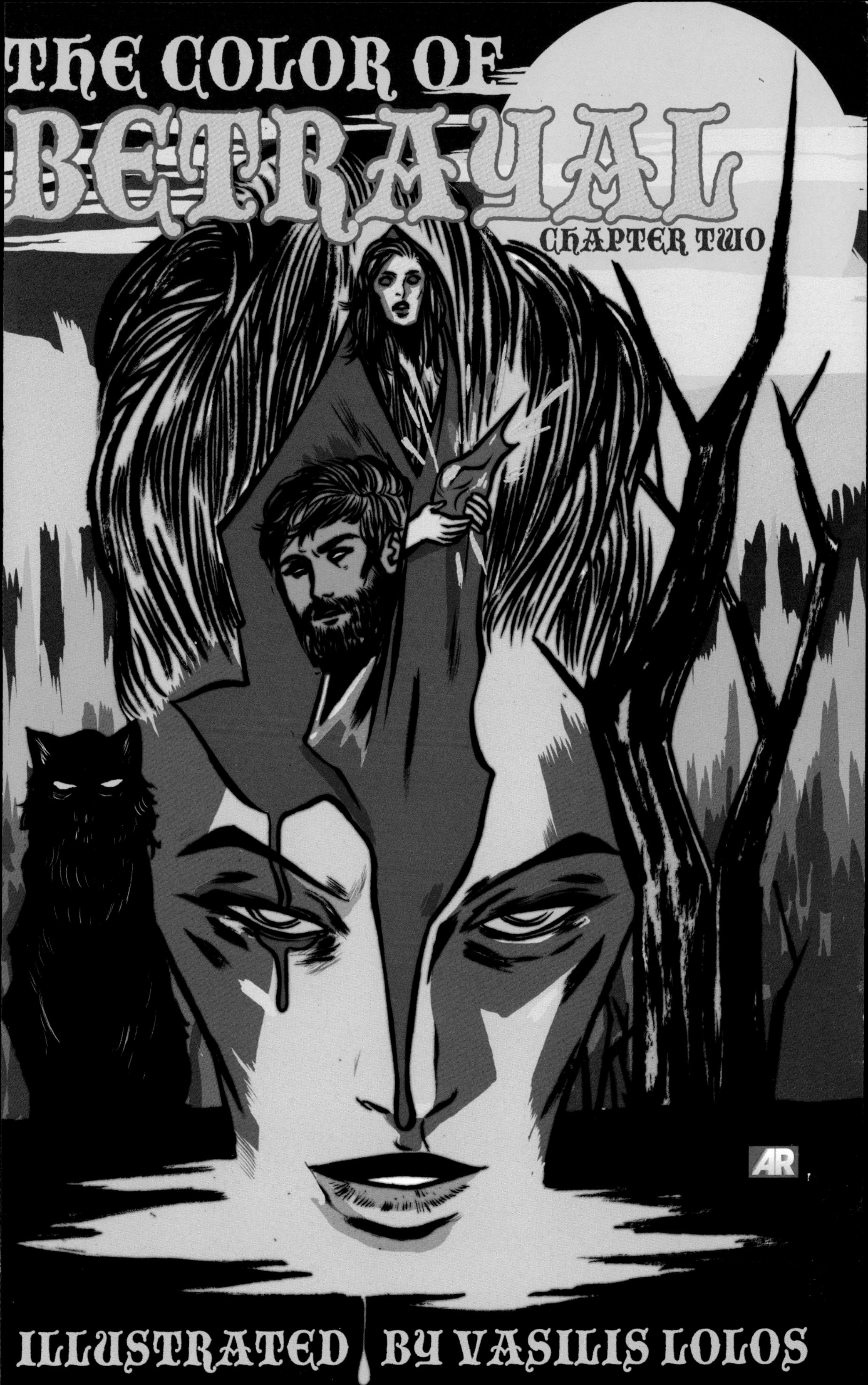
THE COLOR OF
BETRAYAL
CHAPTER TWO
AR
ILLUSTRATED BY VASILIS LOLOS

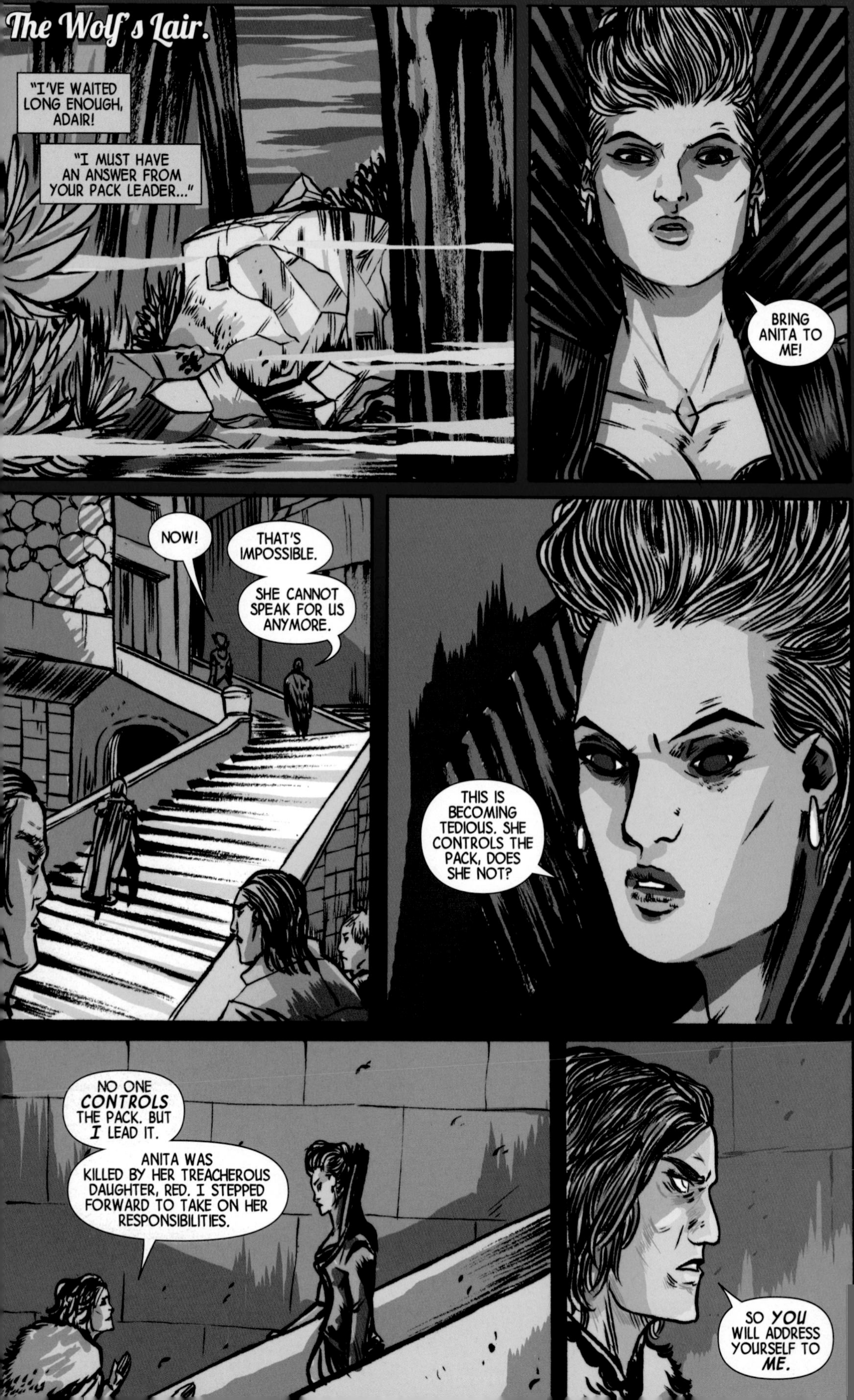
The Wolf's Lair.
"I'VE WAITED LONG ENOUGH, ADAIR!
"I MUST HAVE AN ANSWER FROM YOUR PACK LEADER..."
BRING ANITA TO ME!
NOW!
THAT'S IMPOSSIBLE.
SHE CANNOT SPEAK FOR US ANYMORE.
THIS IS BECOMING TEDIOUS. SHE CONTROLS THE PACK, DOES SHE NOT?
NO ONE CONTROLS THE PACK. BUT I LEAD IT.
ANITA WAS KILLED BY HER TREACHEROUS DAUGHTER, RED. I STEPPED FORWARD TO TAKE ON HER RESPONSIBILITIES.
SO YOU WILL ADDRESS YOURSELF TO ME.

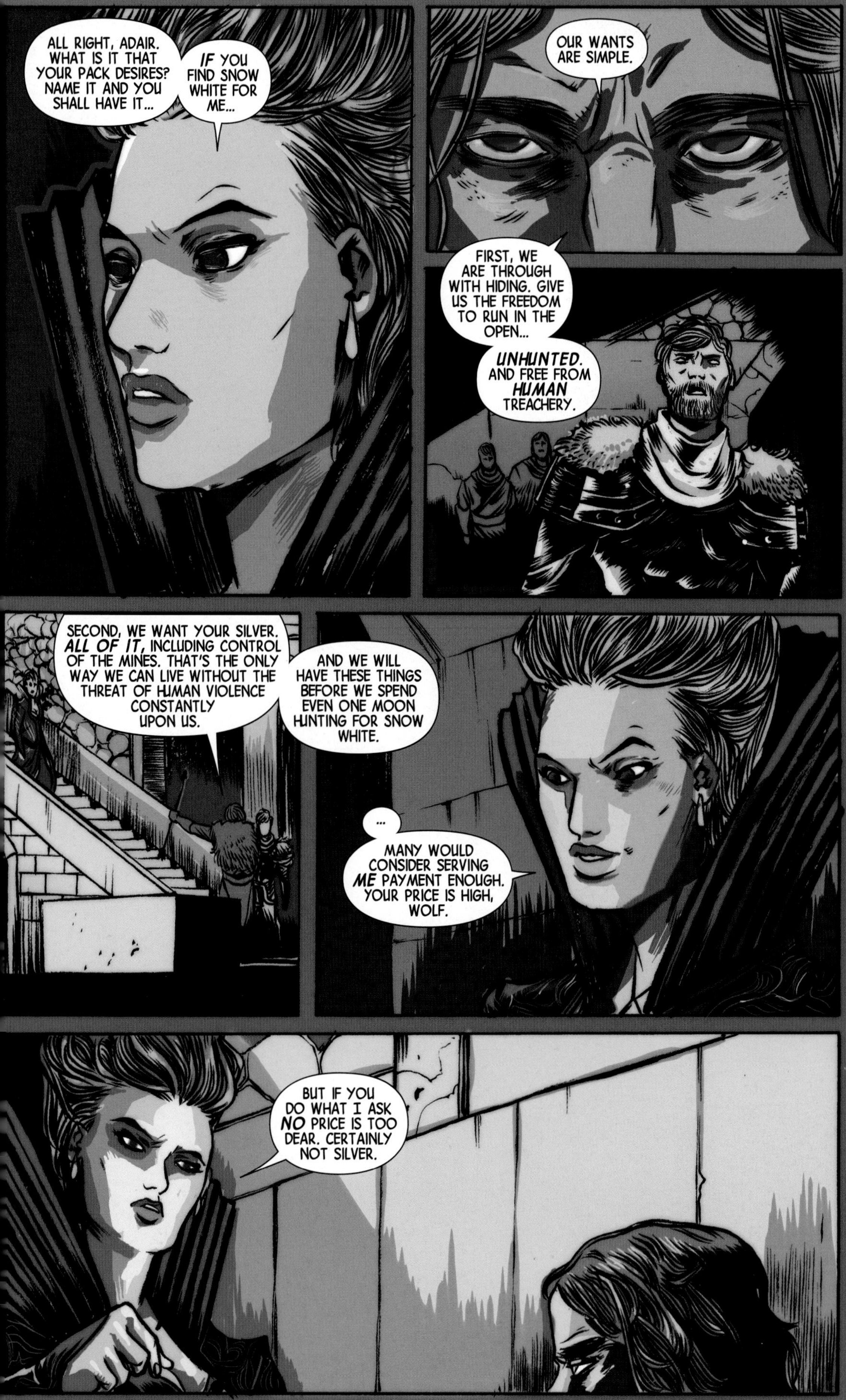
ALL RIGHT, ADAIR. WHAT IS IT THAT YOUR PACK DESIRES? NAME IT AND YOU SHALL HAVE IT...
IF YOU FIND SNOW WHITE FOR ME...
OUR WANTS ARE SIMPLE.
FIRST, WE ARE THROUGH WITH HIDING. GIVE US THE FREEDOM TO RUN IN THE OPEN...
UNHUNTED. AND FREE FROM HUMAN TREACHERY.
SECOND, WE WANT YOUR SILVER. ALL OF IT, INCLUDING CONTROL OF THE MINES. THAT'S THE ONLY WAY WE CAN LIVE WITHOUT THE THREAT OF HUMAN VIOLENCE CONSTANTLY UPON US.
AND WE WILL HAVE THESE THINGS BEFORE WE SPEND EVEN ONE MOON HUNTING FOR SNOW WHITE.
...
MANY WOULD CONSIDER SERVING ME PAYMENT ENOUGH. YOUR PRICE IS HIGH, WOLF.
BUT IF YOU DO WHAT I ASK NO PRICE IS TOO DEAR. CERTAINLY NOT SILVER.

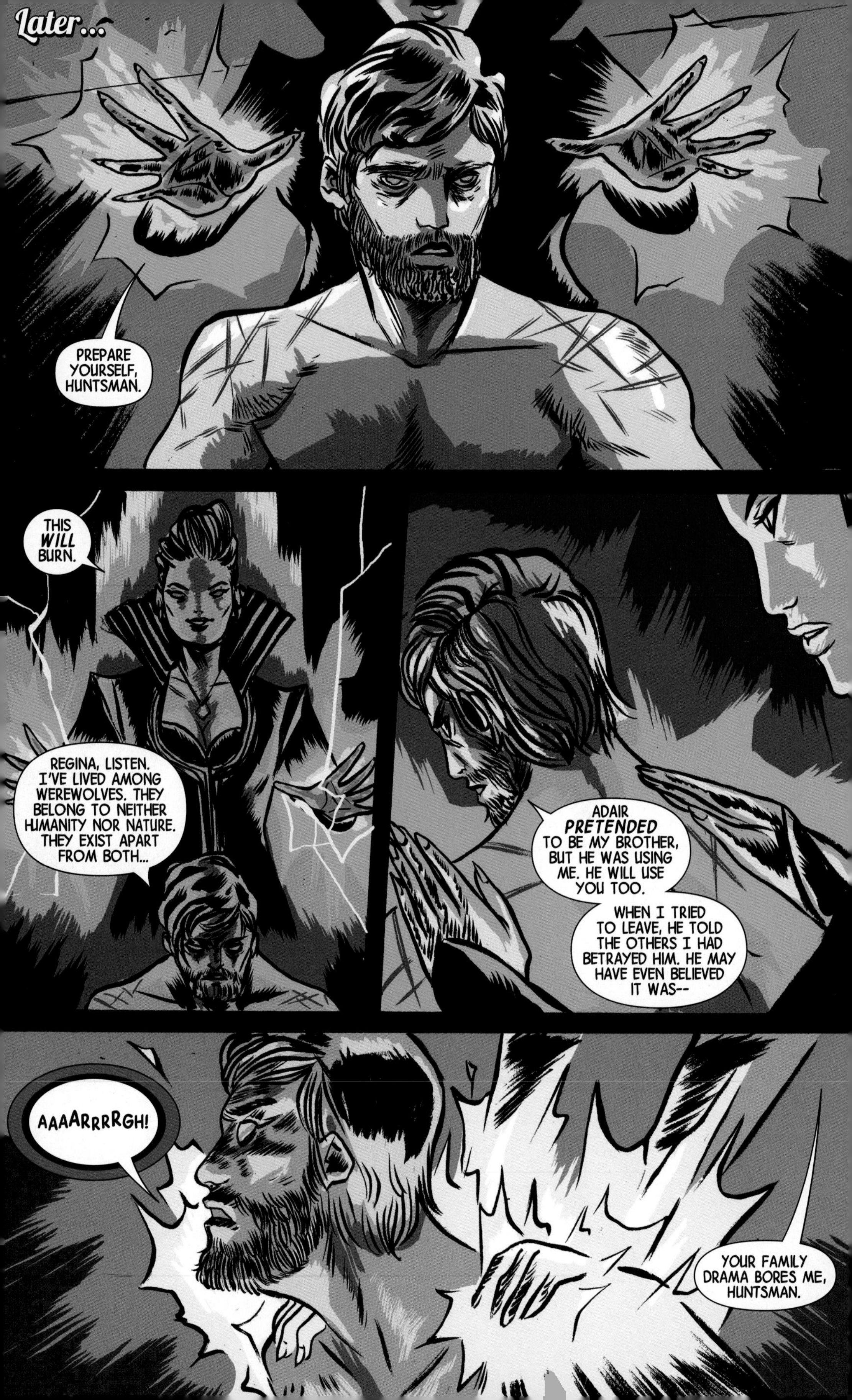
Later...
PREPARE YOURSELF, HUNTSMAN.
THIS WILL BURN.
REGINA, LISTEN. I'VE LIVED AMONG WEREWOLVES. THEY BELONG TO NEITHER HUMANITY NOR NATURE. THEY EXIST APART FROM BOTH...
ADAIR PRETENDED TO BE MY BROTHER, BUT HE WAS USING ME. HE WILL USE YOU TOO.
WHEN I TRIED TO LEAVE, HE TOLD THE OTHERS I HAD BETRAYED HIM. HE MAY HAVE EVEN BELIEVED IT WAS--
AAAARRRRGH!
YOUR FAMILY DRAMA BORES ME, HUNTSMAN.

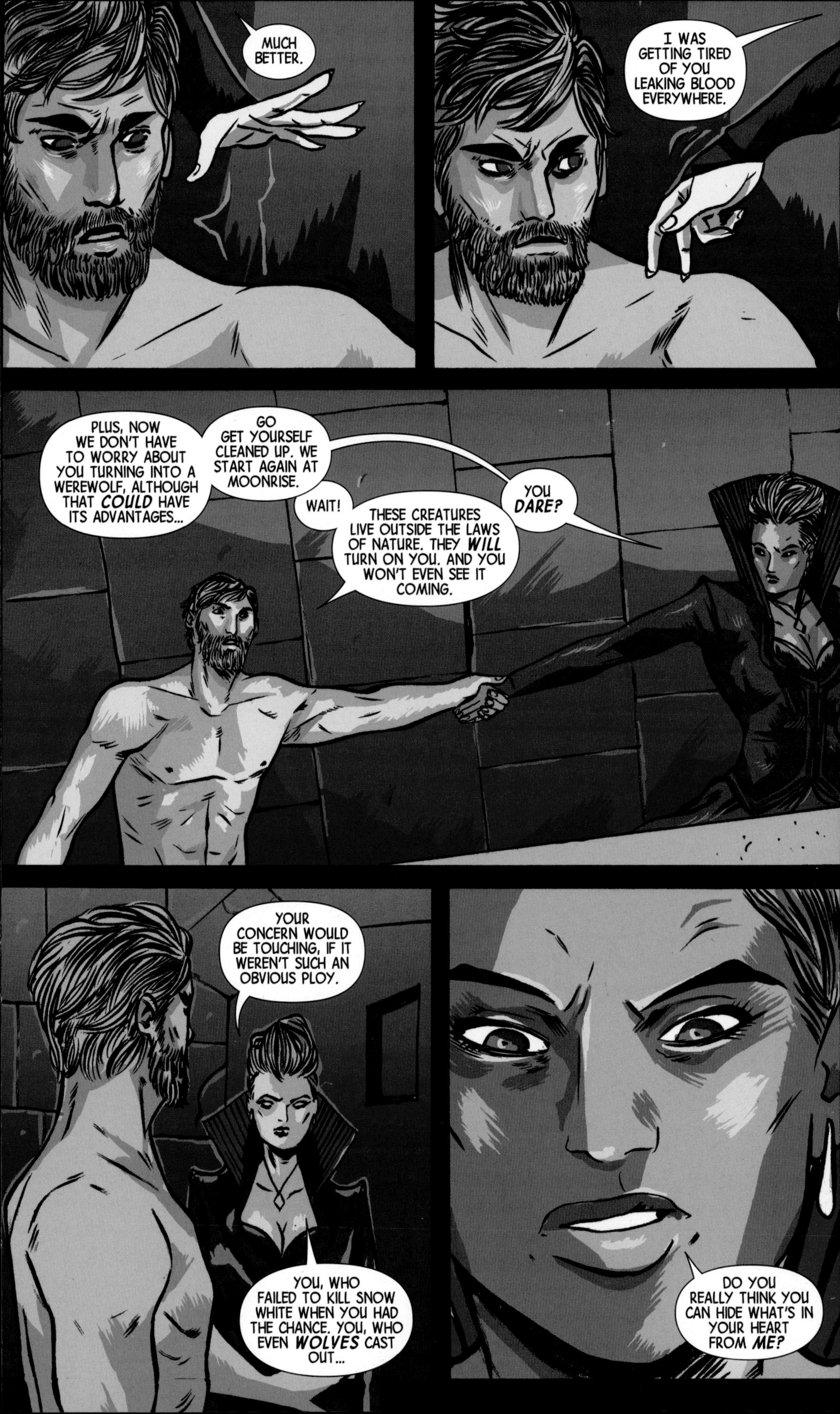
MUCH BETTER.
I WAS GETTING TIRED OF YOU LEAKING BLOOD EVERYWHERE.
PLUS, NOW WE DON'T HAVE TO WORRY ABOUT YOU TURNING INTO A WEREWOLF, ALTHOUGH THAT COULD HAVE ITS ADVANTAGES...
GO GET YOURSELF CLEANED UP. WE START AGAIN AT MOONRISE.
WAIT!
THESE CREATURES LIVE OUTSIDE THE LAWS OF NATURE. THEY WILL TURN ON YOU. AND YOU WON'T EVEN SEE IT COMING.
YOU DARE?
YOUR CONCERN WOULD BE TOUCHING, IF IT WEREN'T SUCH AN OBVIOUS PLOY.
YOU, WHO FAILED TO KILL SNOW WHITE WHEN YOU HAD THE CHANCE. YOU, WHO EVEN WOLVES CAST OUT...
DO YOU REALLY THINK YOU CAN HIDE WHAT'S IN YOUR HEART FROM ME?

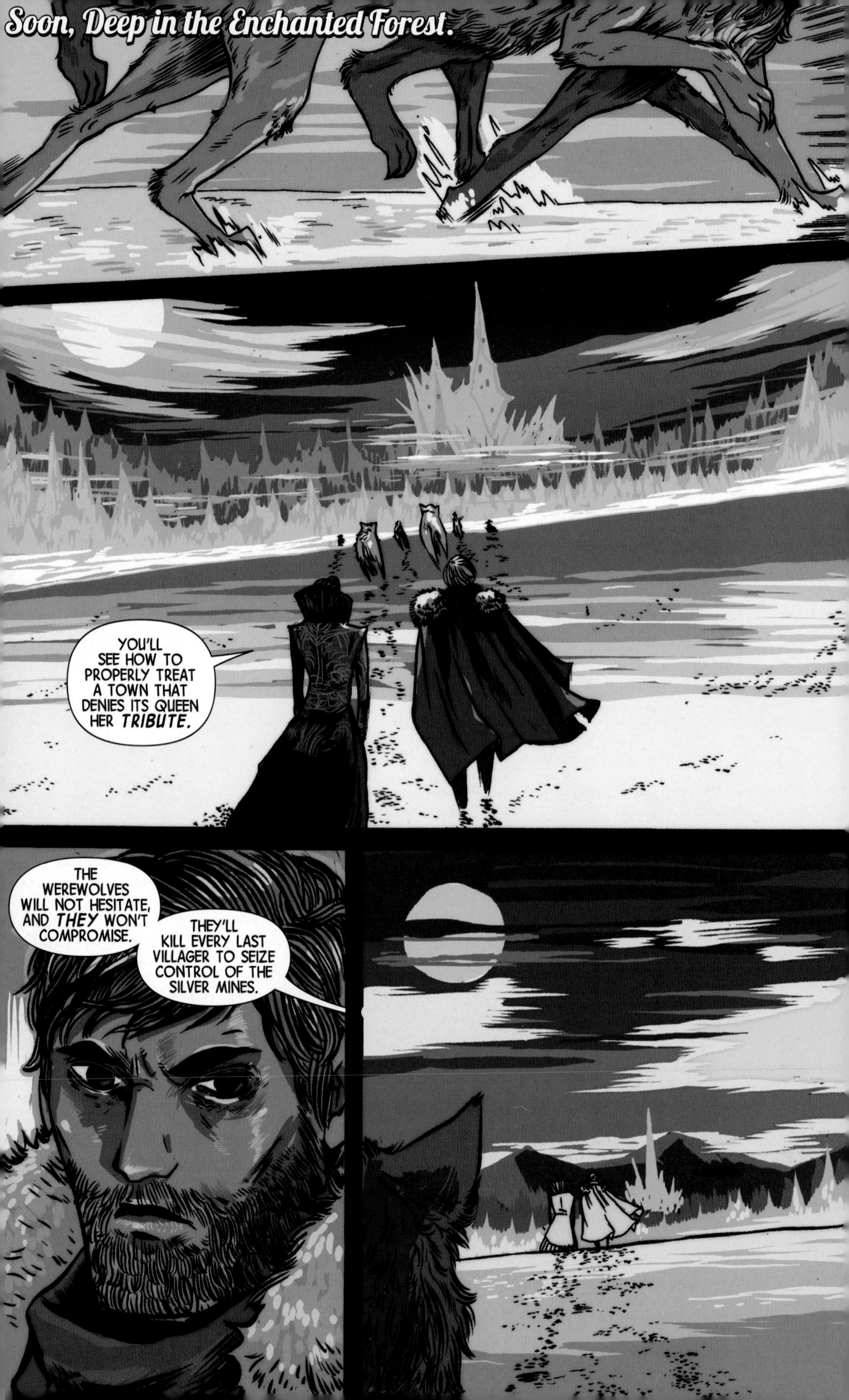
Soon, Deep in the Enchanted Forest.
YOU'LL SEE HOW TO PROPERLY TREAT A TOWN THAT DENIES ITS QUEEN HER *TRIBUTE.*
THE WEREWOLVES WILL NOT HESITATE, AND *THEY* WON'T COMPROMISE.
THEY'LL KILL EVERY LAST VILLAGER TO SEIZE CONTROL OF THE SILVER MINES.

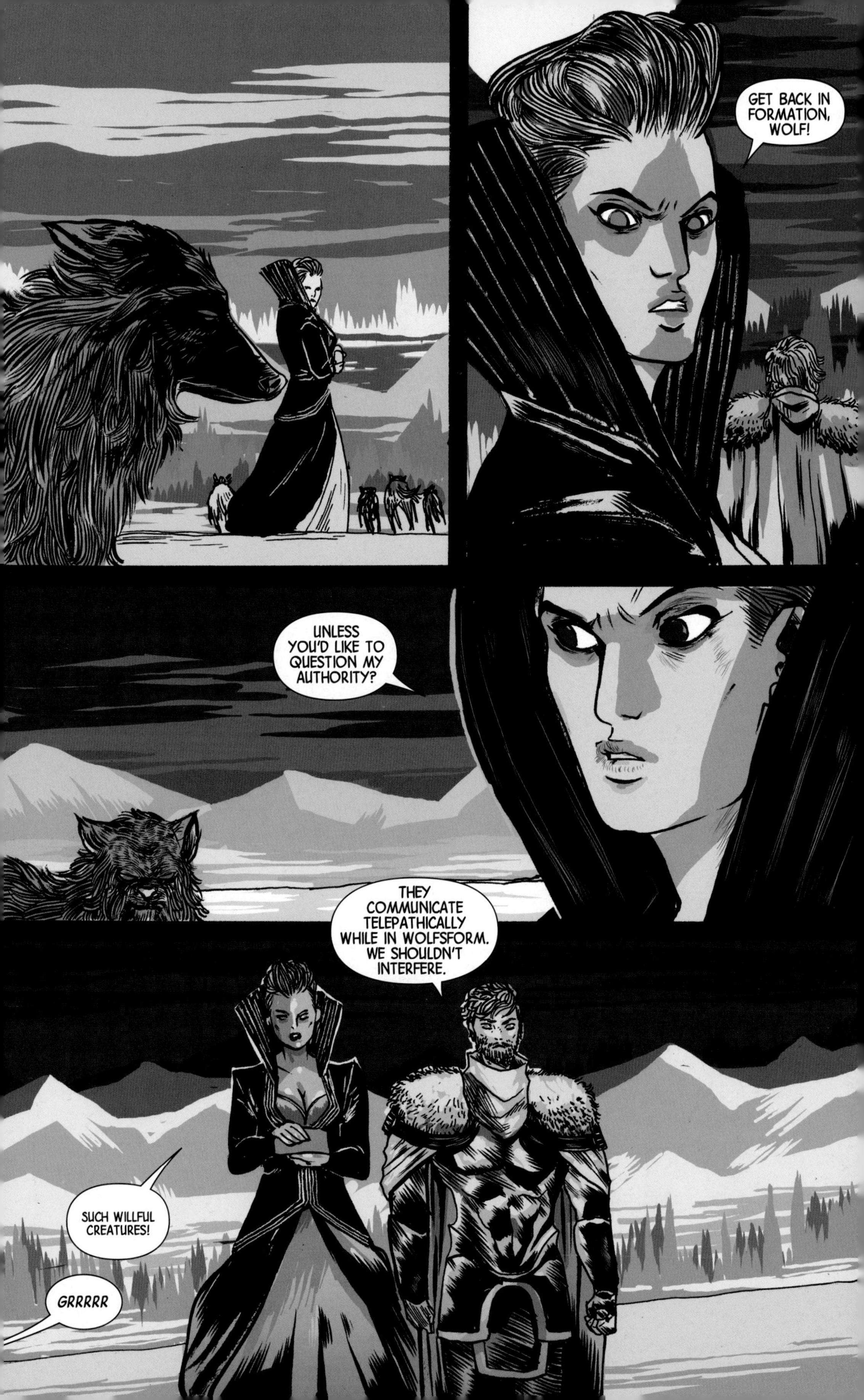
GET BACK IN FORMATION, WOLF!
UNLESS YOU'D LIKE TO QUESTION MY AUTHORITY?
THEY COMMUNICATE TELEPATHICALLY WHILE IN WOLFSFORM. WE SHOULDN'T INTERFERE.
SUCH WILLFUL CREATURES!
GRRRRR

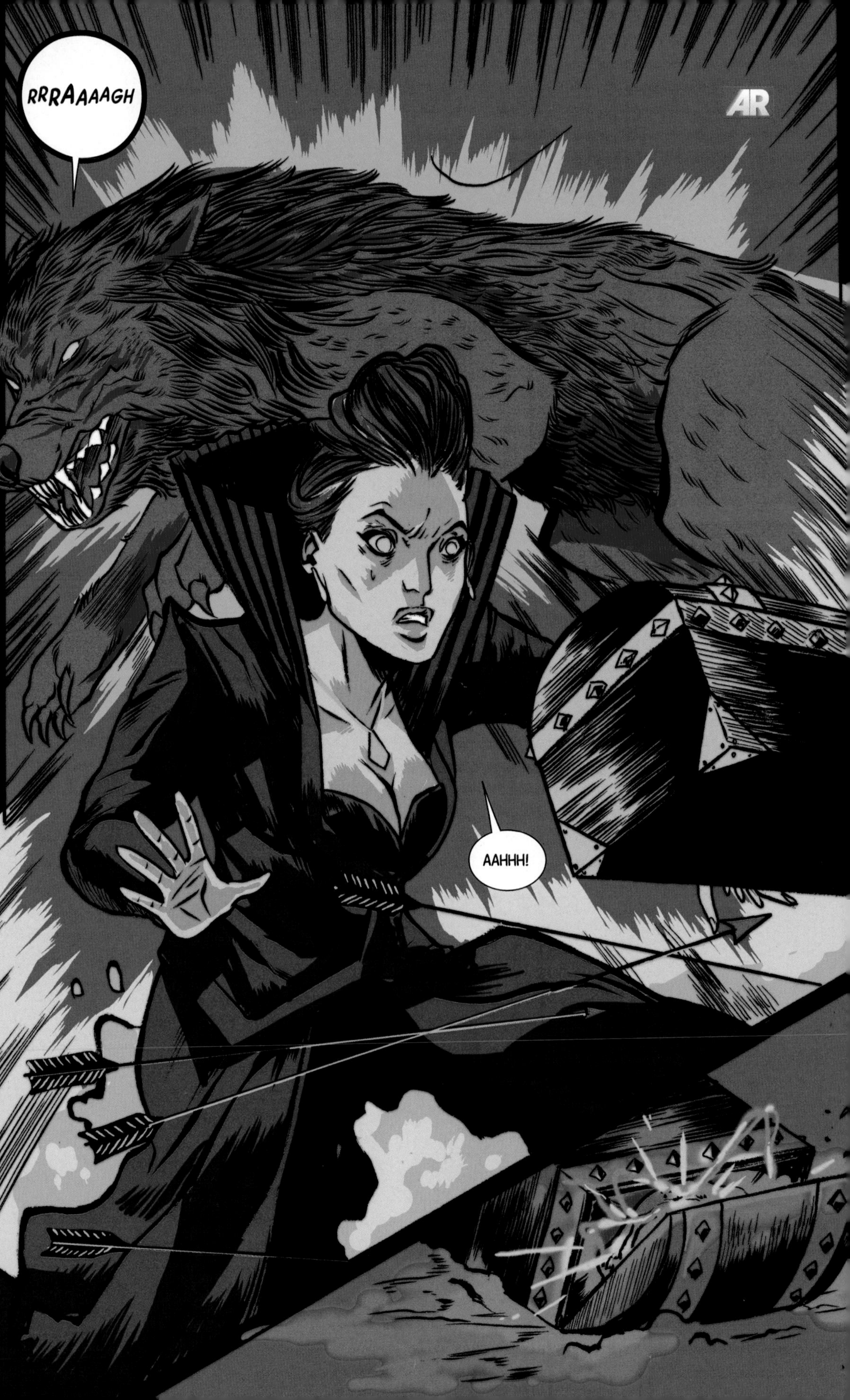
RRRAAAAGH
AAHHH!

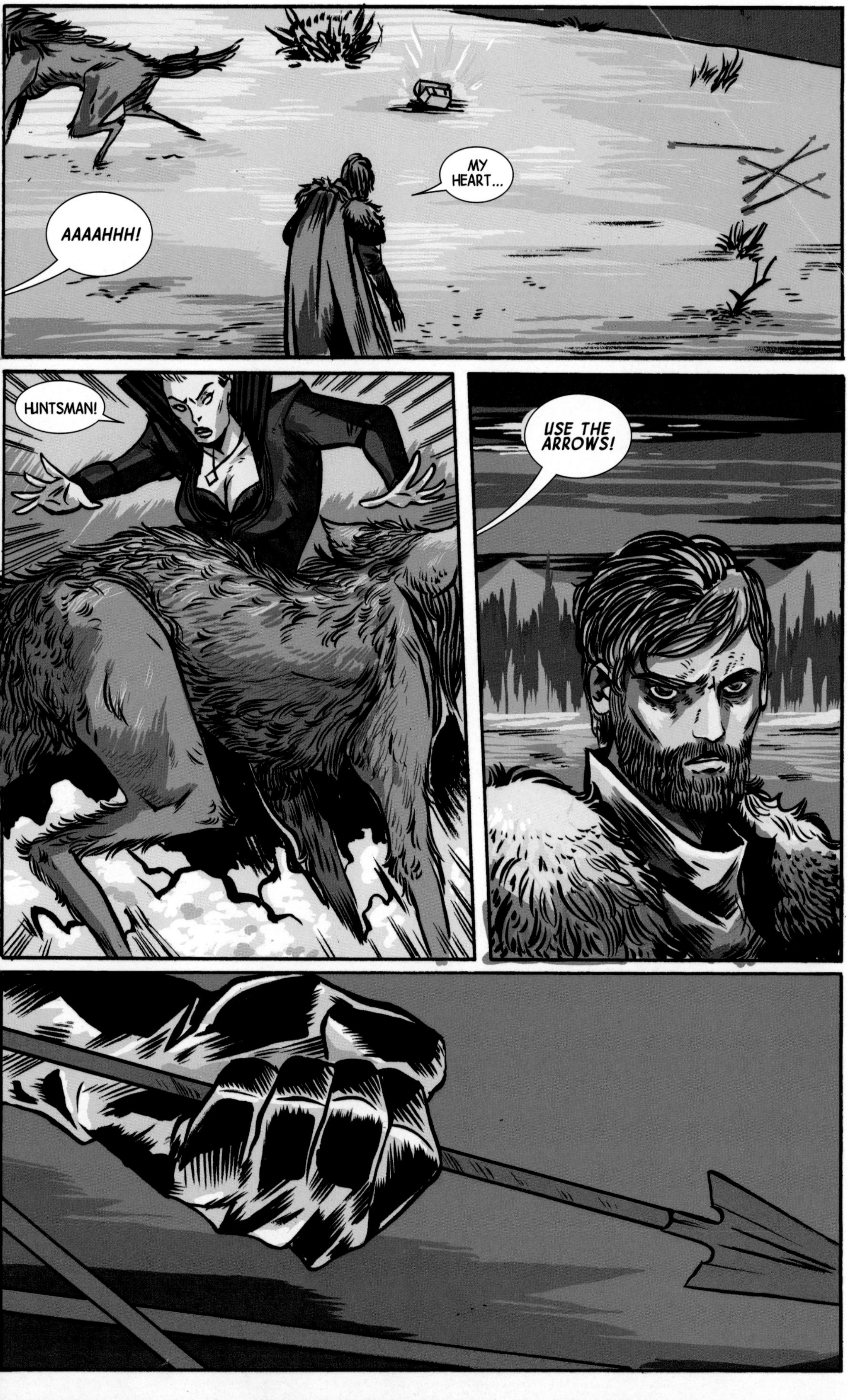
MY HEART...
AAAAHHH!
HUNTSMAN!
USE THE ARROWS!

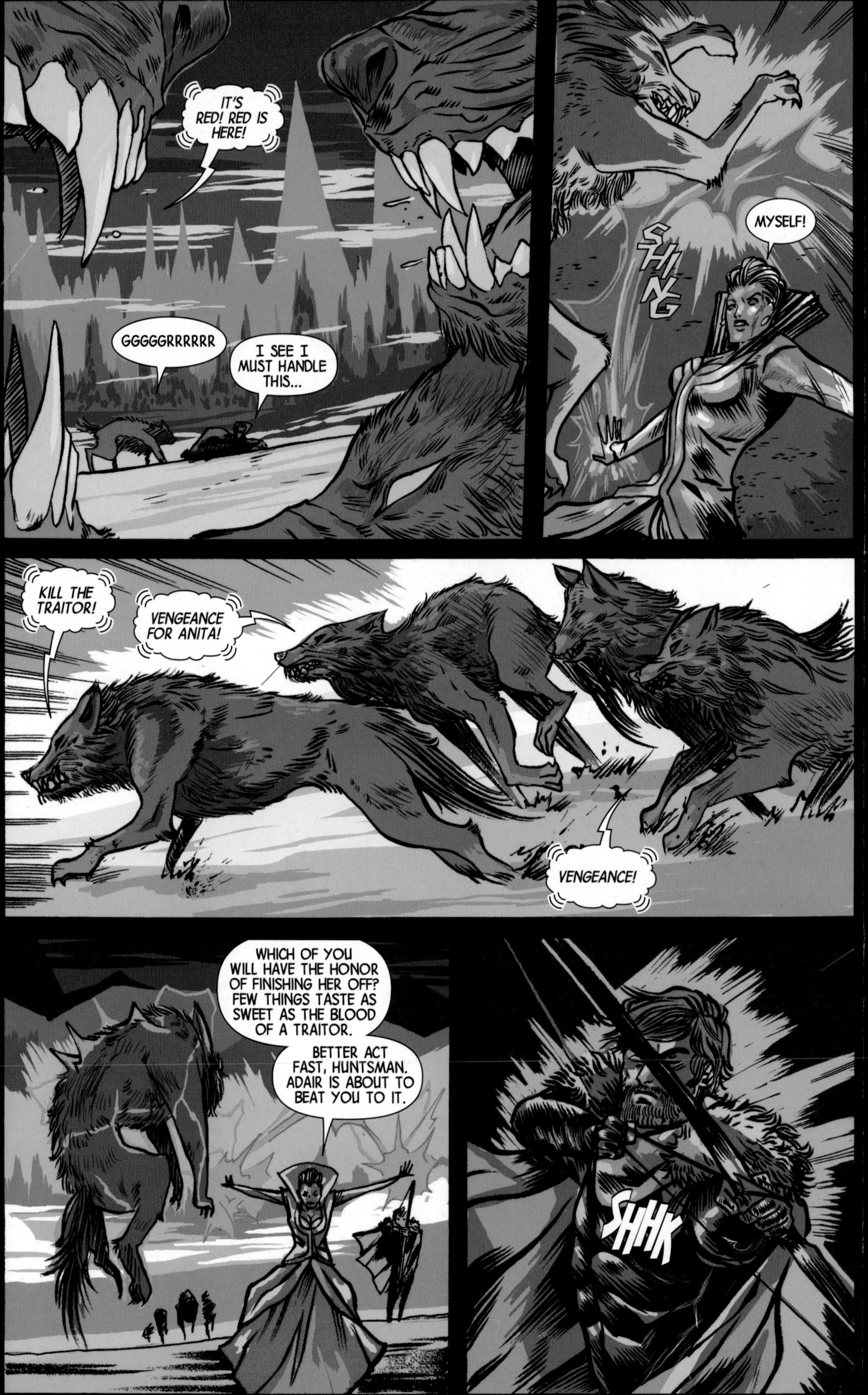
IT'S RED! RED IS HERE!
GGGGGRRRRRR
I SEE I MUST HANDLE THIS...
MYSELF!
SHING
KILL THE TRAITOR!
VENGEANCE FOR ANITA!
VENGEANCE!
WHICH OF YOU WILL HAVE THE HONOR OF FINISHING HER OFF? FEW THINGS TASTE AS SWEET AS THE BLOOD OF A TRAITOR.
BETTER ACT FAST, HUNTSMAN. ADAIR IS ABOUT TO BEAT YOU TO IT.
SHHK

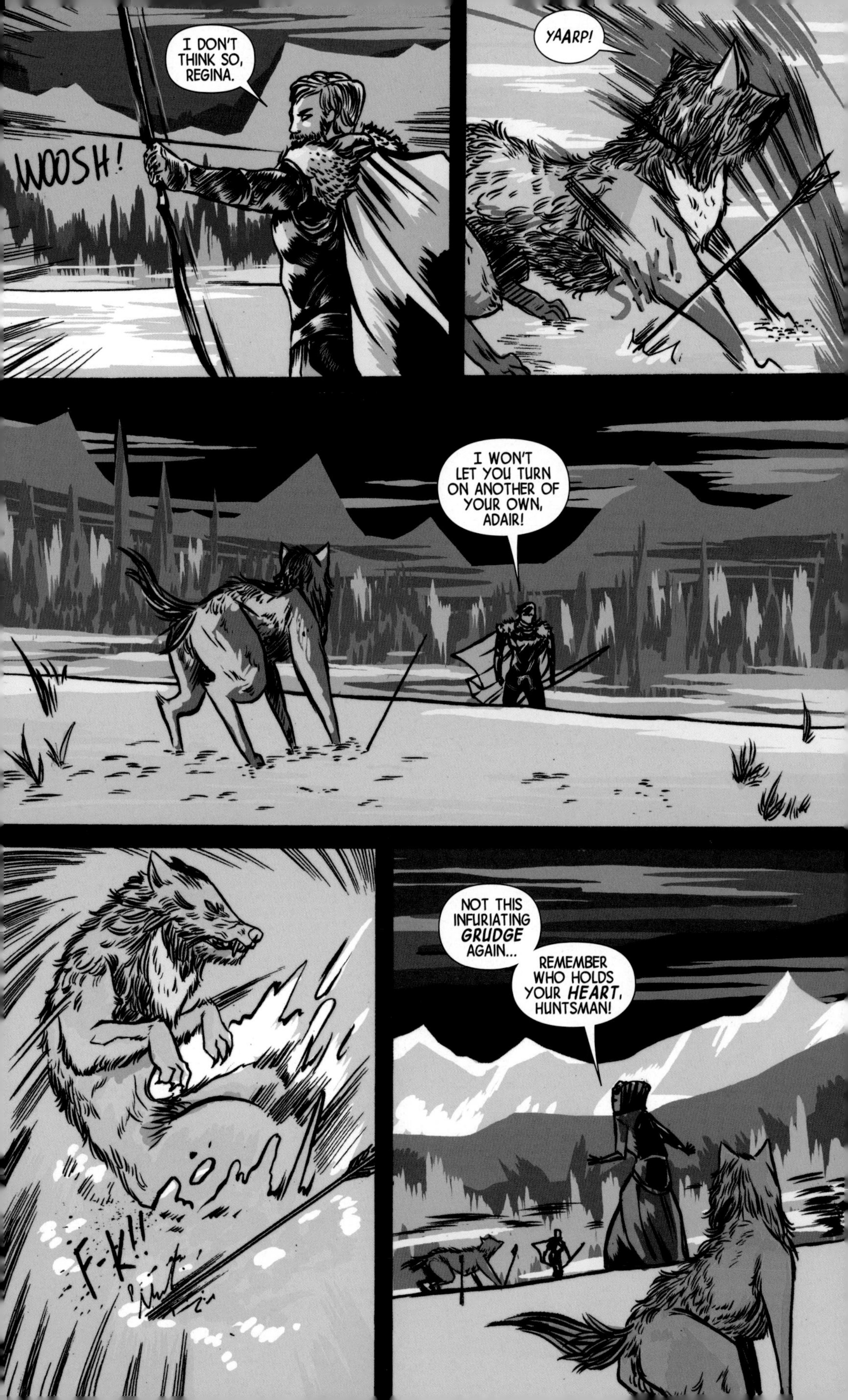
I DON'T THINK SO, REGINA.
WOOSH!
YAARP!
SHK!
I WON'T LET YOU TURN ON ANOTHER OF YOUR OWN, ADAIR!
F-K!!
NOT THIS INFURIATING GRUDGE AGAIN...
REMEMBER WHO HOLDS YOUR HEART, HUNTSMAN!

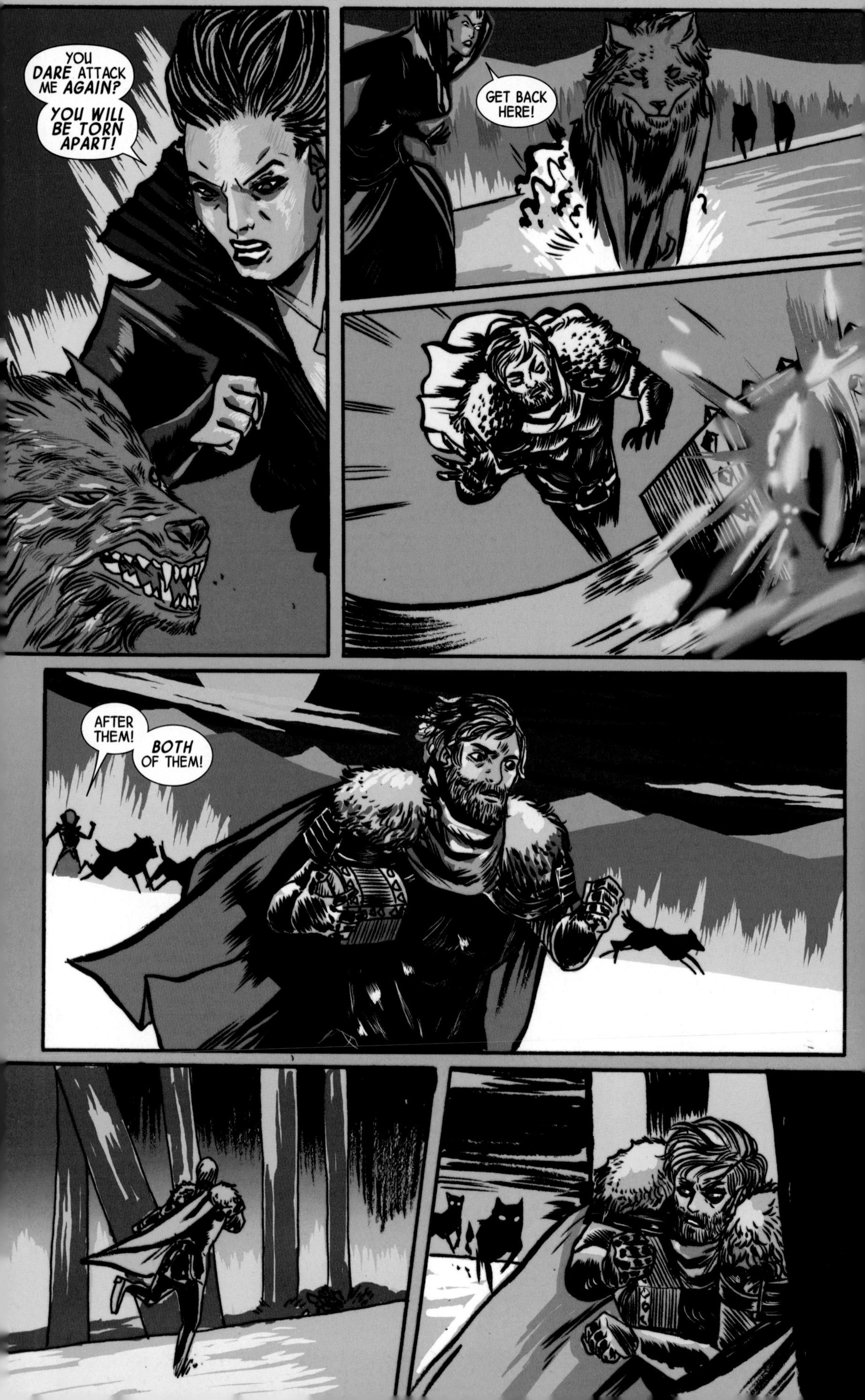
YOU DARE ATTACK ME AGAIN?
YOU WILL BE TORN APART!
GET BACK HERE!
AFTER THEM!
BOTH OF THEM!

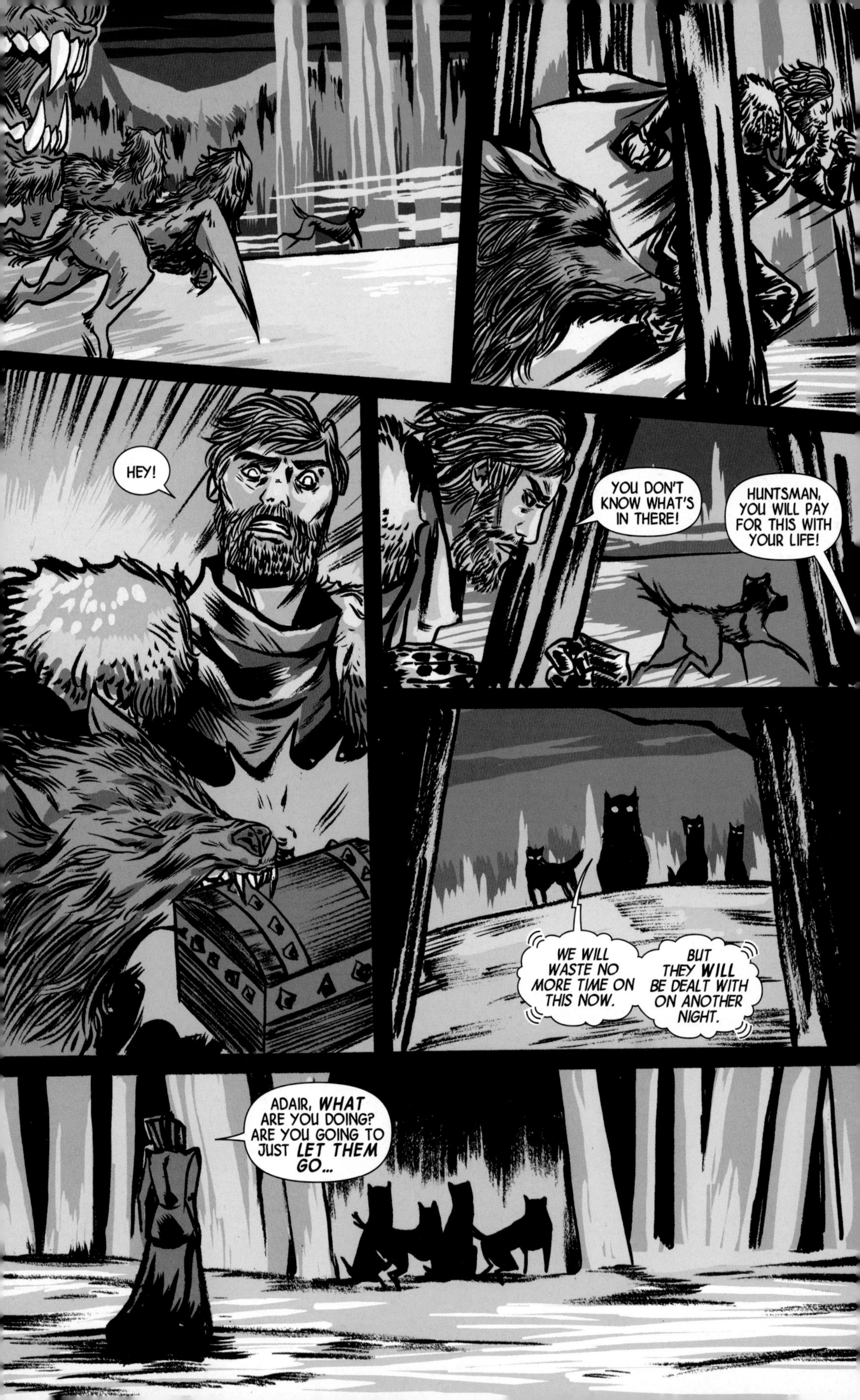
HEY!
YOU DON'T KNOW WHAT'S IN THERE!
HUNTSMAN, YOU WILL PAY FOR THIS WITH YOUR LIFE!
WE WILL WASTE NO MORE TIME ON THIS NOW.
BUT THEY WILL BE DEALT WITH ON ANOTHER NIGHT.
ADAIR, WHAT ARE YOU DOING? ARE YOU GOING TO JUST LET THEM GO...

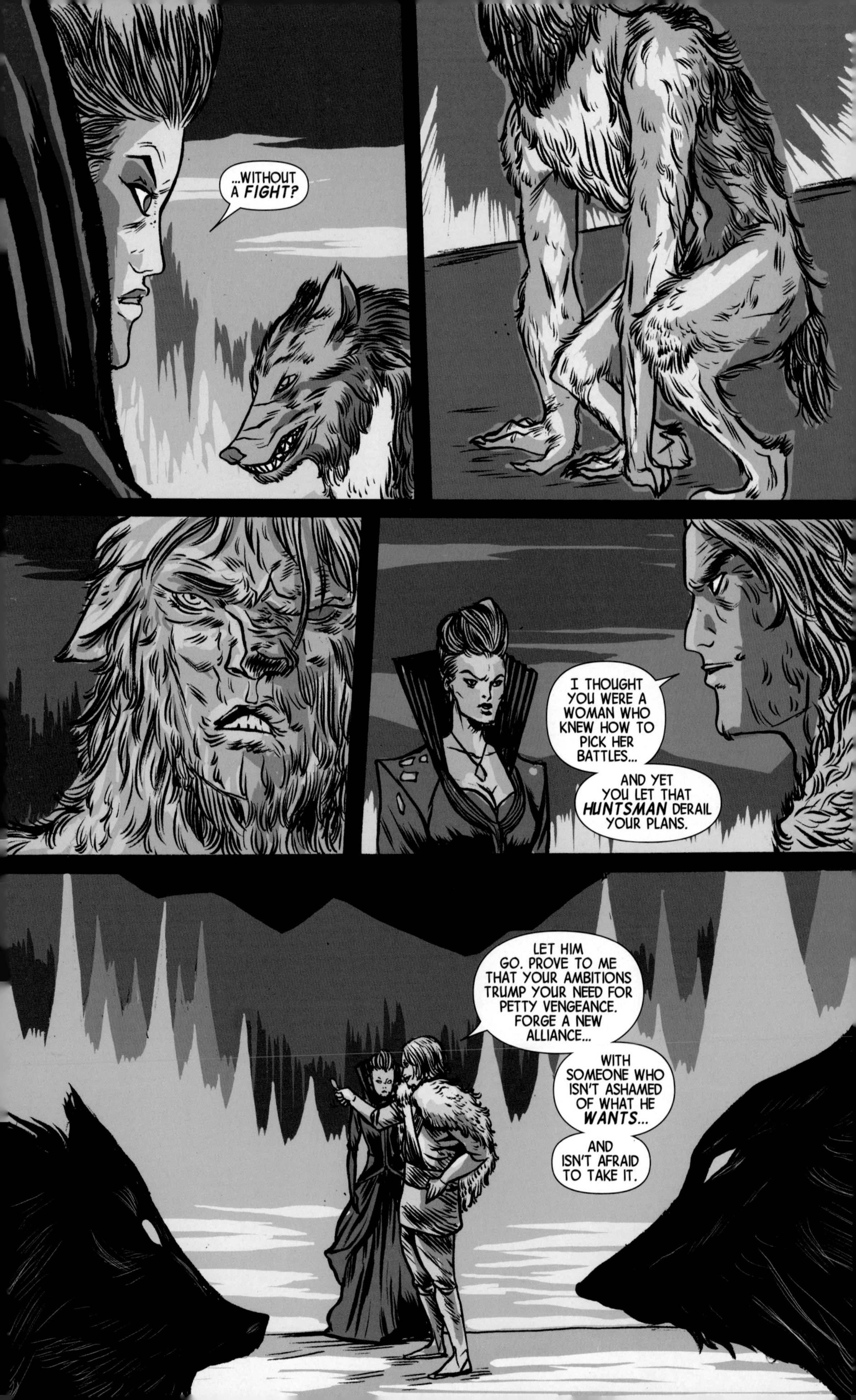
...WITHOUT A FIGHT?
I THOUGHT YOU WERE A WOMAN WHO KNEW HOW TO PICK HER BATTLES...
AND YET YOU LET THAT HUNTSMAN DERAIL YOUR PLANS.
LET HIM GO. PROVE TO ME THAT YOUR AMBITIONS TRUMP YOUR NEED FOR PETTY VENGEANCE. FORGE A NEW ALLIANCE...
WITH SOMEONE WHO ISN'T ASHAMED OF WHAT HE WANTS...
AND ISN'T AFRAID TO TAKE IT.

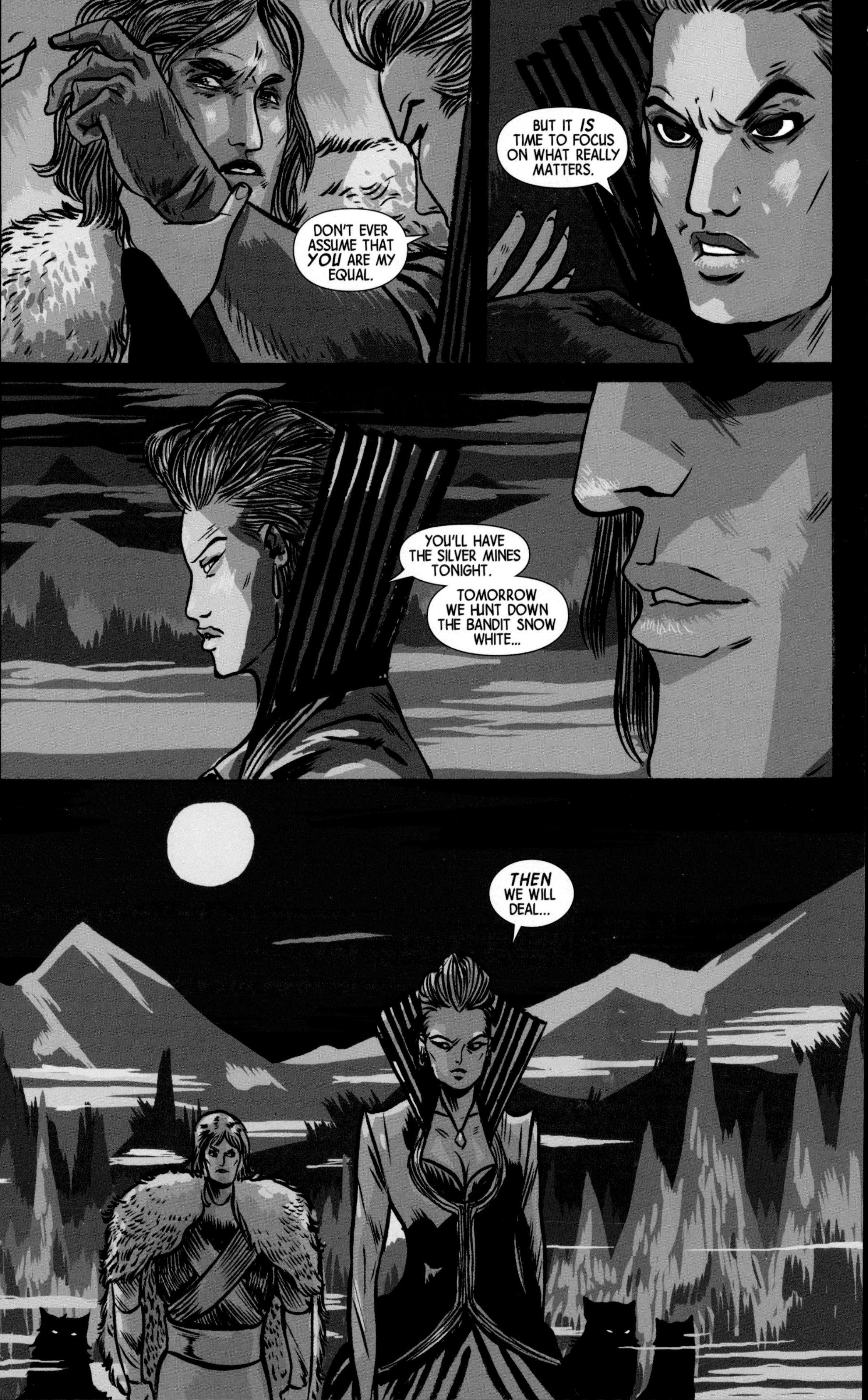
DON'T EVER ASSUME THAT *YOU* ARE MY EQUAL.
BUT IT *IS* TIME TO FOCUS ON WHAT REALLY MATTERS.
YOU'LL HAVE THE SILVER MINES TONIGHT.
TOMORROW WE HUNT DOWN THE BANDIT SNOW WHITE...
THEN WE WILL DEAL...

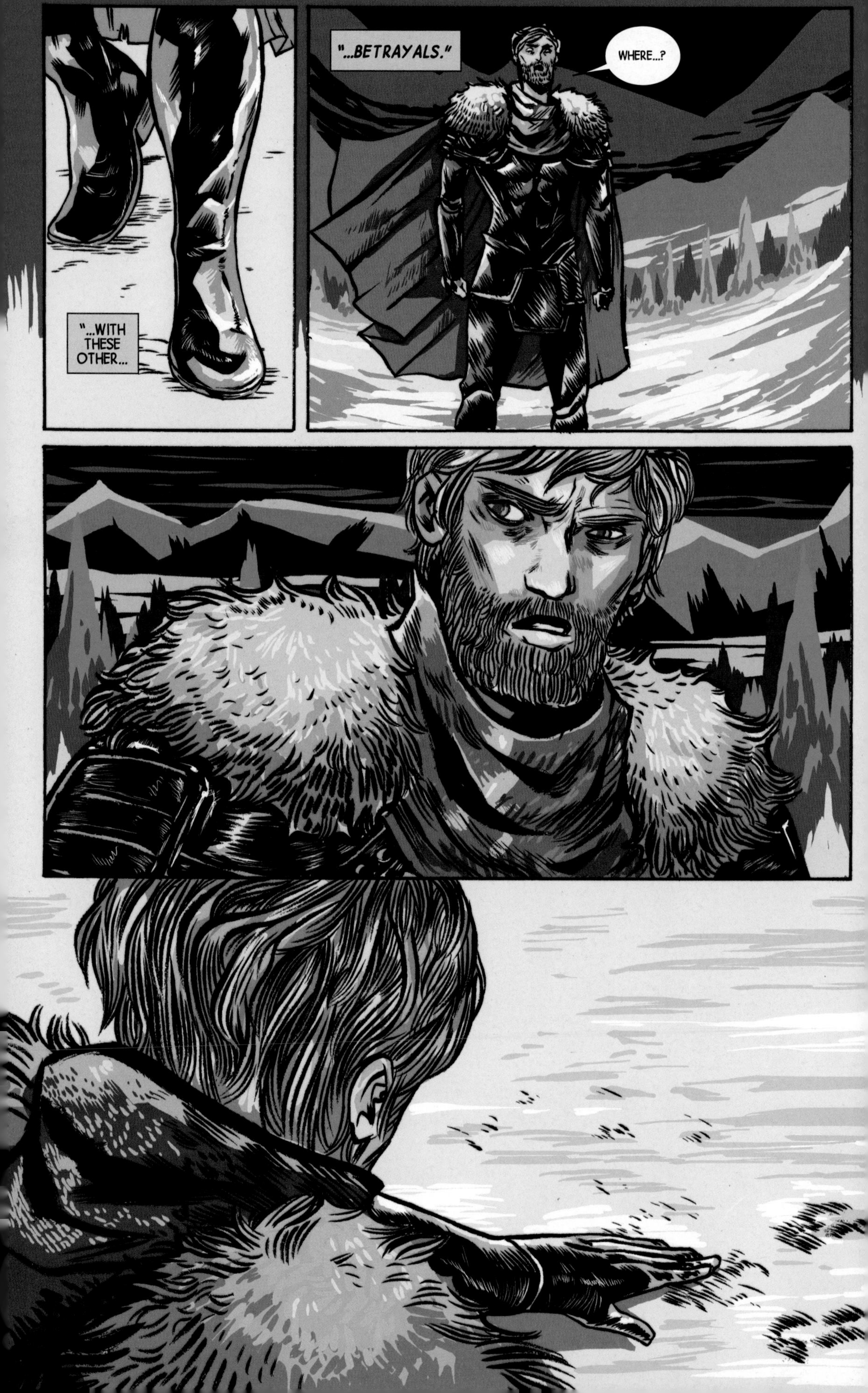
"...WITH THESE OTHER...
"...BETRAYALS."
WHERE...?

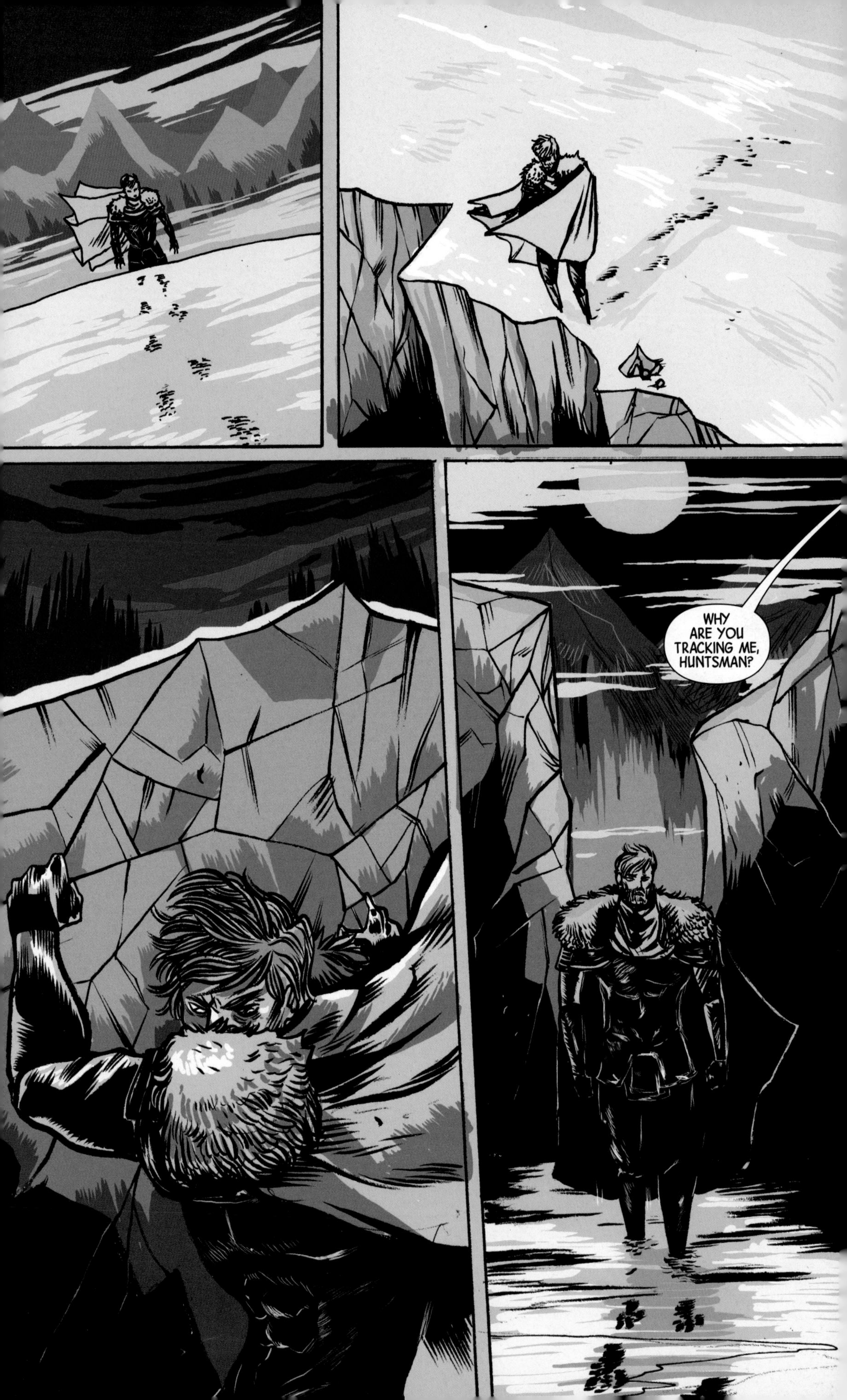
WHY ARE YOU TRACKING ME, HUNTSMAN?

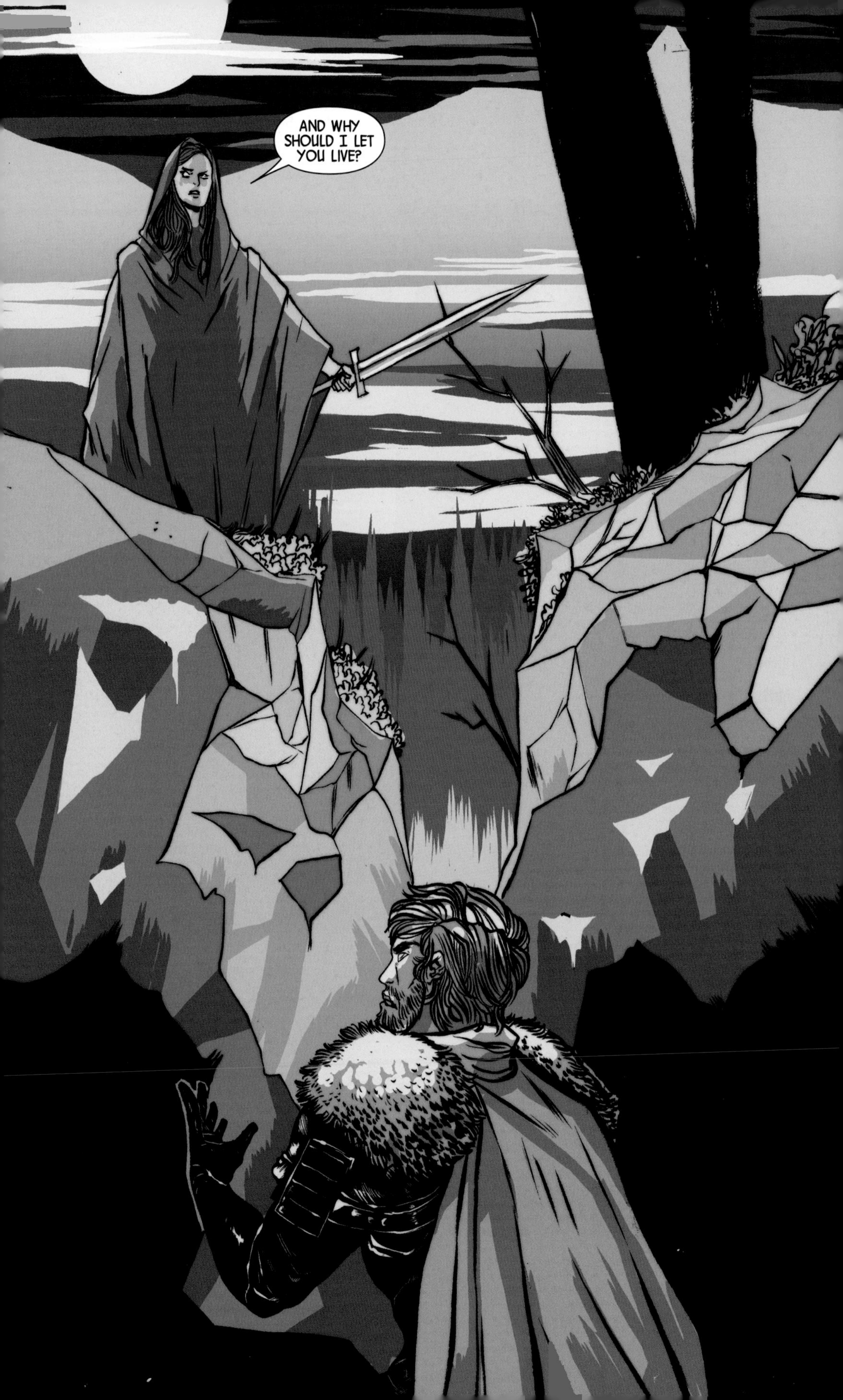
AND WHY SHOULD I LET YOU LIVE?

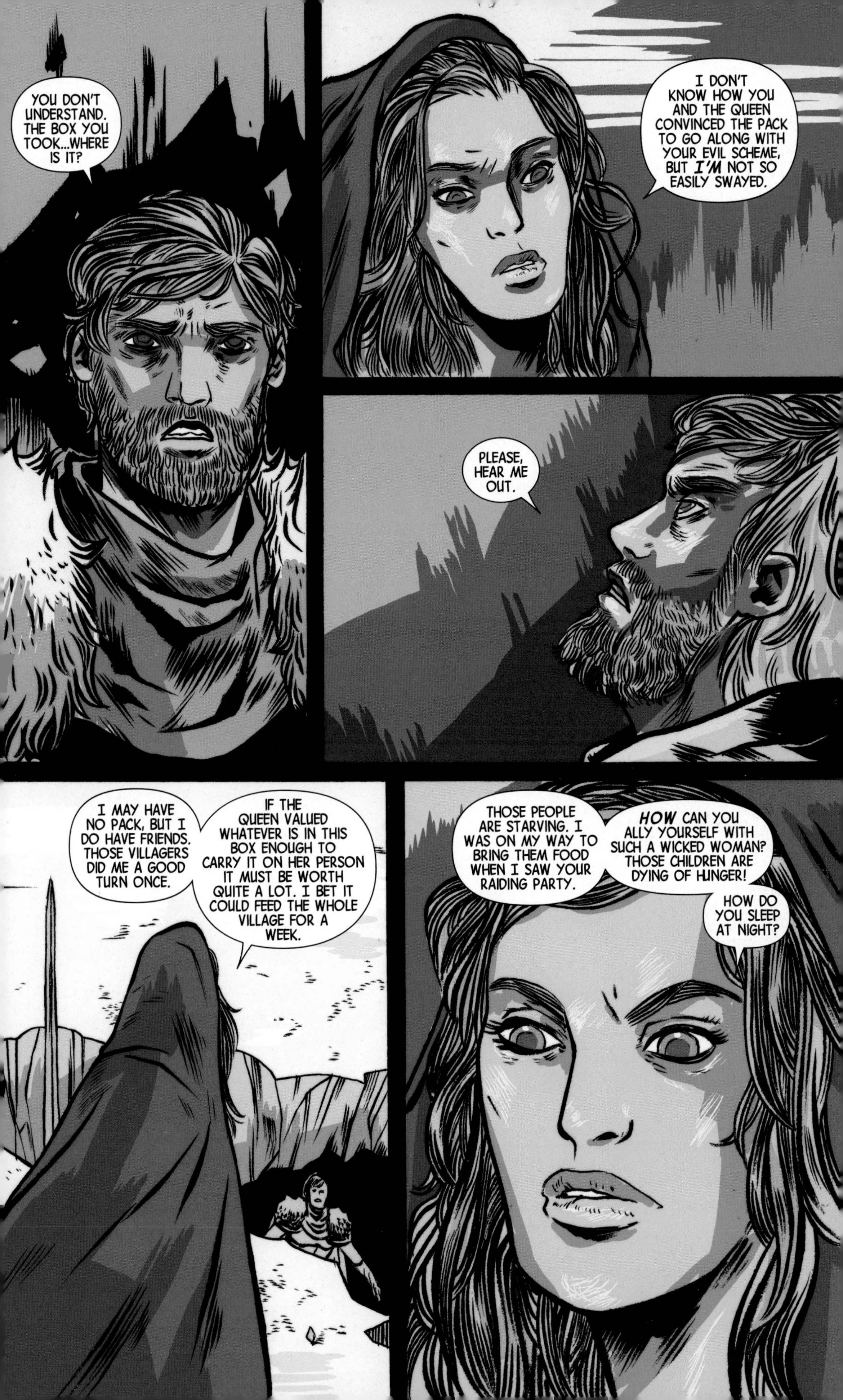
YOU DON'T UNDERSTAND. THE BOX YOU TOOK...WHERE IS IT?
I DON'T KNOW HOW YOU AND THE QUEEN CONVINCED THE PACK TO GO ALONG WITH YOUR EVIL SCHEME, BUT I'M NOT SO EASILY SWAYED.
PLEASE, HEAR ME OUT.
I MAY HAVE NO PACK, BUT I DO HAVE FRIENDS. THOSE VILLAGERS DID ME A GOOD TURN ONCE.
IF THE QUEEN VALUED WHATEVER IS IN THIS BOX ENOUGH TO CARRY IT ON HER PERSON IT MUST BE WORTH QUITE A LOT. I BET IT COULD FEED THE WHOLE VILLAGE FOR A WEEK.
THOSE PEOPLE ARE STARVING. I WAS ON MY WAY TO BRING THEM FOOD WHEN I SAW YOUR RAIDING PARTY.
HOW CAN YOU ALLY YOURSELF WITH SUCH A WICKED WOMAN? THOSE CHILDREN ARE DYING OF HUNGER!
HOW DO YOU SLEEP AT NIGHT?

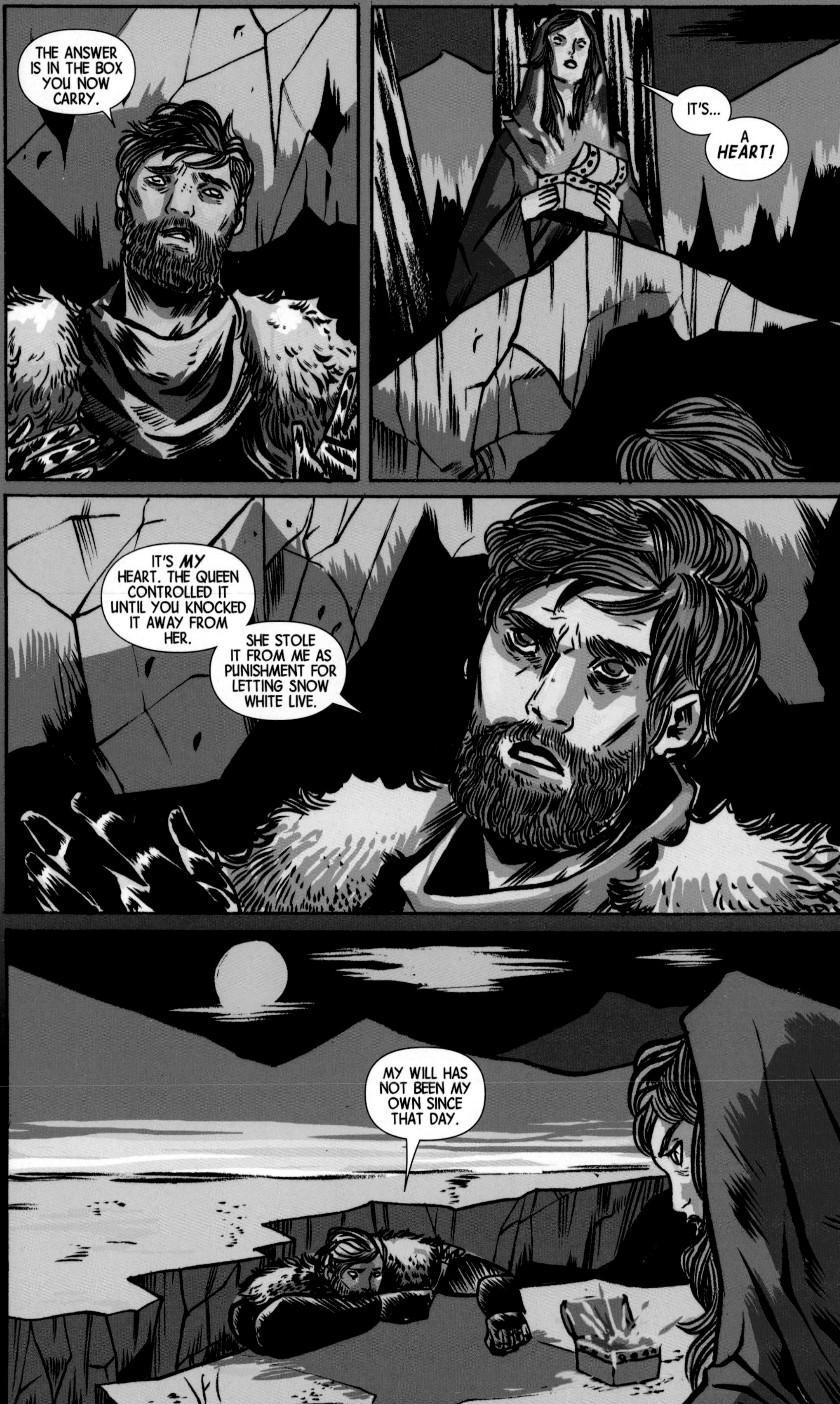
THE ANSWER IS IN THE BOX YOU NOW CARRY.
IT'S...
A HEART!
IT'S MY HEART. THE QUEEN CONTROLLED IT UNTIL YOU KNOCKED IT AWAY FROM HER.
SHE STOLE IT FROM ME AS PUNISHMENT FOR LETTING SNOW WHITE LIVE.
MY WILL HAS NOT BEEN MY OWN SINCE THAT DAY.

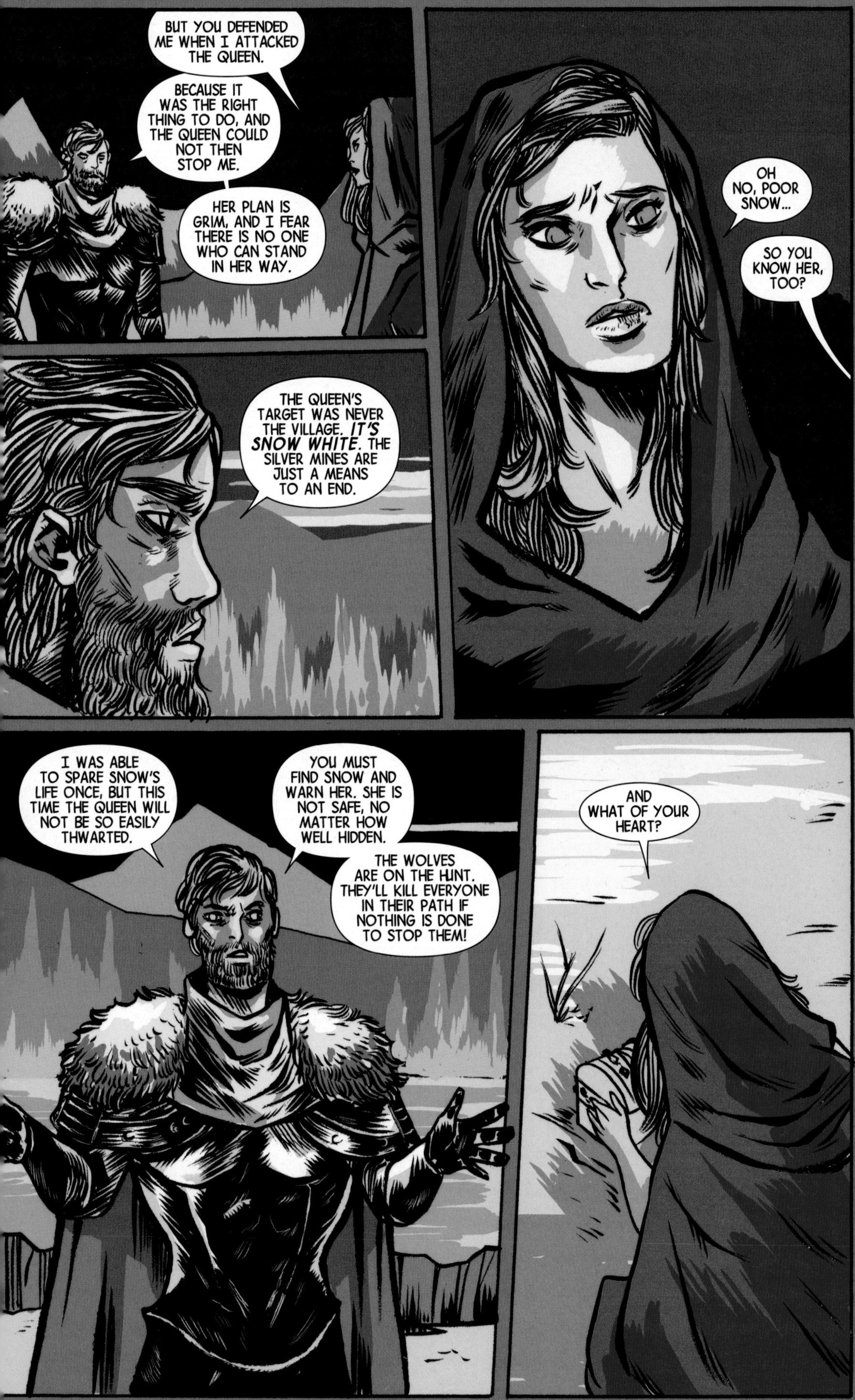
BUT YOU DEFENDED ME WHEN I ATTACKED THE QUEEN.
BECAUSE IT WAS THE RIGHT THING TO DO, AND THE QUEEN COULD NOT THEN STOP ME.
HER PLAN IS GRIM, AND I FEAR THERE IS NO ONE WHO CAN STAND IN HER WAY.
OH NO, POOR SNOW...
SO YOU KNOW HER, TOO?
THE QUEEN'S TARGET WAS NEVER THE VILLAGE. *IT'S SNOW WHITE.* THE SILVER MINES ARE JUST A MEANS TO AN END.
I WAS ABLE TO SPARE SNOW'S LIFE ONCE, BUT THIS TIME THE QUEEN WILL NOT BE SO EASILY THWARTED.
YOU MUST FIND SNOW AND WARN HER. SHE IS NOT SAFE, NO MATTER HOW WELL HIDDEN.
THE WOLVES ARE ON THE HUNT. THEY'LL KILL EVERYONE IN THEIR PATH IF NOTHING IS DONE TO STOP THEM!
AND WHAT OF YOUR HEART?

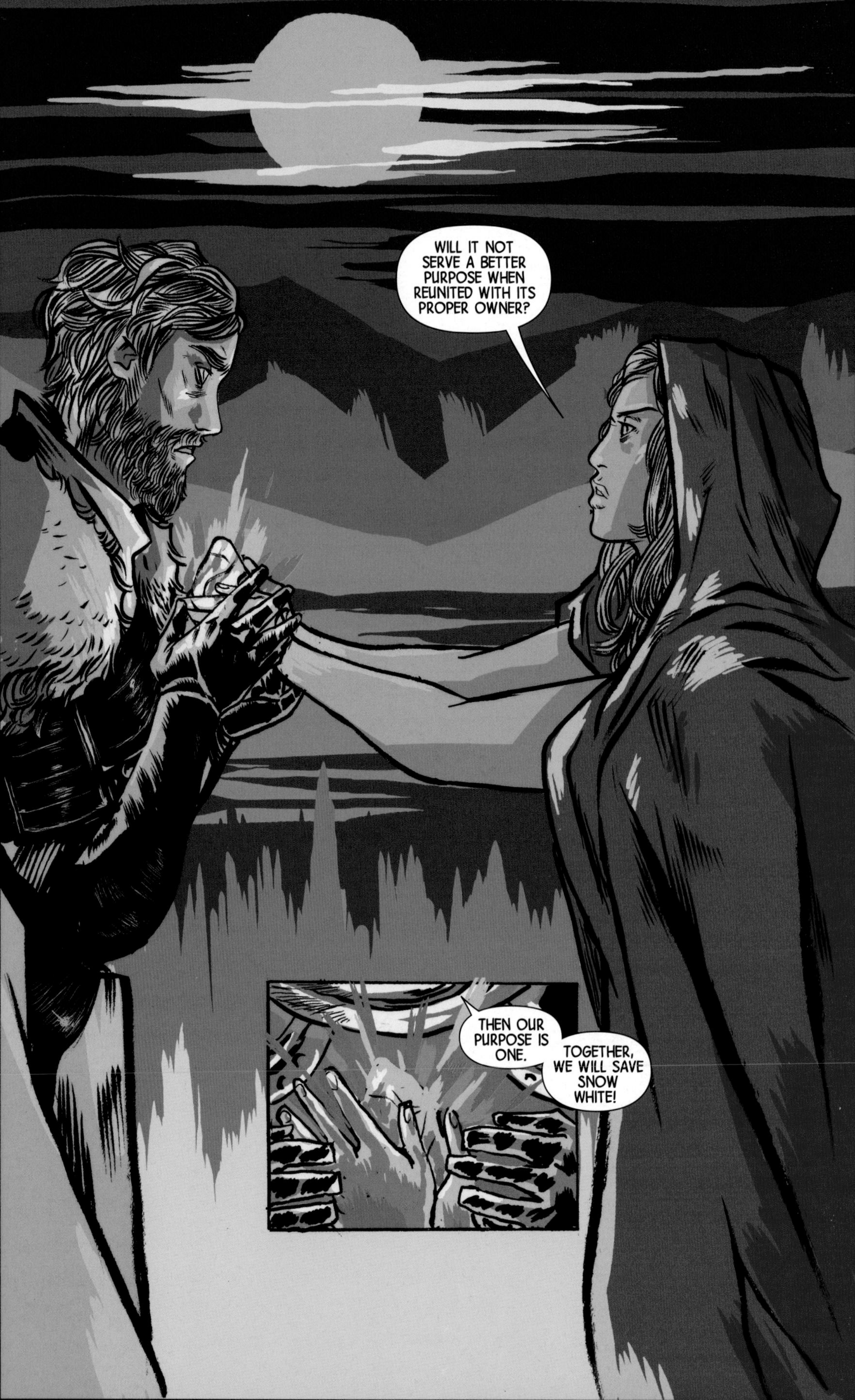
WILL IT NOT SERVE A BETTER PURPOSE WHEN REUNITED WITH ITS PROPER OWNER?
THEN OUR PURPOSE IS ONE.
TOGETHER, WE WILL SAVE SNOW WHITE!

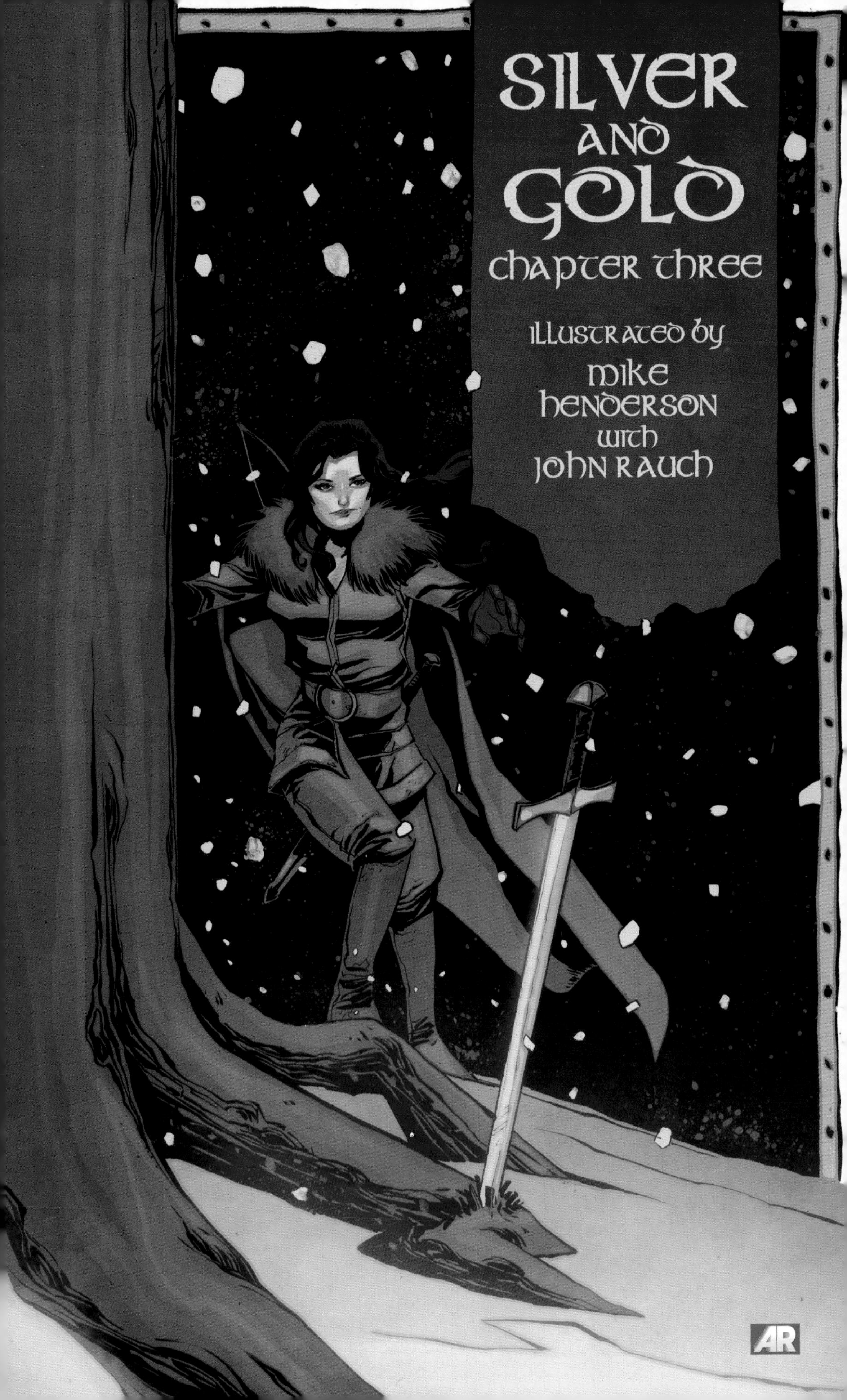
SILVER AND GOLD
CHAPTER THREE
ILLUSTRATED BY
MIKE HENDERSON
WITH
JOHN RAUCH
AR

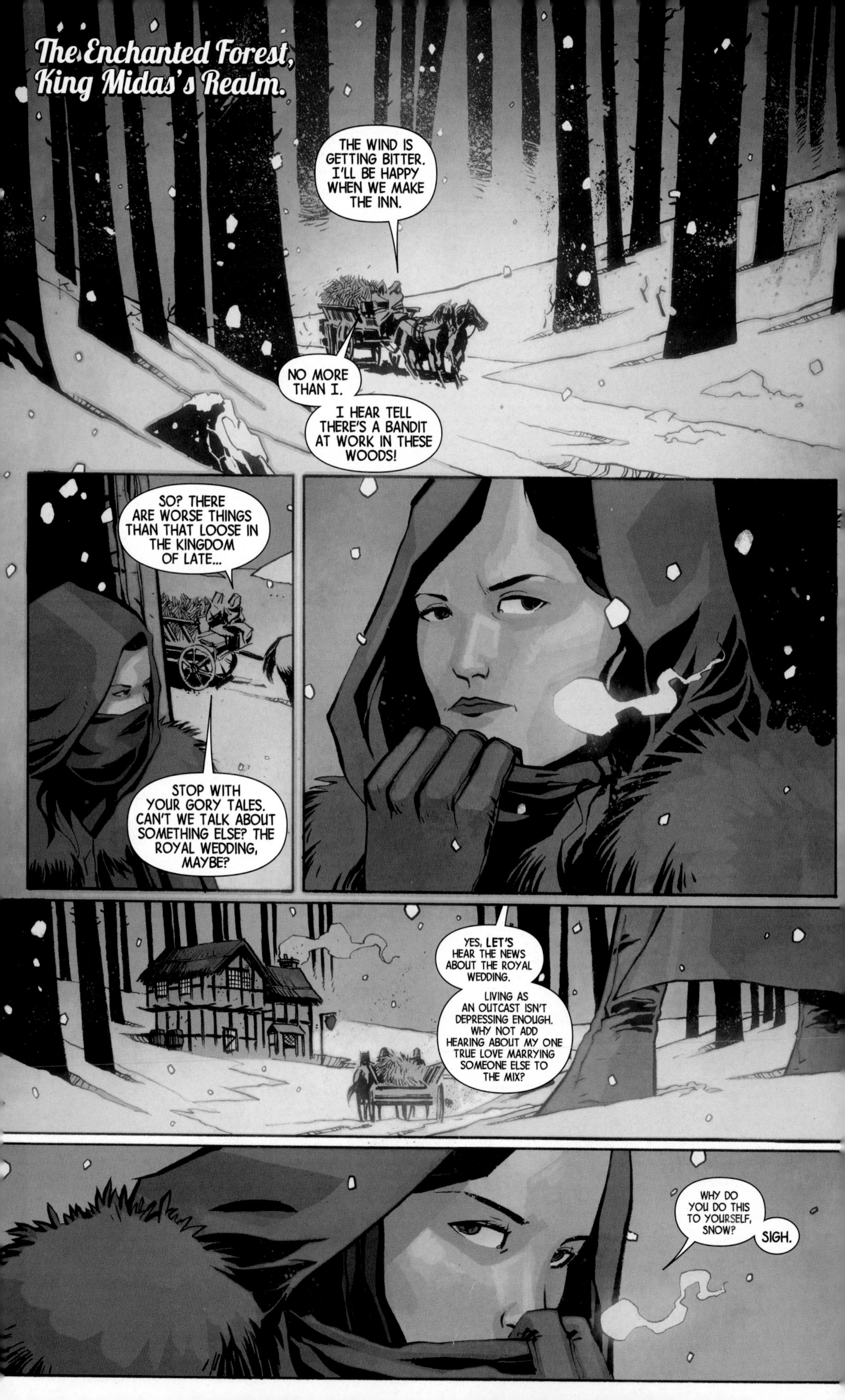
The Enchanted Forest, King Midas's Realm.
THE WIND IS GETTING BITTER. I'LL BE HAPPY WHEN WE MAKE THE INN.
NO MORE THAN I.
I HEAR TELL THERE'S A BANDIT AT WORK IN THESE WOODS!
SO? THERE ARE WORSE THINGS THAN THAT LOOSE IN THE KINGDOM OF LATE...
STOP WITH YOUR GORY TALES. CAN'T WE TALK ABOUT SOMETHING ELSE? THE ROYAL WEDDING, MAYBE?
YES, LET'S HEAR THE NEWS ABOUT THE ROYAL WEDDING.
LIVING AS AN OUTCAST ISN'T DEPRESSING ENOUGH. WHY NOT ADD HEARING ABOUT MY ONE TRUE LOVE MARRYING SOMEONE ELSE TO THE MIX?
WHY DO YOU DO THIS TO YOURSELF, SNOW?
SIGH.

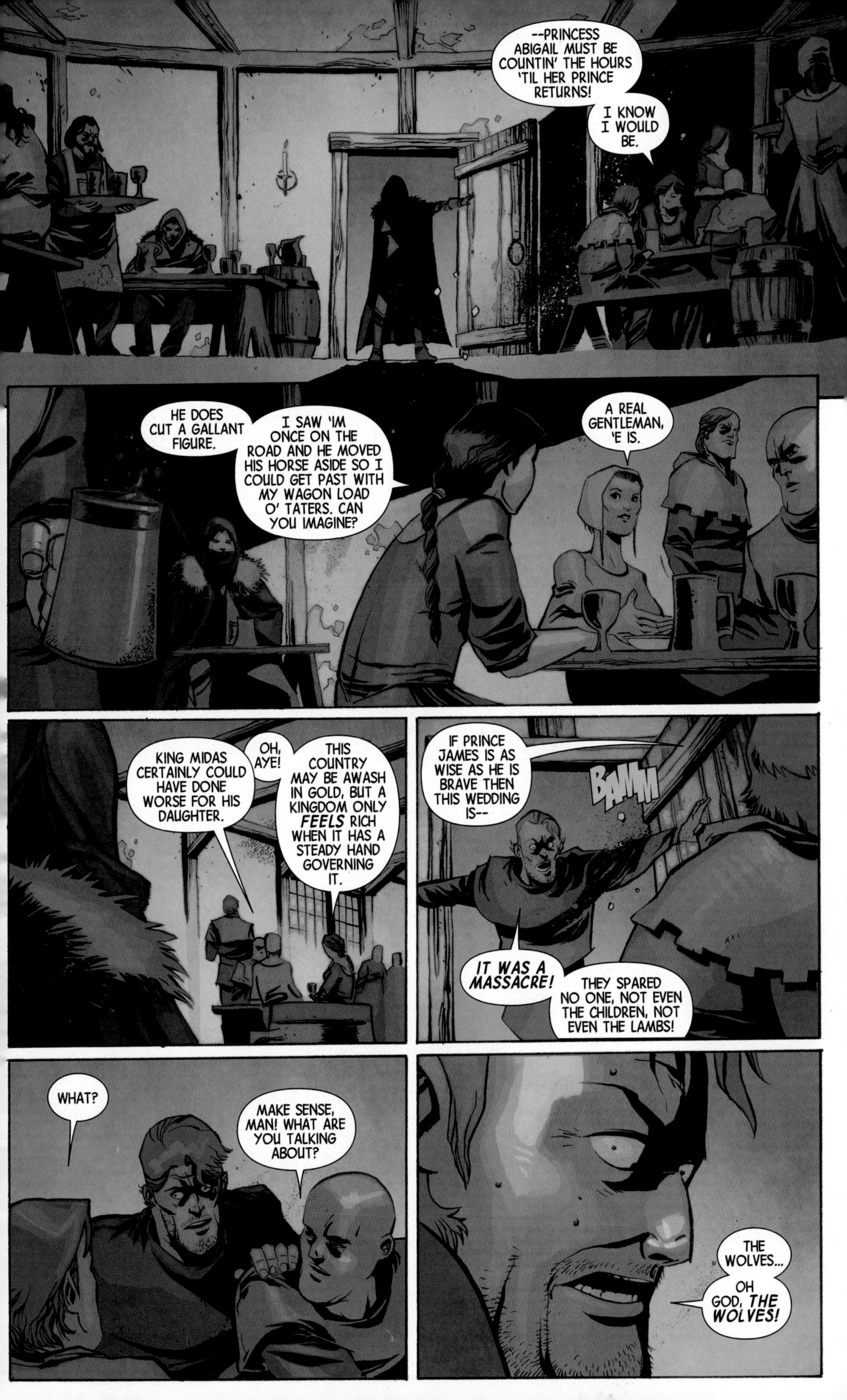
--PRINCESS ABIGAIL MUST BE COUNTIN' THE HOURS 'TIL HER PRINCE RETURNS!
I KNOW I WOULD BE.
HE DOES CUT A GALLANT FIGURE.
I SAW 'IM ONCE ON THE ROAD AND HE MOVED HIS HORSE ASIDE SO I COULD GET PAST WITH MY WAGON LOAD O' TATERS. CAN YOU IMAGINE?
A REAL GENTLEMAN, 'E IS.
KING MIDAS CERTAINLY COULD HAVE DONE WORSE FOR HIS DAUGHTER.
OH, AYE!
THIS COUNTRY MAY BE AWASH IN GOLD, BUT A KINGDOM ONLY FEELS RICH WHEN IT HAS A STEADY HAND GOVERNING IT.
IF PRINCE JAMES IS AS WISE AS HE IS BRAVE THEN THIS WEDDING IS--
BAMM
IT WAS A MASSACRE!
THEY SPARED NO ONE, NOT EVEN THE CHILDREN, NOT EVEN THE LAMBS!
WHAT?
MAKE SENSE, MAN! WHAT ARE YOU TALKING ABOUT?
THE WOLVES...
OH GOD, THE WOLVES!

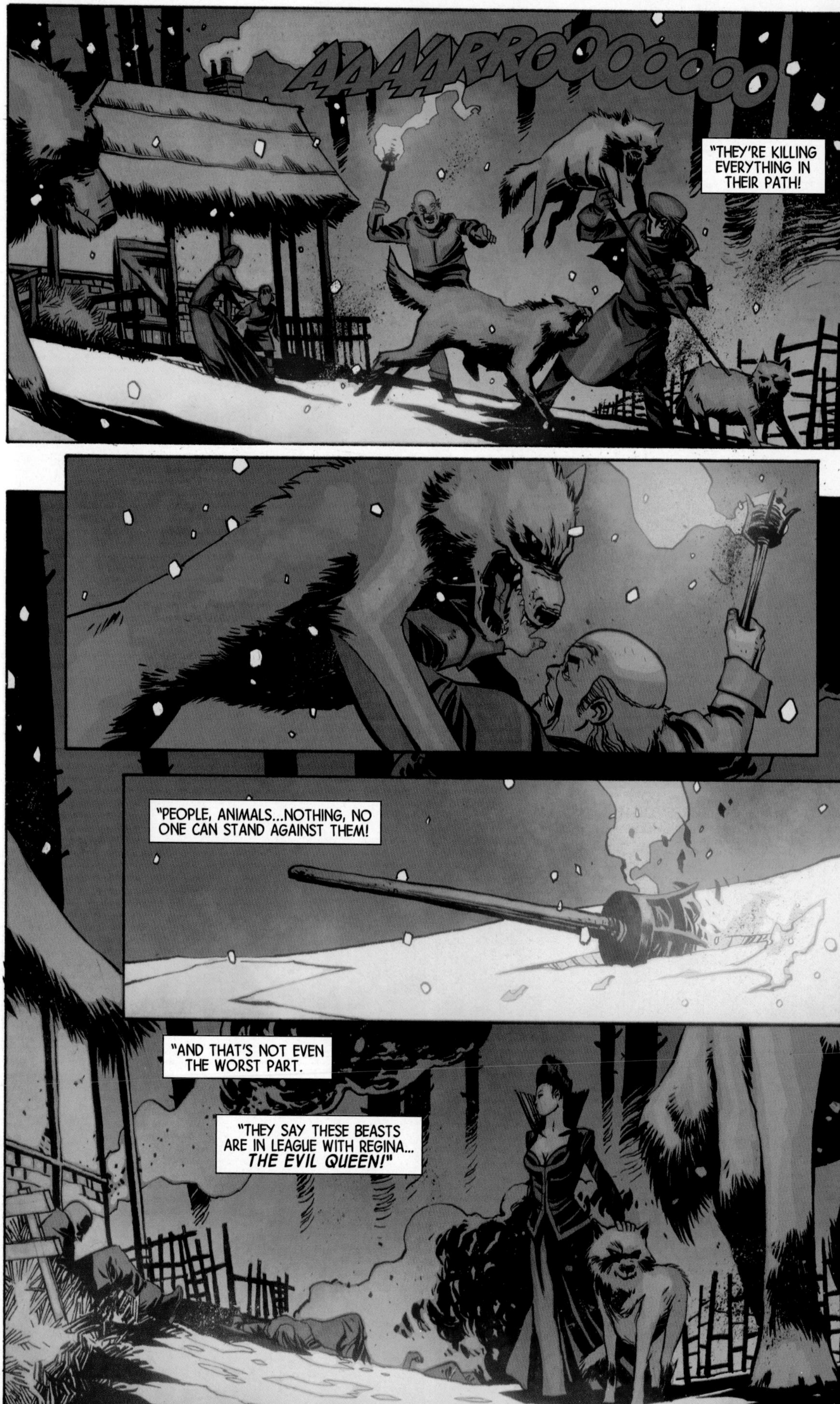
AAAARROOOOOOOO
"THEY'RE KILLING EVERYTHING IN THEIR PATH!
"PEOPLE, ANIMALS...NOTHING, NO ONE CAN STAND AGAINST THEM!
"AND THAT'S NOT EVEN THE WORST PART.
"THEY SAY THESE BEASTS ARE IN LEAGUE WITH REGINA... THE EVIL QUEEN!"

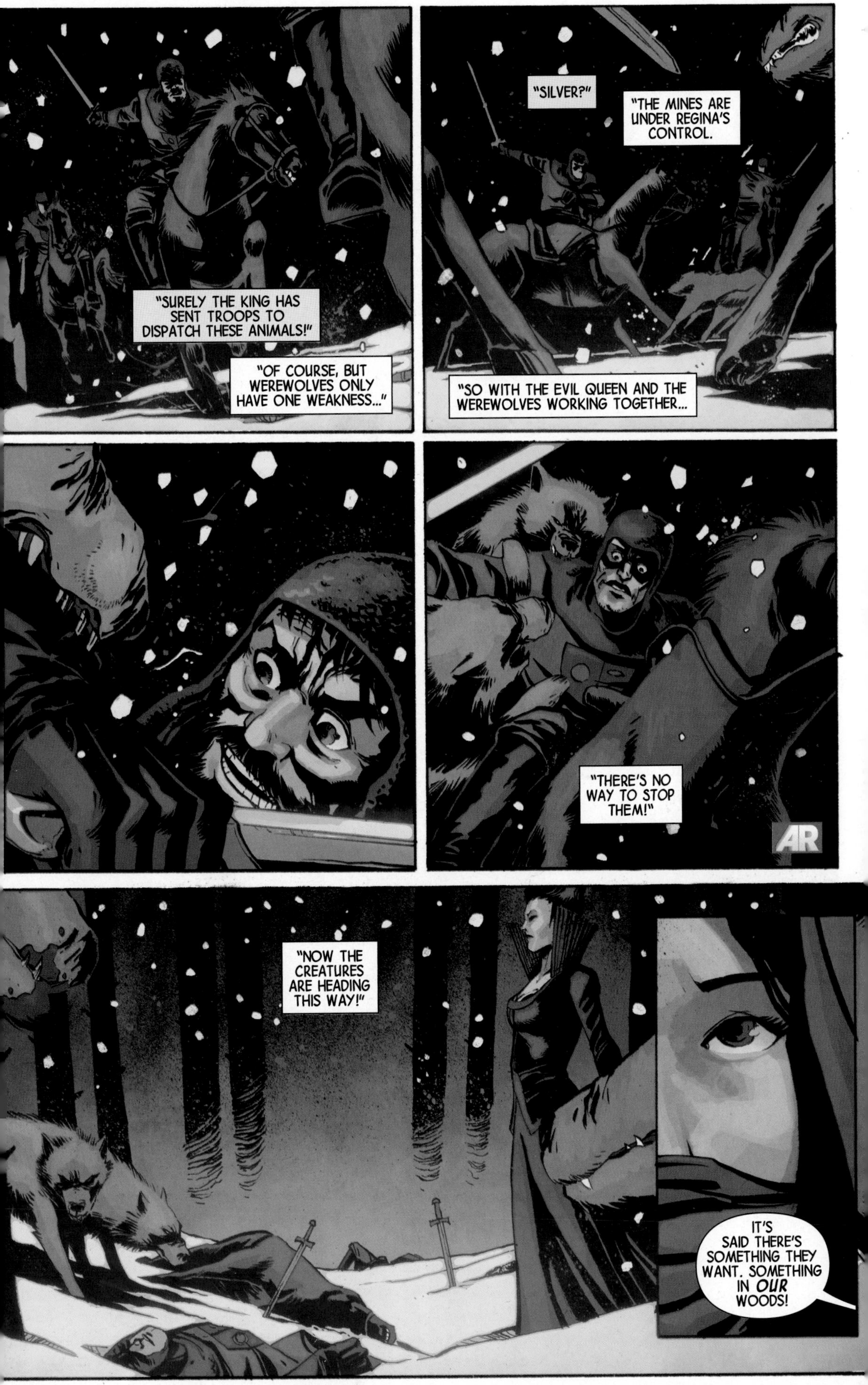
"SURELY THE KING HAS SENT TROOPS TO DISPATCH THESE ANIMALS!"
"OF COURSE, BUT WEREWOLVES ONLY HAVE ONE WEAKNESS..."
"SILVER?"
"THE MINES ARE UNDER REGINA'S CONTROL.
"SO WITH THE EVIL QUEEN AND THE WEREWOLVES WORKING TOGETHER...
"THERE'S NO WAY TO STOP THEM!"
"NOW THE CREATURES ARE HEADING THIS WAY!"
IT'S SAID THERE'S SOMETHING THEY WANT. SOMETHING IN OUR WOODS!

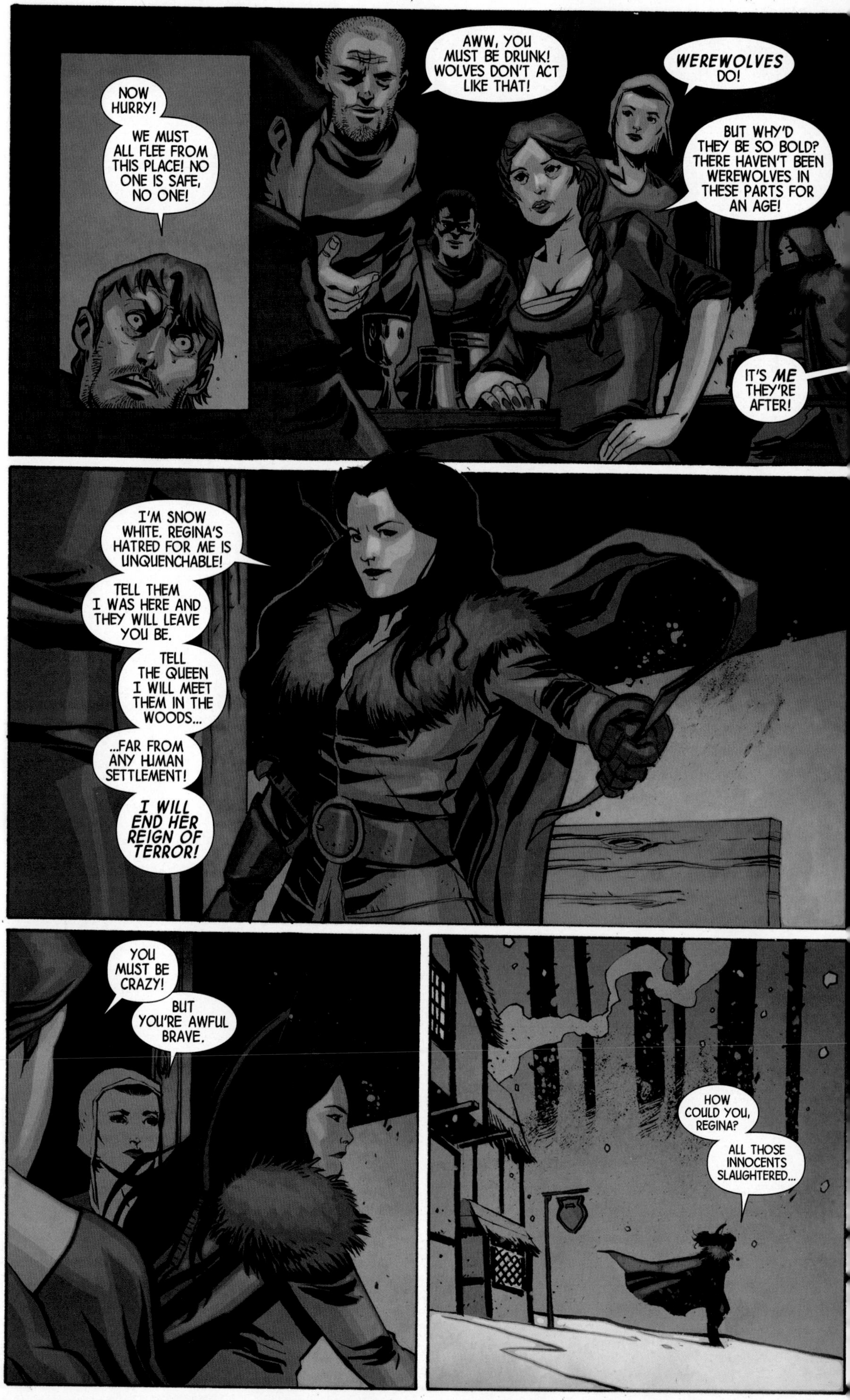
NOW HURRY!
WE MUST ALL FLEE FROM THIS PLACE! NO ONE IS SAFE, NO ONE!
AWW, YOU MUST BE DRUNK! WOLVES DON'T ACT LIKE THAT!
WEREWOLVES DO!
BUT WHY'D THEY BE SO BOLD? THERE HAVEN'T BEEN WEREWOLVES IN THESE PARTS FOR AN AGE!
IT'S ME THEY'RE AFTER!
I'M SNOW WHITE. REGINA'S HATRED FOR ME IS UNQUENCHABLE!
TELL THEM I WAS HERE AND THEY WILL LEAVE YOU BE.
TELL THE QUEEN I WILL MEET THEM IN THE WOODS...
...FAR FROM ANY HUMAN SETTLEMENT!
I WILL END HER REIGN OF TERROR!
YOU MUST BE CRAZY!
BUT YOU'RE AWFUL BRAVE.
HOW COULD YOU, REGINA?
ALL THOSE INNOCENTS SLAUGHTERED...

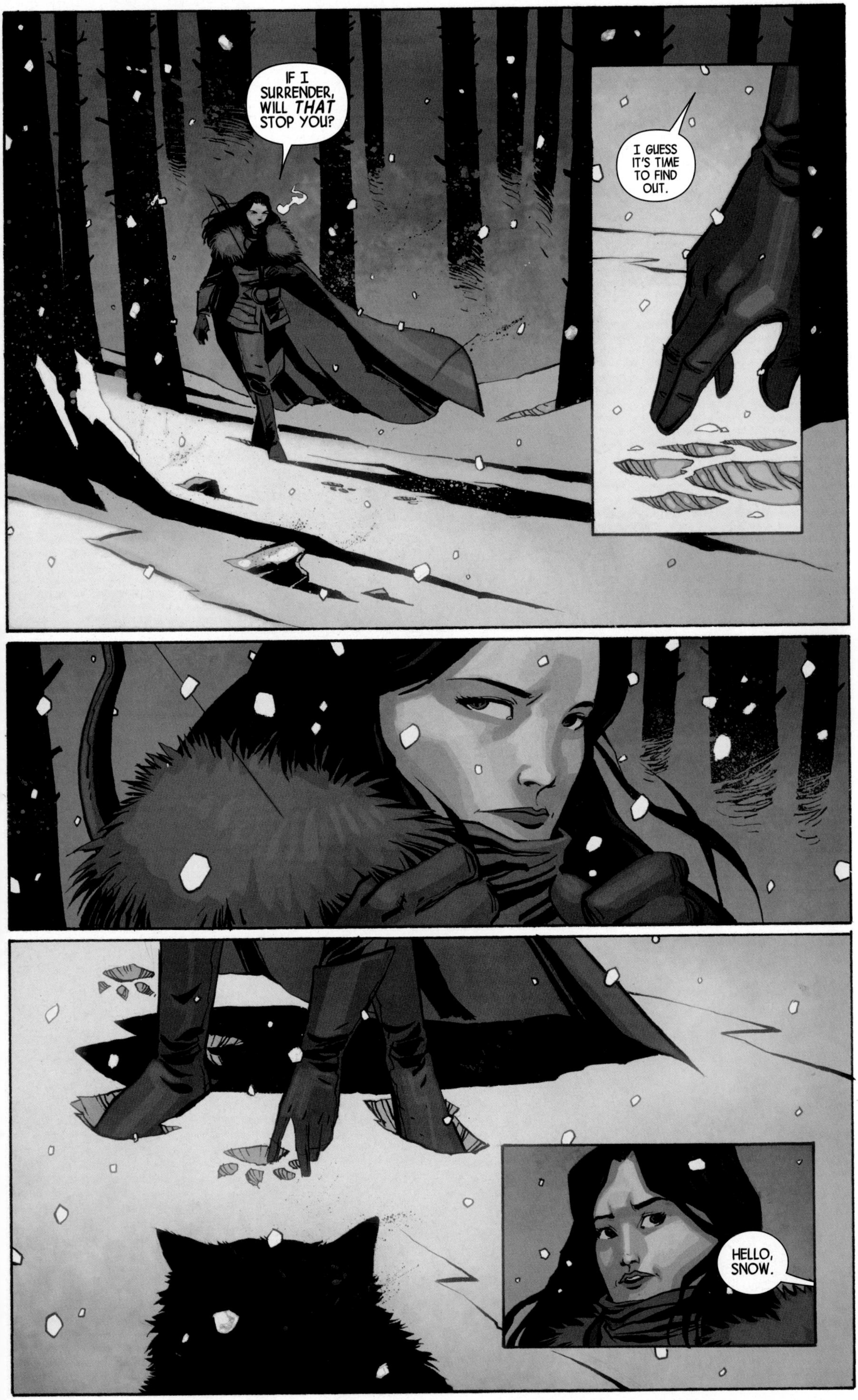
IF I SURRENDER, WILL *THAT* STOP YOU?
I GUESS IT'S TIME TO FIND OUT.
HELLO, SNOW.

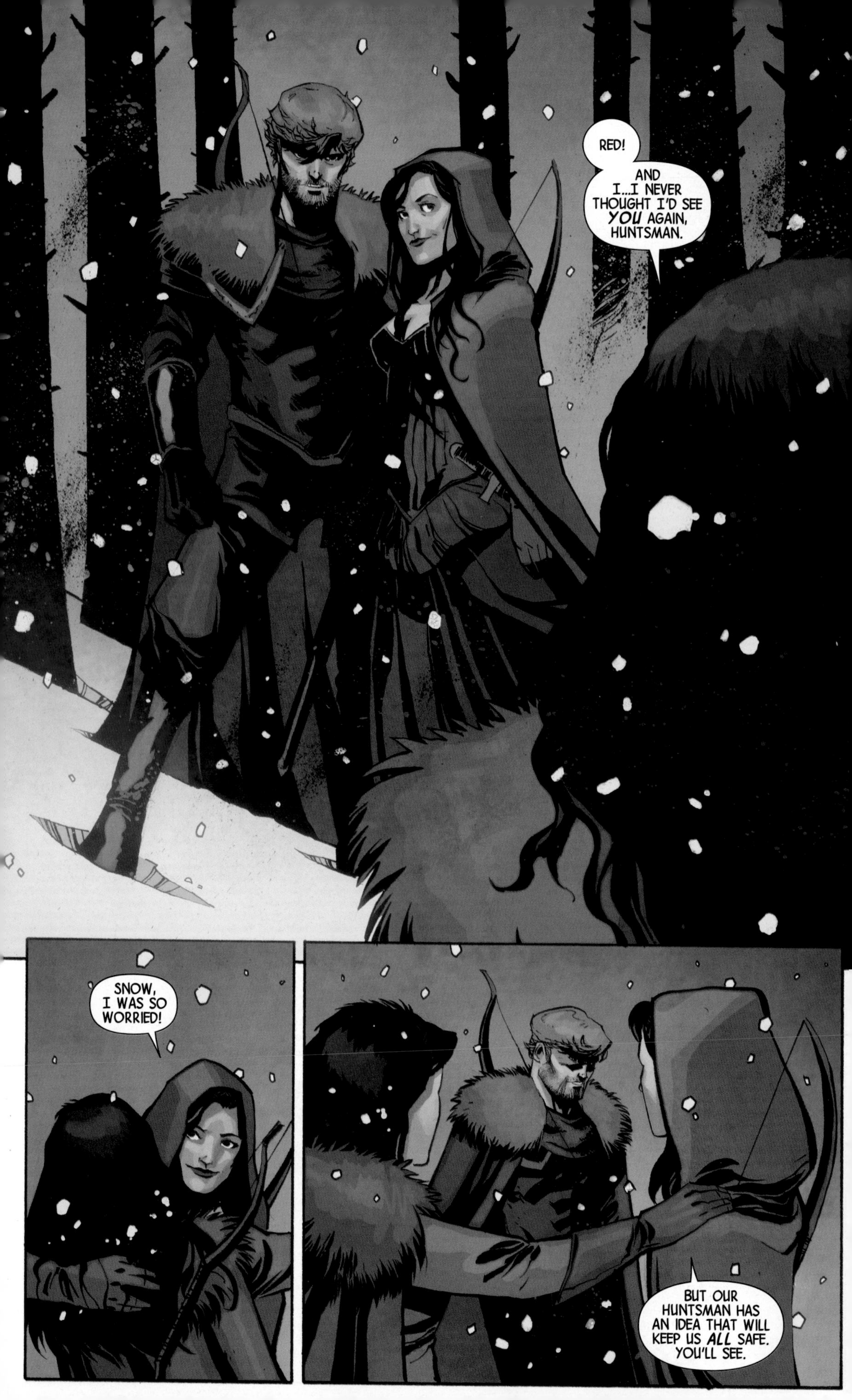
RED!
AND I...I NEVER THOUGHT I'D SEE *YOU* AGAIN, HUNTSMAN.
SNOW, I WAS SO WORRIED!
BUT OUR HUNTSMAN HAS AN IDEA THAT WILL KEEP US *ALL* SAFE. YOU'LL SEE.

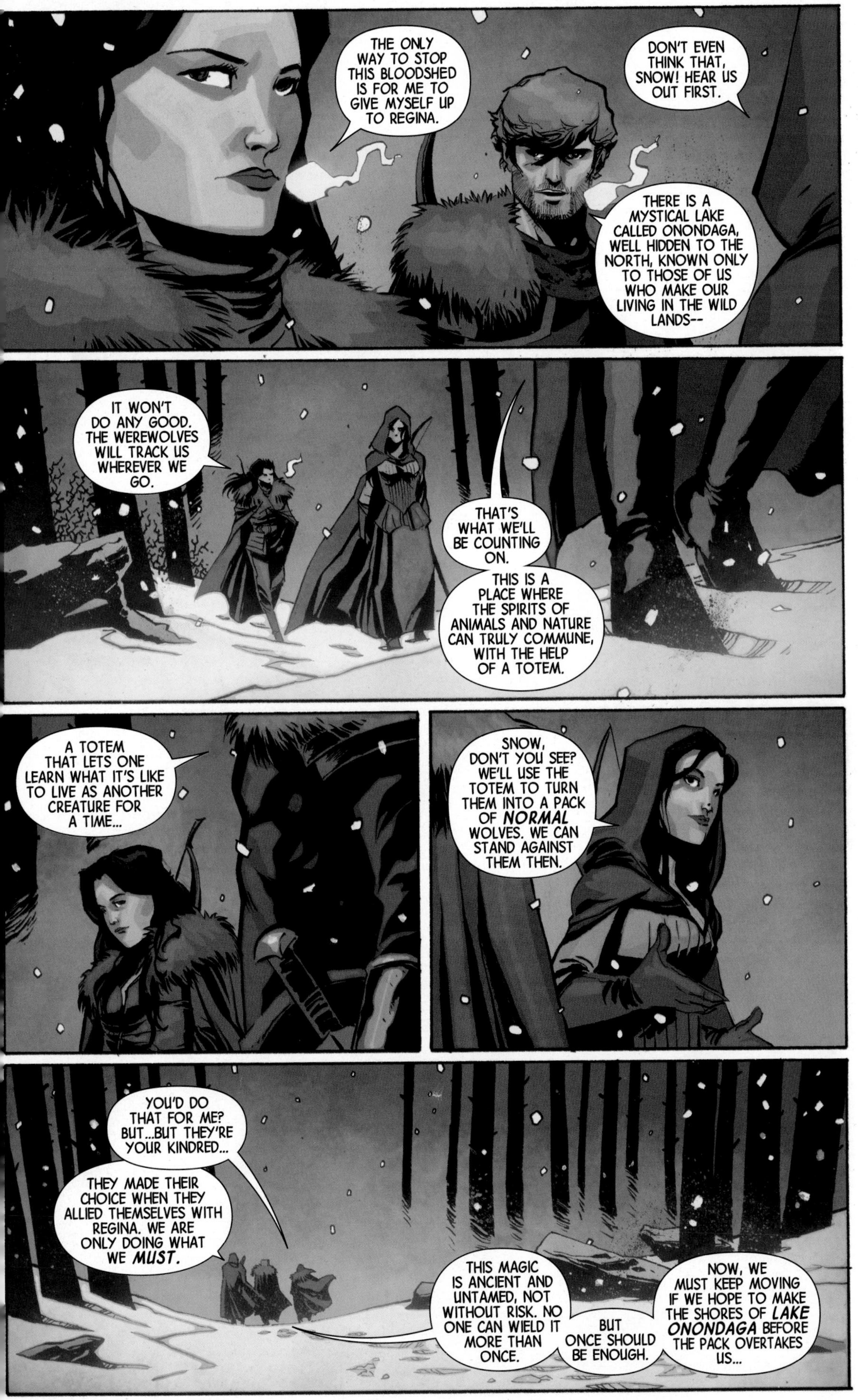
THE ONLY WAY TO STOP THIS BLOODSHED IS FOR ME TO GIVE MYSELF UP TO REGINA.
DON'T EVEN THINK THAT, SNOW! HEAR US OUT FIRST.
THERE IS A MYSTICAL LAKE CALLED ONONDAGA, WELL HIDDEN TO THE NORTH, KNOWN ONLY TO THOSE OF US WHO MAKE OUR LIVING IN THE WILD LANDS--
IT WON'T DO ANY GOOD. THE WEREWOLVES WILL TRACK US WHEREVER WE GO.
THAT'S WHAT WE'LL BE COUNTING ON.
THIS IS A PLACE WHERE THE SPIRITS OF ANIMALS AND NATURE CAN TRULY COMMUNE, WITH THE HELP OF A TOTEM.
A TOTEM THAT LETS ONE LEARN WHAT IT'S LIKE TO LIVE AS ANOTHER CREATURE FOR A TIME...
SNOW, DON'T YOU SEE? WE'LL USE THE TOTEM TO TURN THEM INTO A PACK OF ***NORMAL*** WOLVES. WE CAN STAND AGAINST THEM THEN.
YOU'D DO THAT FOR ME? BUT...BUT THEY'RE YOUR KINDRED...
THEY MADE THEIR CHOICE WHEN THEY ALLIED THEMSELVES WITH REGINA. WE ARE ONLY DOING WHAT WE ***MUST.***
THIS MAGIC IS ANCIENT AND UNTAMED, NOT WITHOUT RISK. NO ONE CAN WIELD IT MORE THAN ONCE.
BUT ONCE SHOULD BE ENOUGH.
NOW, WE MUST KEEP MOVING IF WE HOPE TO MAKE THE SHORES OF ***LAKE ONONDAGA*** BEFORE THE PACK OVERTAKES US...

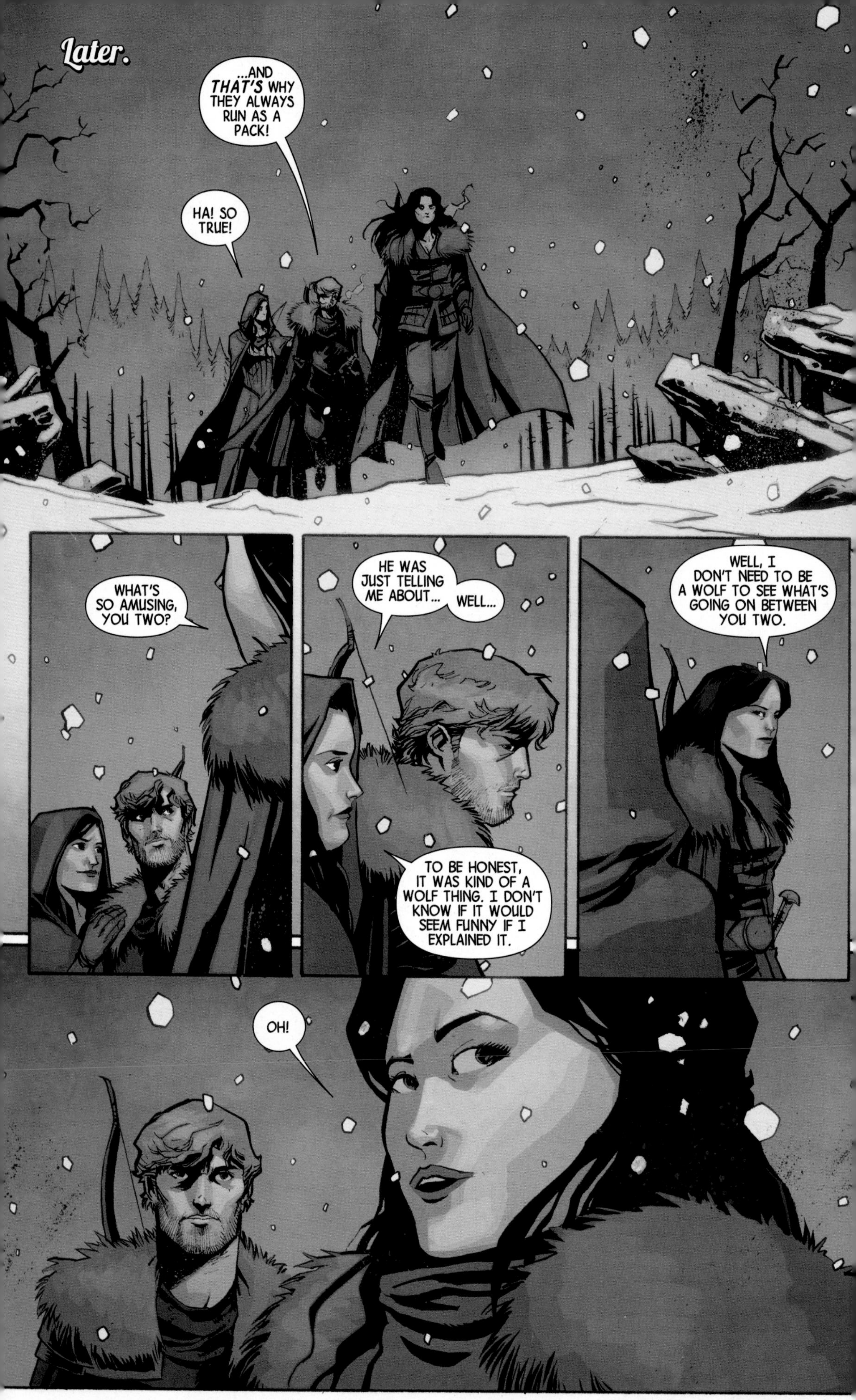
Later.
...AND THAT'S WHY THEY ALWAYS RUN AS A PACK!
HA! SO TRUE!
WHAT'S SO AMUSING, YOU TWO?
HE WAS JUST TELLING ME ABOUT...
WELL...
TO BE HONEST, IT WAS KIND OF A WOLF THING. I DON'T KNOW IF IT WOULD SEEM FUNNY IF I EXPLAINED IT.
WELL, I DON'T NEED TO BE A WOLF TO SEE WHAT'S GOING ON BETWEEN YOU TWO.
OH!

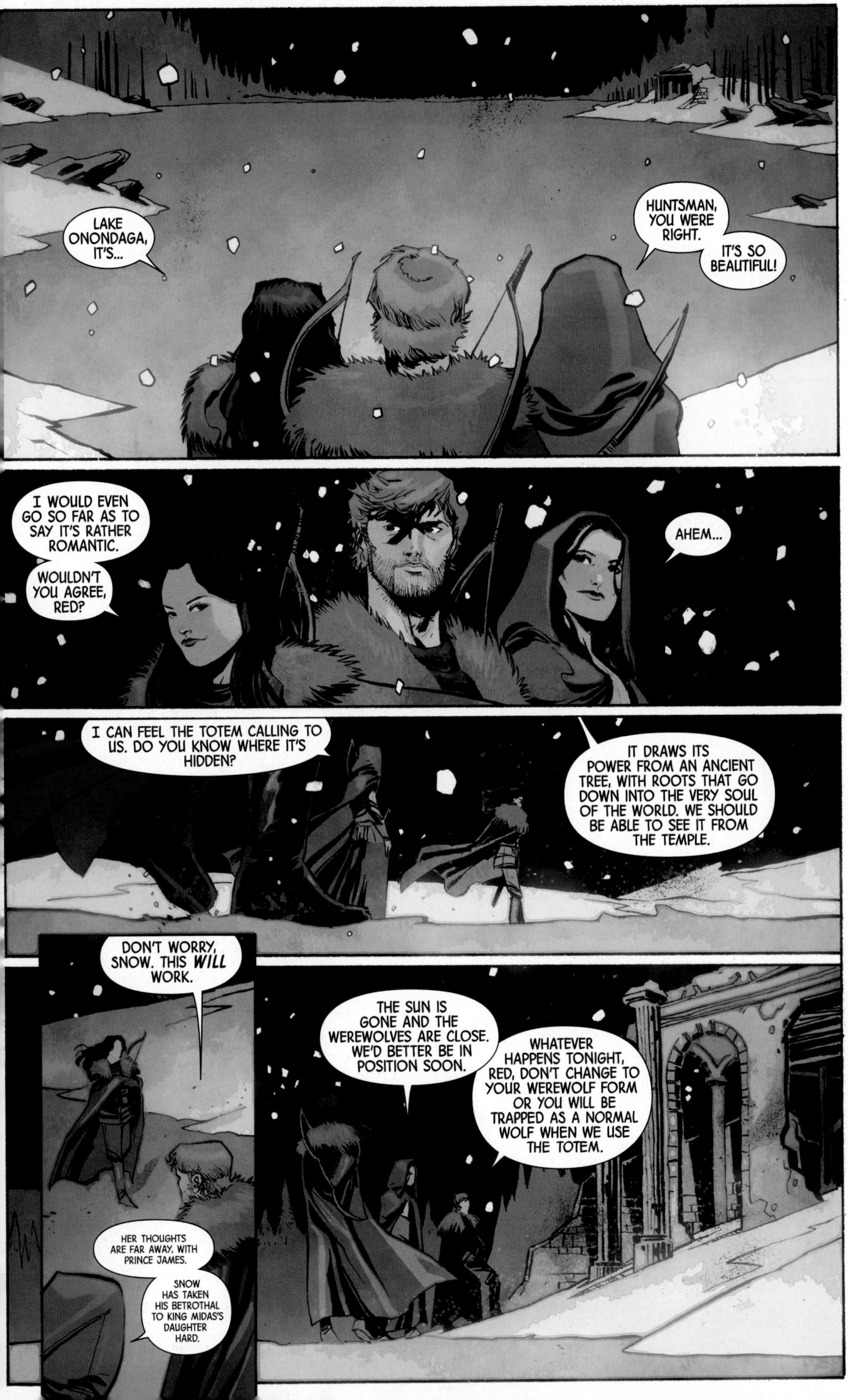
LAKE ONONDAGA, IT'S...
HUNTSMAN, YOU WERE RIGHT.
IT'S SO BEAUTIFUL!
I WOULD EVEN GO SO FAR AS TO SAY IT'S RATHER ROMANTIC.
WOULDN'T YOU AGREE, RED?
AHEM...
I CAN FEEL THE TOTEM CALLING TO US. DO YOU KNOW WHERE IT'S HIDDEN?
IT DRAWS ITS POWER FROM AN ANCIENT TREE, WITH ROOTS THAT GO DOWN INTO THE VERY SOUL OF THE WORLD. WE SHOULD BE ABLE TO SEE IT FROM THE TEMPLE.
DON'T WORRY, SNOW. THIS WILL WORK.
HER THOUGHTS ARE FAR AWAY, WITH PRINCE JAMES.
SNOW HAS TAKEN HIS BETROTHAL TO KING MIDAS'S DAUGHTER HARD.
THE SUN IS GONE AND THE WEREWOLVES ARE CLOSE. WE'D BETTER BE IN POSITION SOON.
WHATEVER HAPPENS TONIGHT, RED, DON'T CHANGE TO YOUR WEREWOLF FORM OR YOU WILL BE TRAPPED AS A NORMAL WOLF WHEN WE USE THE TOTEM.

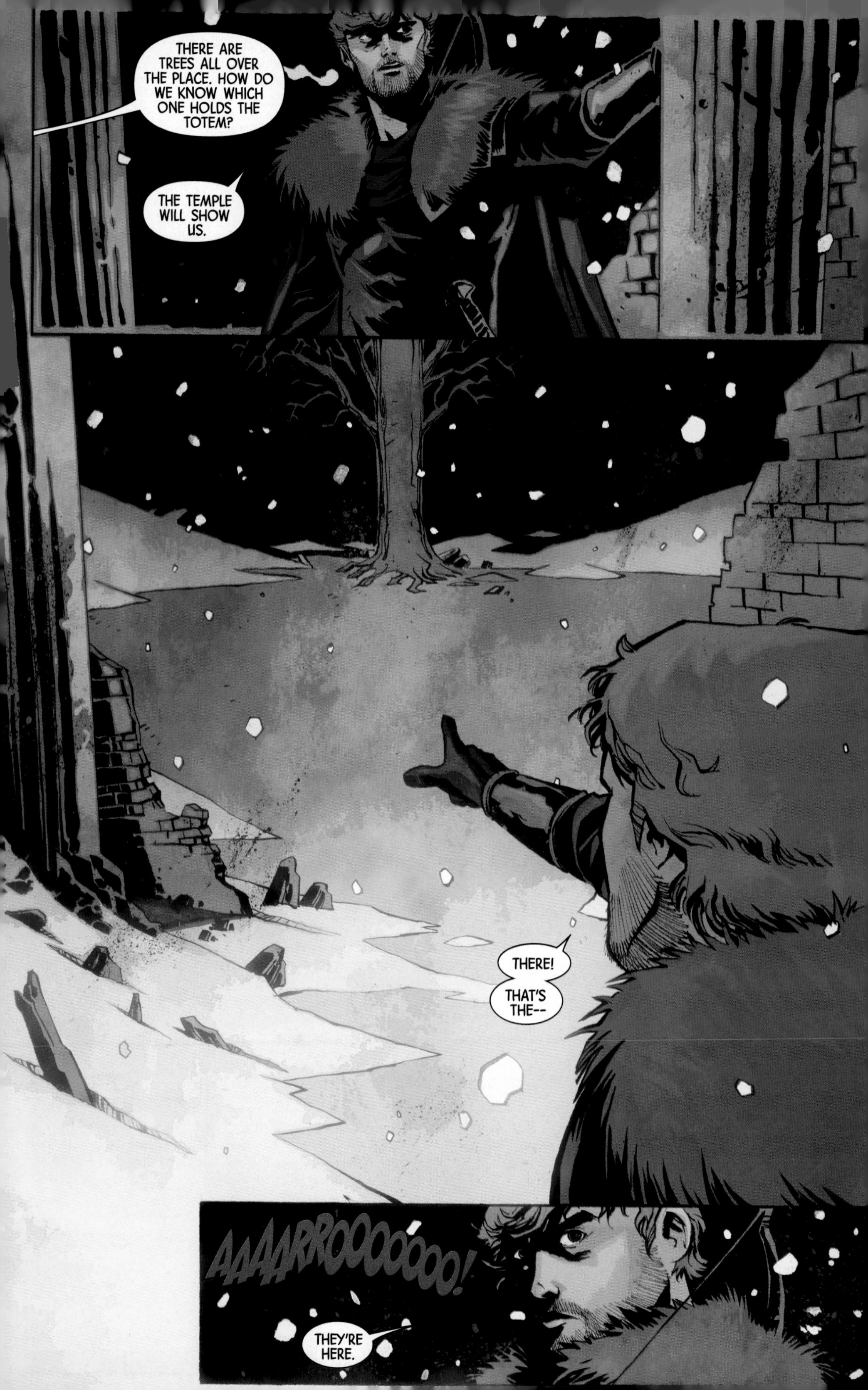
THERE ARE TREES ALL OVER THE PLACE. HOW DO WE KNOW WHICH ONE HOLDS THE TOTEM?
THE TEMPLE WILL SHOW US.
THERE!
THAT'S THE--
AAAARROOOOOOO!
THEY'RE HERE.

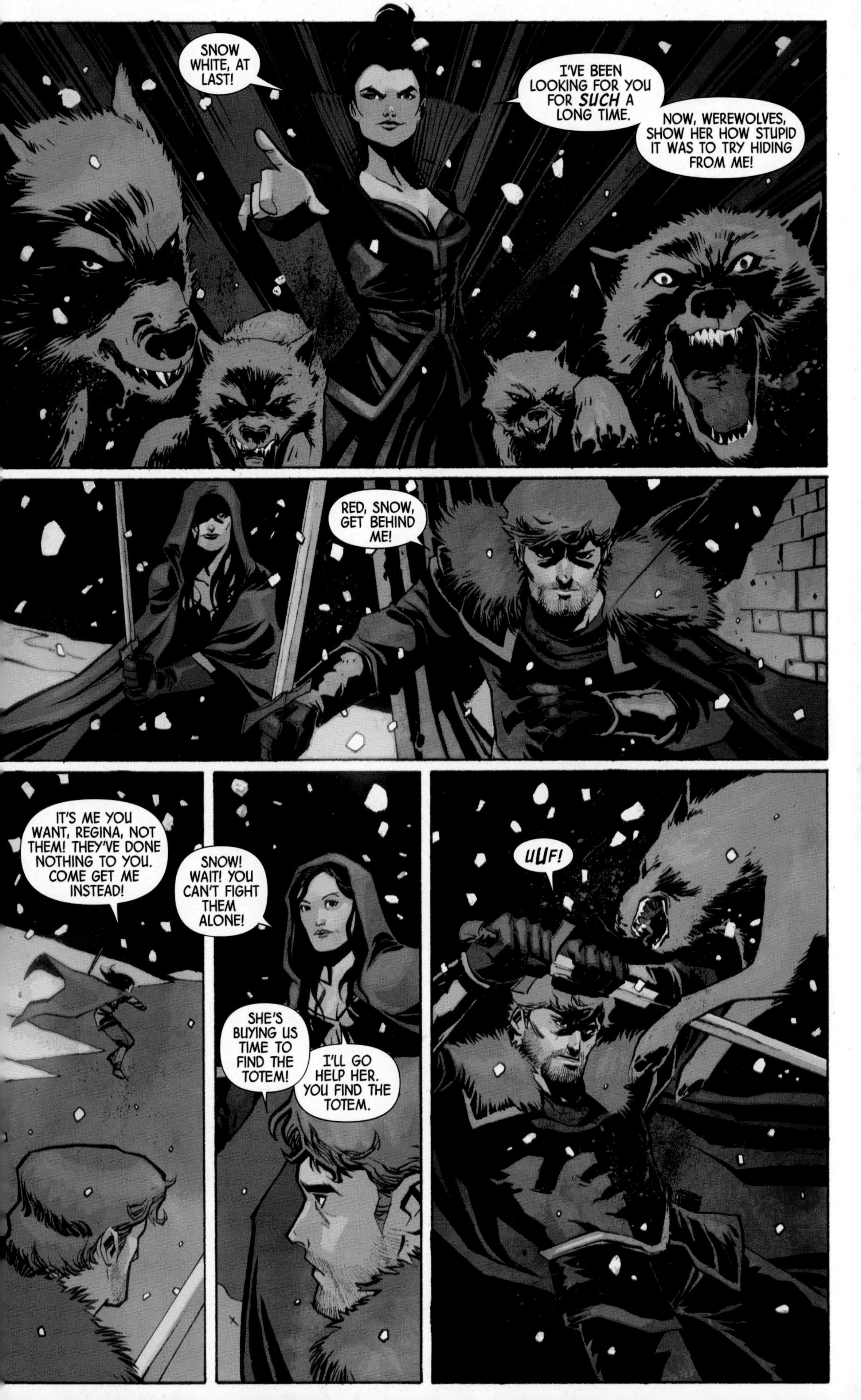
SNOW WHITE, AT LAST!
I'VE BEEN LOOKING FOR YOU FOR SUCH A LONG TIME.
NOW, WEREWOLVES, SHOW HER HOW STUPID IT WAS TO TRY HIDING FROM ME!
RED, SNOW, GET BEHIND ME!
IT'S ME YOU WANT, REGINA, NOT THEM! THEY'VE DONE NOTHING TO YOU. COME GET ME INSTEAD!
SNOW! WAIT! YOU CAN'T FIGHT THEM ALONE!
SHE'S BUYING US TIME TO FIND THE TOTEM!
I'LL GO HELP HER. YOU FIND THE TOTEM.
UUF!

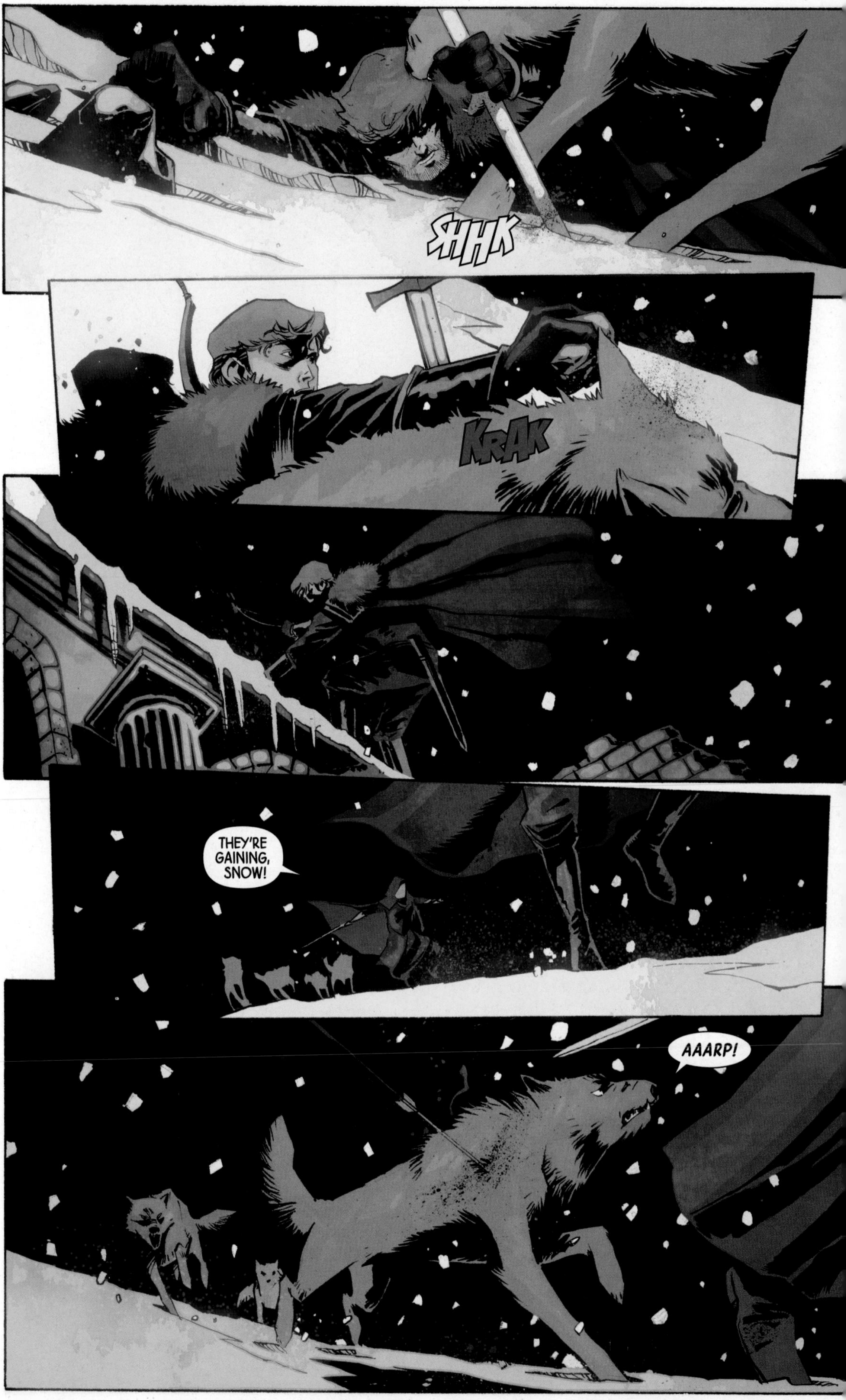
SHHK
KRAK
THEY'RE GAINING, SNOW!
AAARP!

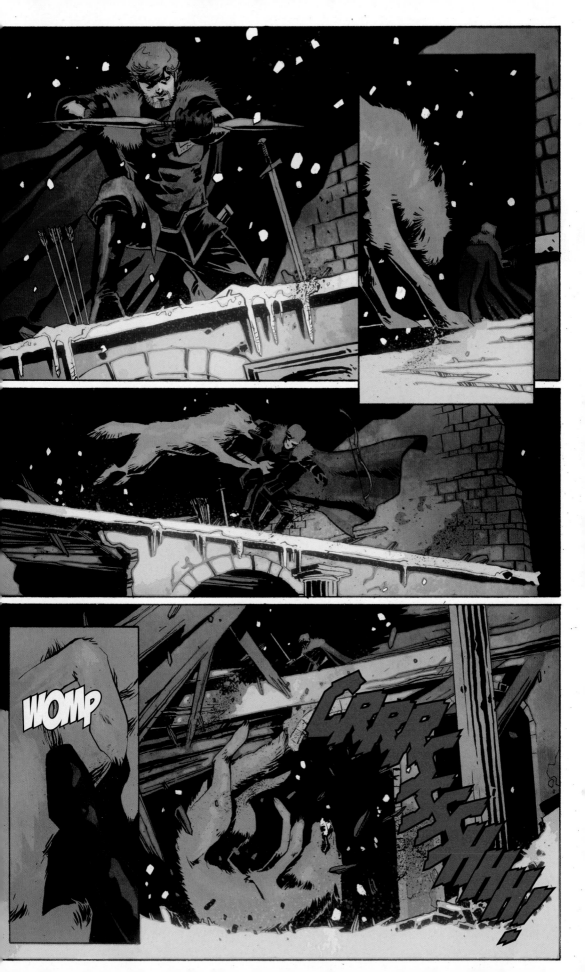

WOMP

CRRRSCHHH!

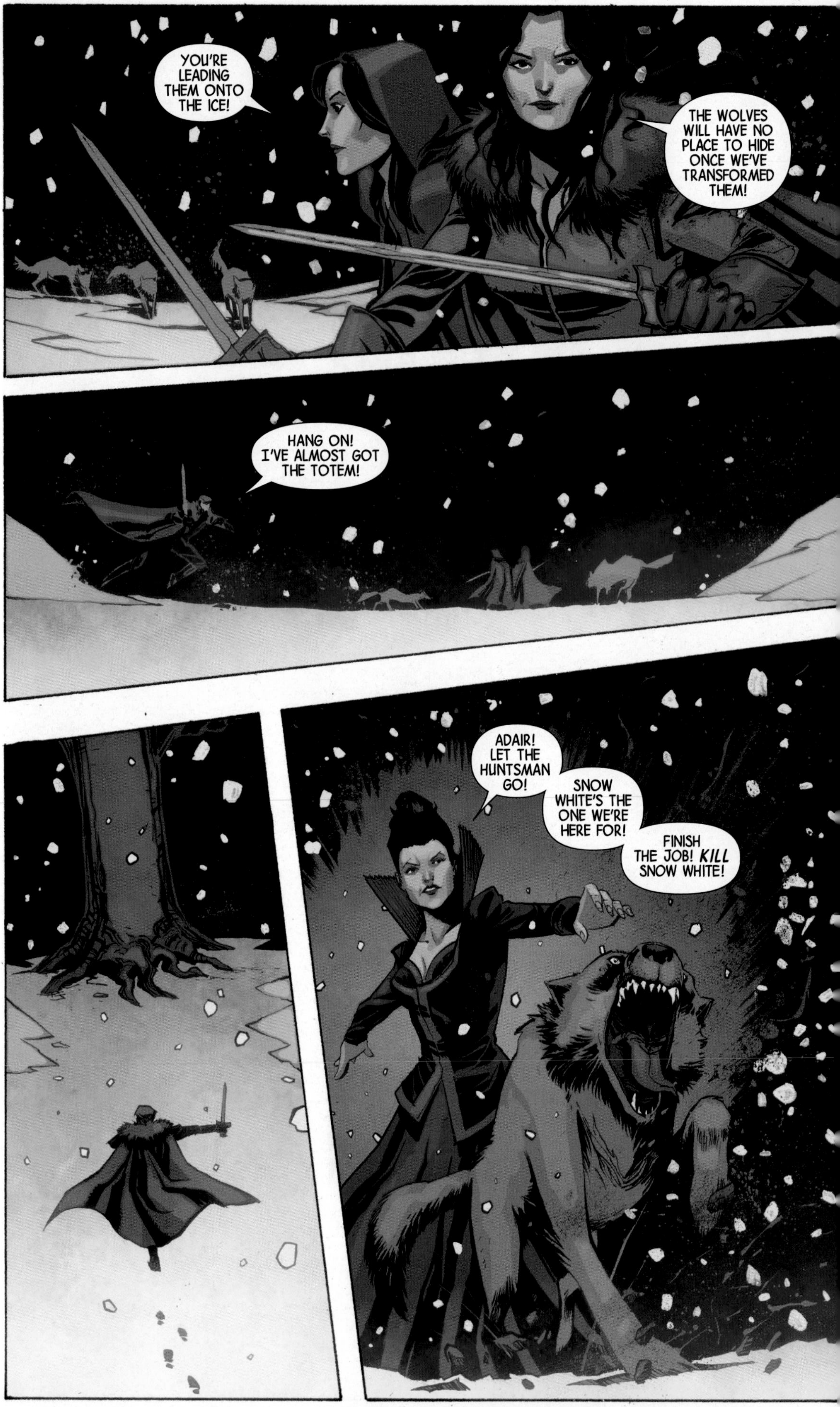
YOU'RE LEADING THEM ONTO THE ICE!
THE WOLVES WILL HAVE NO PLACE TO HIDE ONCE WE'VE TRANSFORMED THEM!
HANG ON! I'VE ALMOST GOT THE TOTEM!
ADAIR! LET THE HUNTSMAN GO!
SNOW WHITE'S THE ONE WE'RE HERE FOR!
FINISH THE JOB! *KILL* SNOW WHITE!

GRRRRRR

CCRKKKK

CCRKKK

CCRKKKK

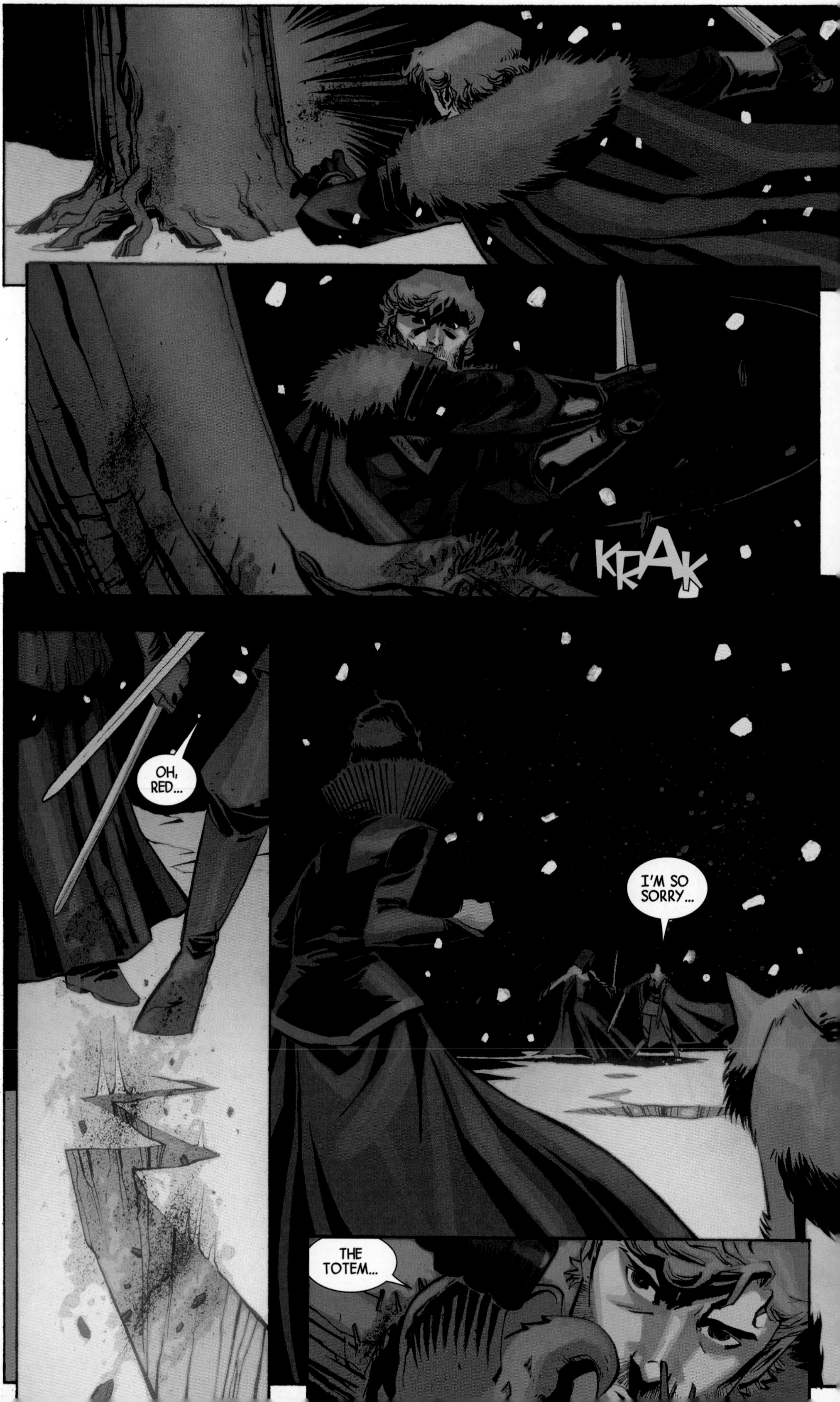
KRAK
OH, RED...
I'M SO SORRY...
THE TOTEM...

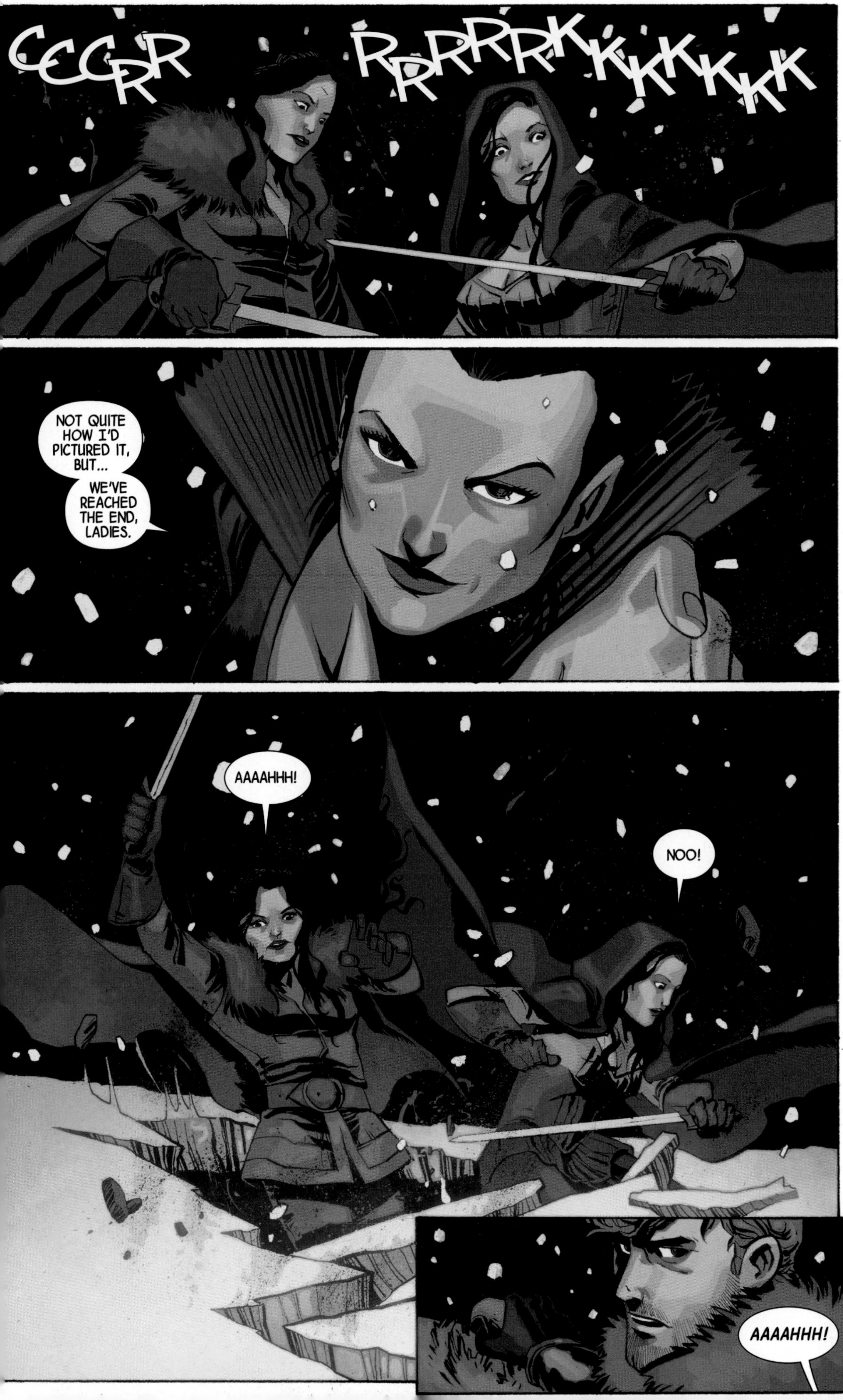
CCCRR
RRRRRRKKKKKKK
NOT QUITE HOW I'D PICTURED IT, BUT...
WE'VE REACHED THE END, LADIES.
AAAAHHH!
NOO!
AAAAHHH!

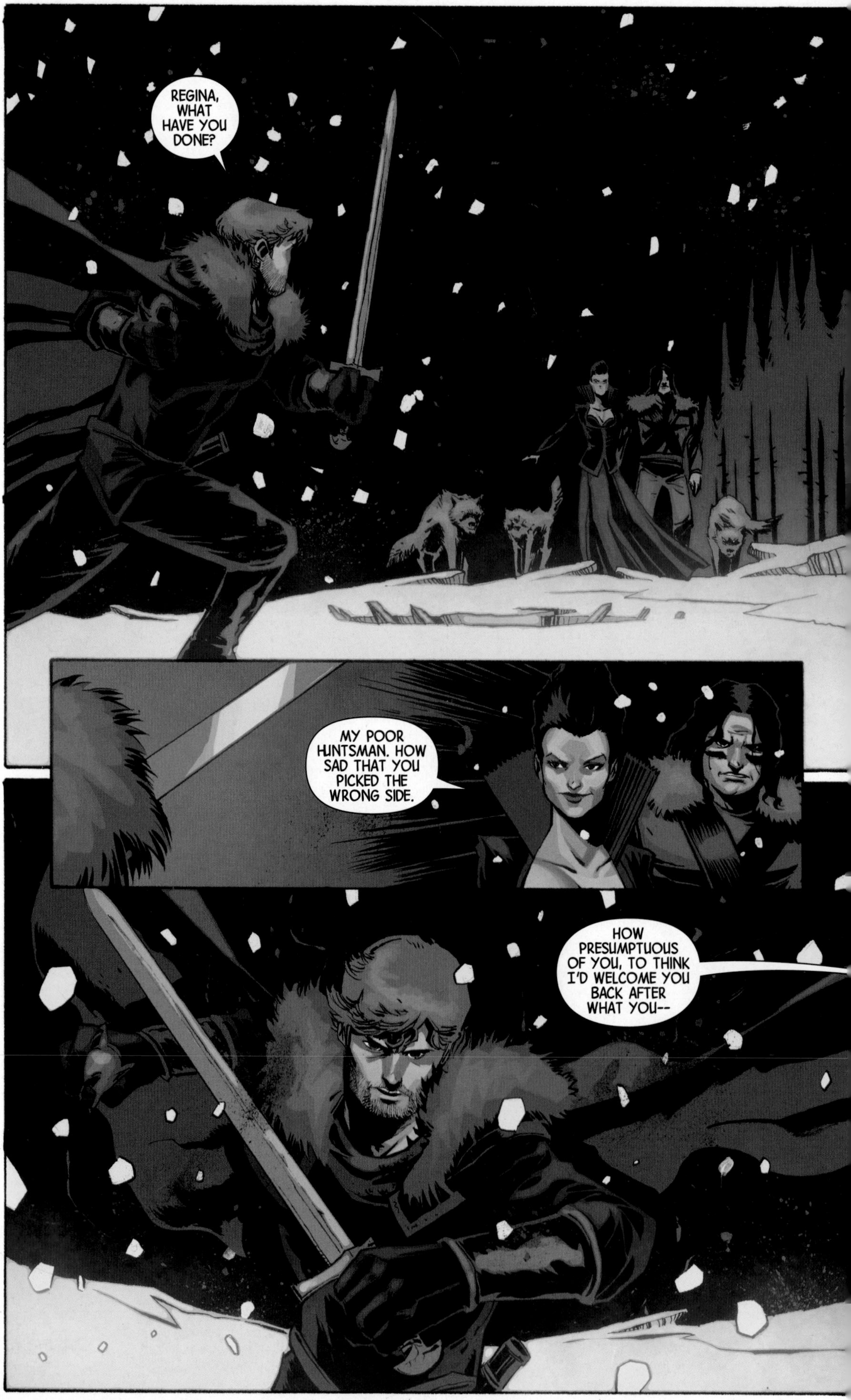
REGINA, WHAT HAVE YOU DONE?
MY POOR HUNTSMAN. HOW SAD THAT YOU PICKED THE WRONG SIDE.
HOW PRESUMPTUOUS OF YOU, TO THINK I'D WELCOME YOU BACK AFTER WHAT YOU--

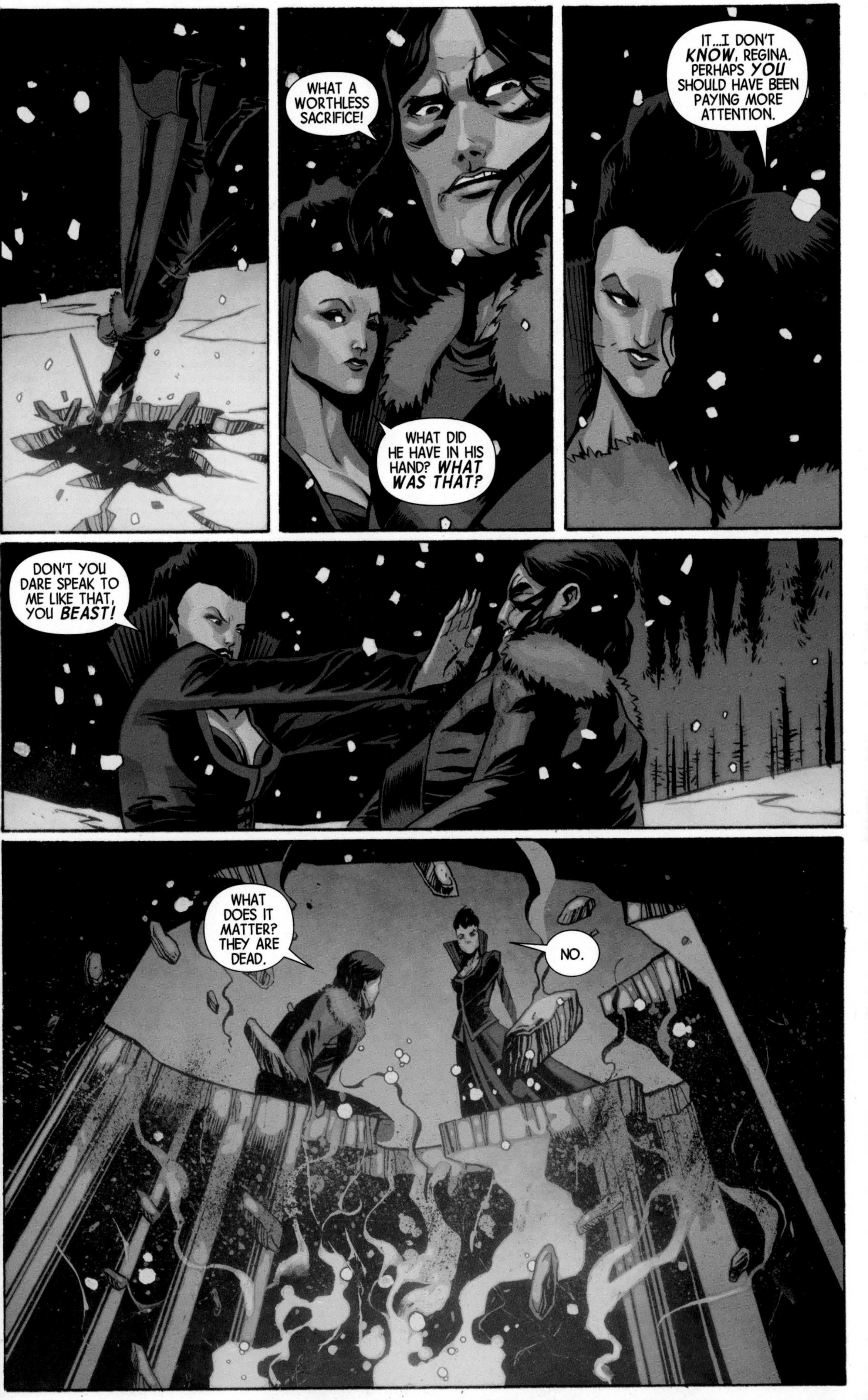
WHAT A WORTHLESS SACRIFICE!
WHAT DID HE HAVE IN HIS HAND? WHAT WAS THAT?
IT...I DON'T KNOW, REGINA. PERHAPS YOU SHOULD HAVE BEEN PAYING MORE ATTENTION.
DON'T YOU DARE SPEAK TO ME LIKE THAT, YOU BEAST!
WHAT DOES IT MATTER? THEY ARE DEAD.
NO.

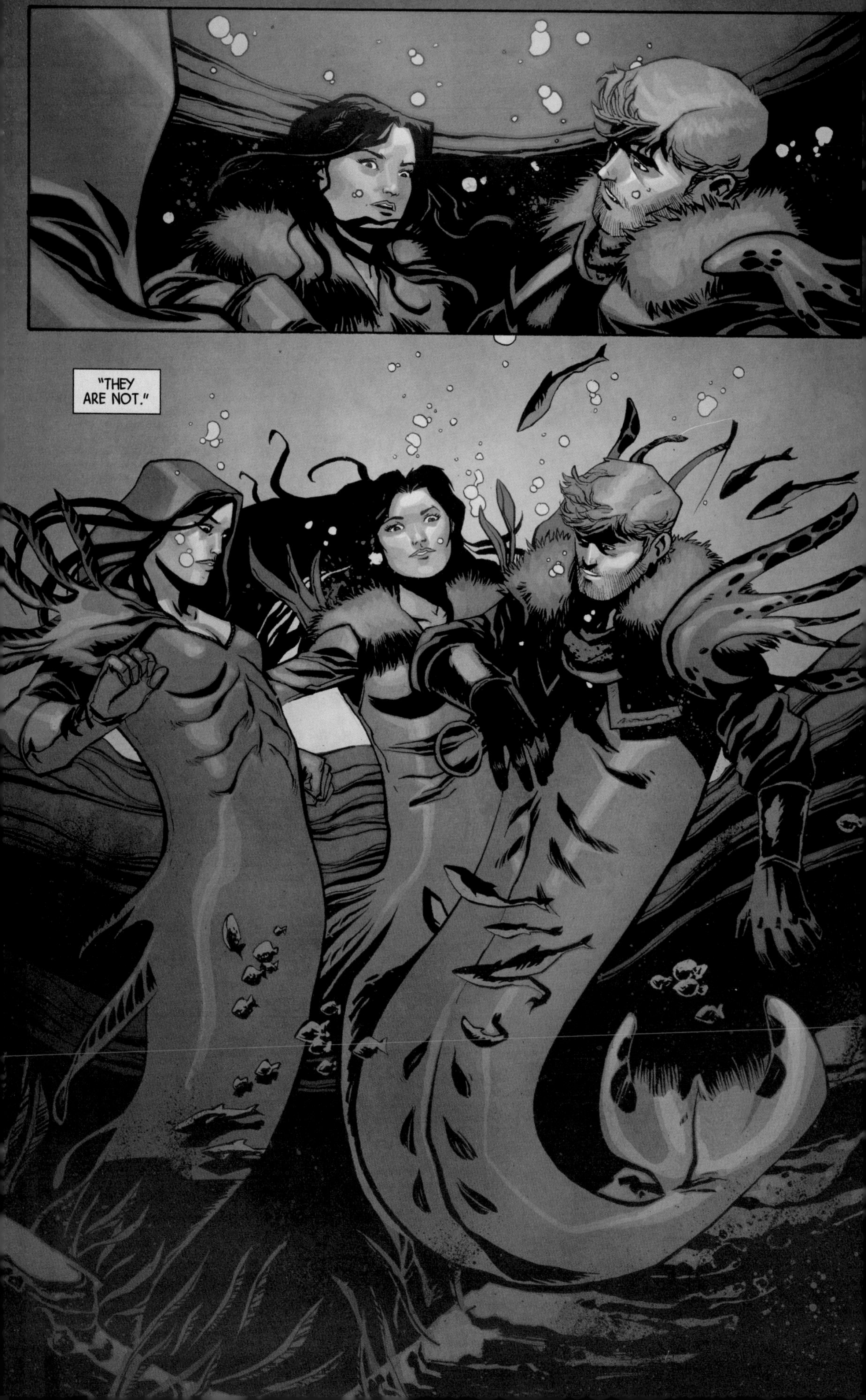
"THEY ARE NOT."

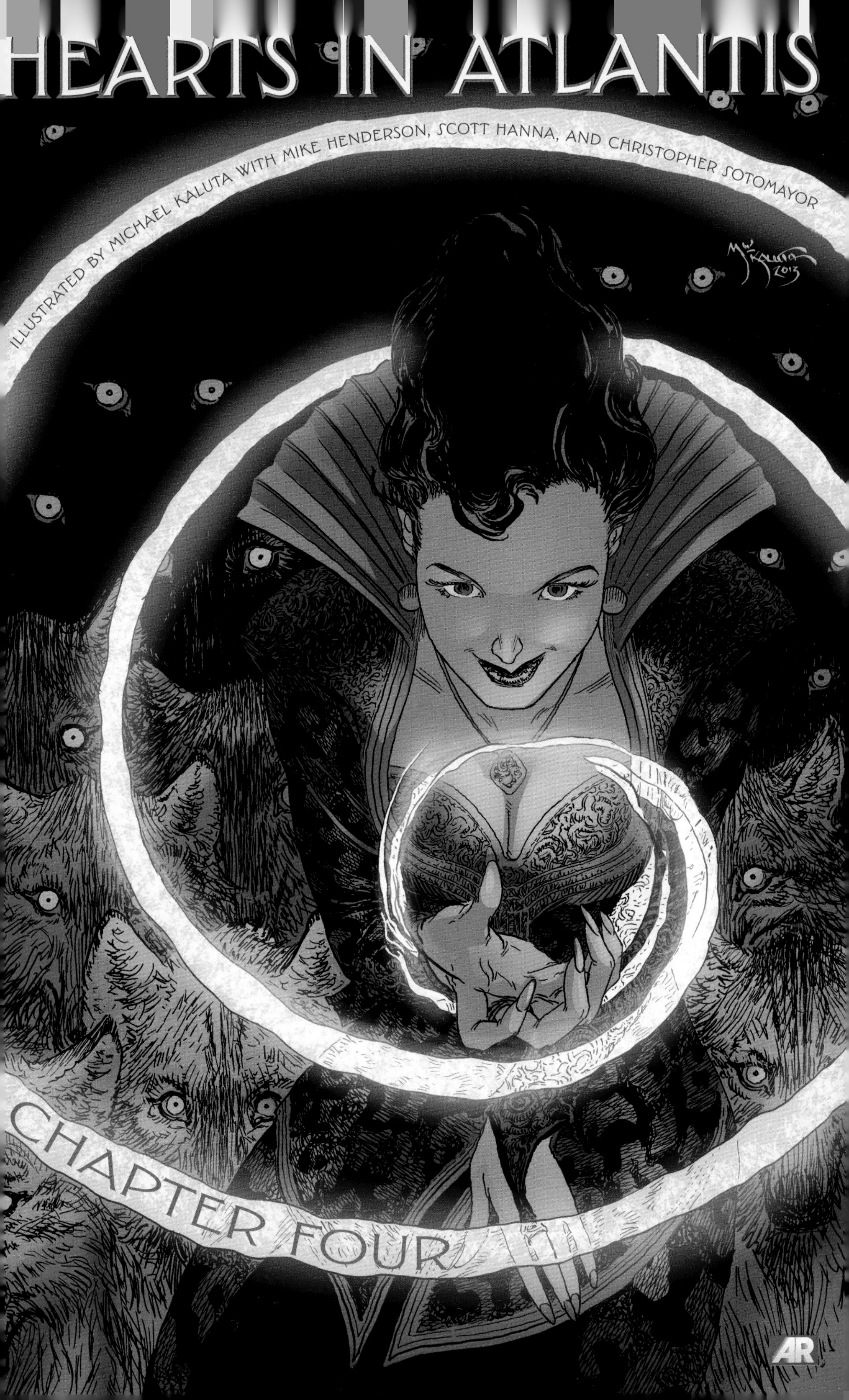
HEARTS IN ATLANTIS
ILLUSTRATED BY MICHAEL KALUTA WITH MIKE HENDERSON, SCOTT HANNA, AND CHRISTOPHER SOTOMAYOR
CHAPTER FOUR

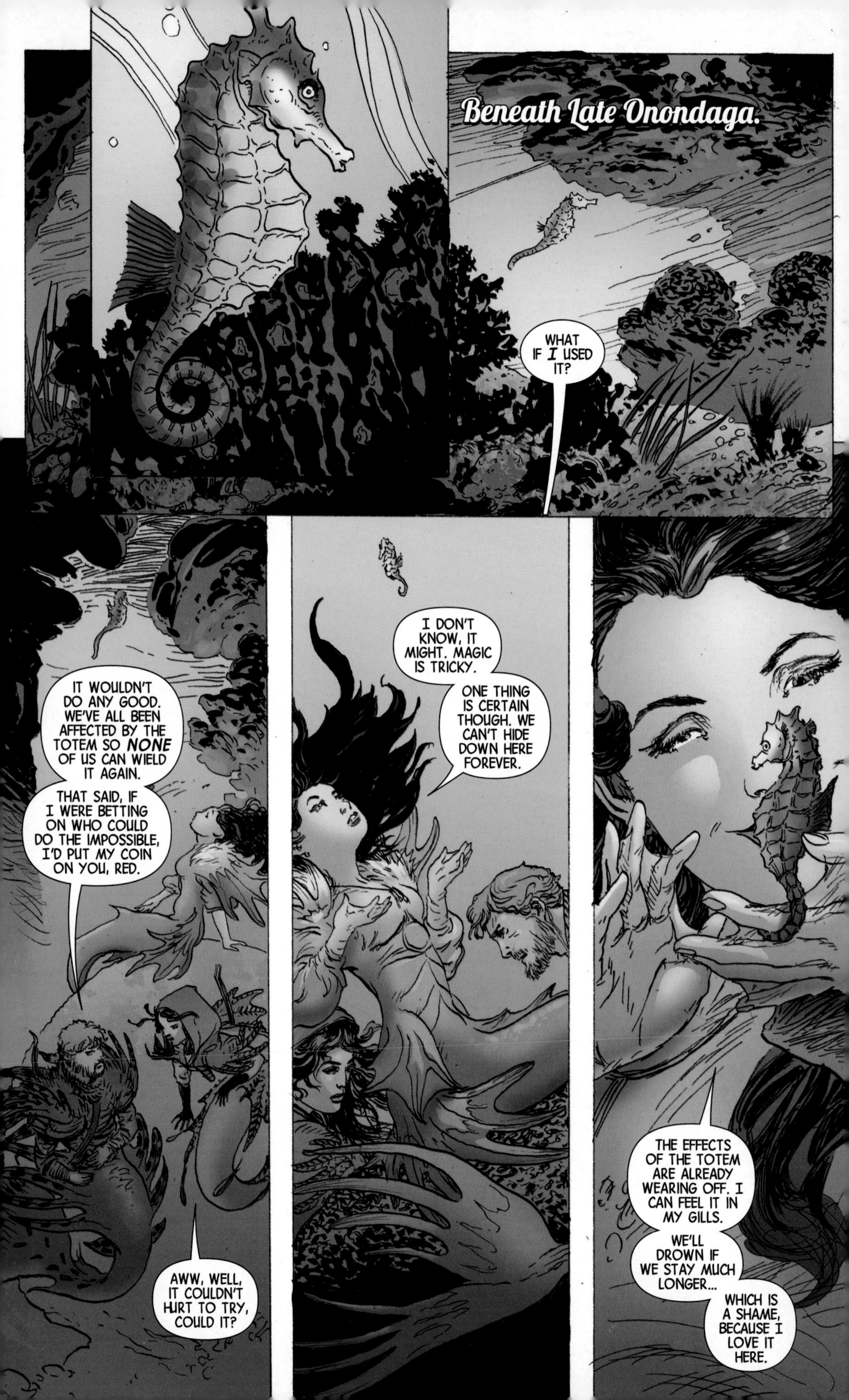

Beneath Late Onondaga.
WHAT IF I USED IT?
IT WOULDN'T DO ANY GOOD. WE'VE ALL BEEN AFFECTED BY THE TOTEM SO NONE OF US CAN WIELD IT AGAIN.
THAT SAID, IF I WERE BETTING ON WHO COULD DO THE IMPOSSIBLE, I'D PUT MY COIN ON YOU, RED.
AWW, WELL, IT COULDN'T HURT TO TRY, COULD IT?
I DON'T KNOW, IT MIGHT. MAGIC IS TRICKY.
ONE THING IS CERTAIN THOUGH. WE CAN'T HIDE DOWN HERE FOREVER.
THE EFFECTS OF THE TOTEM ARE ALREADY WEARING OFF. I CAN FEEL IT IN MY GILLS.
WE'LL DROWN IF WE STAY MUCH LONGER...
WHICH IS A SHAME, BECAUSE I LOVE IT HERE.

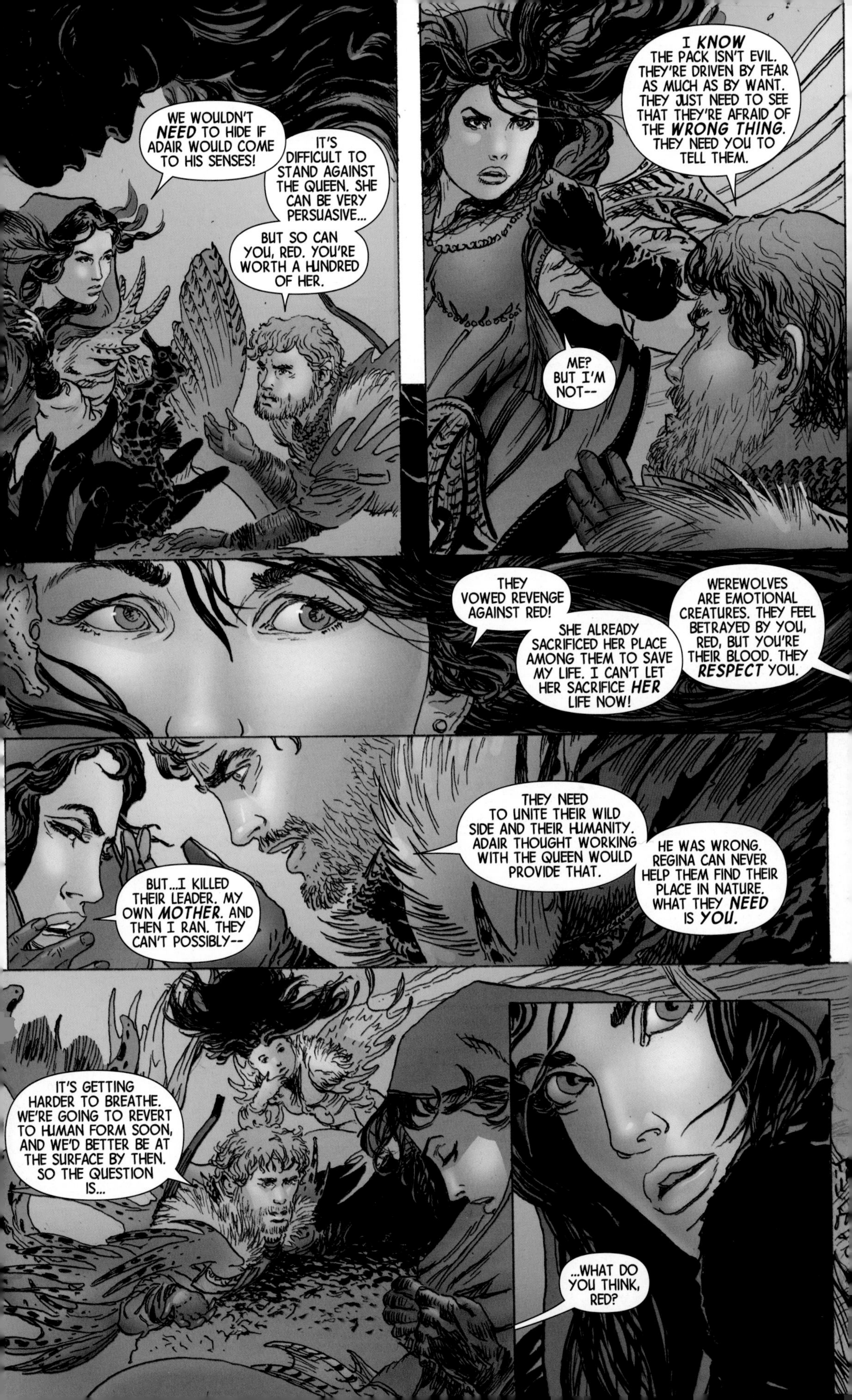
WE WOULDN'T NEED TO HIDE IF ADAIR WOULD COME TO HIS SENSES!
IT'S DIFFICULT TO STAND AGAINST THE QUEEN. SHE CAN BE VERY PERSUASIVE...
BUT SO CAN YOU, RED. YOU'RE WORTH A HUNDRED OF HER.
I KNOW THE PACK ISN'T EVIL. THEY'RE DRIVEN BY FEAR AS MUCH AS BY WANT. THEY JUST NEED TO SEE THAT THEY'RE AFRAID OF THE WRONG THING. THEY NEED YOU TO TELL THEM.
ME? BUT I'M NOT--
THEY VOWED REVENGE AGAINST RED!
SHE ALREADY SACRIFICED HER PLACE AMONG THEM TO SAVE MY LIFE. I CAN'T LET HER SACRIFICE HER LIFE NOW!
WEREWOLVES ARE EMOTIONAL CREATURES. THEY FEEL BETRAYED BY YOU, RED, BUT YOU'RE THEIR BLOOD. THEY RESPECT YOU.
BUT...I KILLED THEIR LEADER. MY OWN MOTHER. AND THEN I RAN. THEY CAN'T POSSIBLY--
THEY NEED TO UNITE THEIR WILD SIDE AND THEIR HUMANITY. ADAIR THOUGHT WORKING WITH THE QUEEN WOULD PROVIDE THAT.
HE WAS WRONG. REGINA CAN NEVER HELP THEM FIND THEIR PLACE IN NATURE. WHAT THEY NEED IS YOU.
IT'S GETTING HARDER TO BREATHE. WE'RE GOING TO REVERT TO HUMAN FORM SOON, AND WE'D BETTER BE AT THE SURFACE BY THEN. SO THE QUESTION IS...
...WHAT DO YOU THINK, RED?

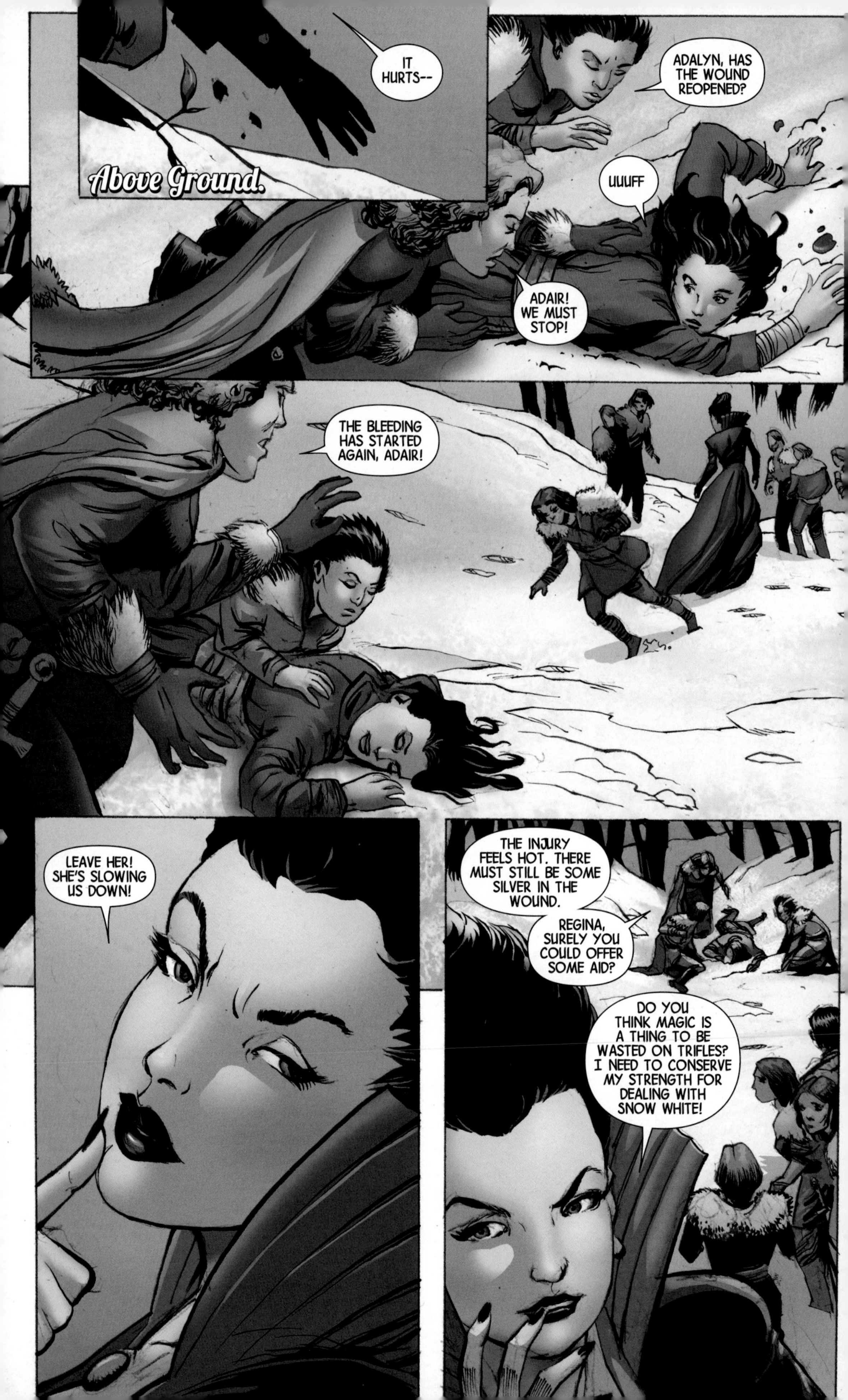
IT HURTS--
Above Ground.
ADALYN, HAS THE WOUND REOPENED?
UUUFF
ADAIR! WE MUST STOP!
THE BLEEDING HAS STARTED AGAIN, ADAIR!
LEAVE HER! SHE'S SLOWING US DOWN!
THE INJURY FEELS HOT. THERE MUST STILL BE SOME SILVER IN THE WOUND.
REGINA, SURELY YOU COULD OFFER SOME AID?
DO YOU THINK MAGIC IS A THING TO BE WASTED ON TRIFLES? I NEED TO CONSERVE MY STRENGTH FOR DEALING WITH SNOW WHITE!

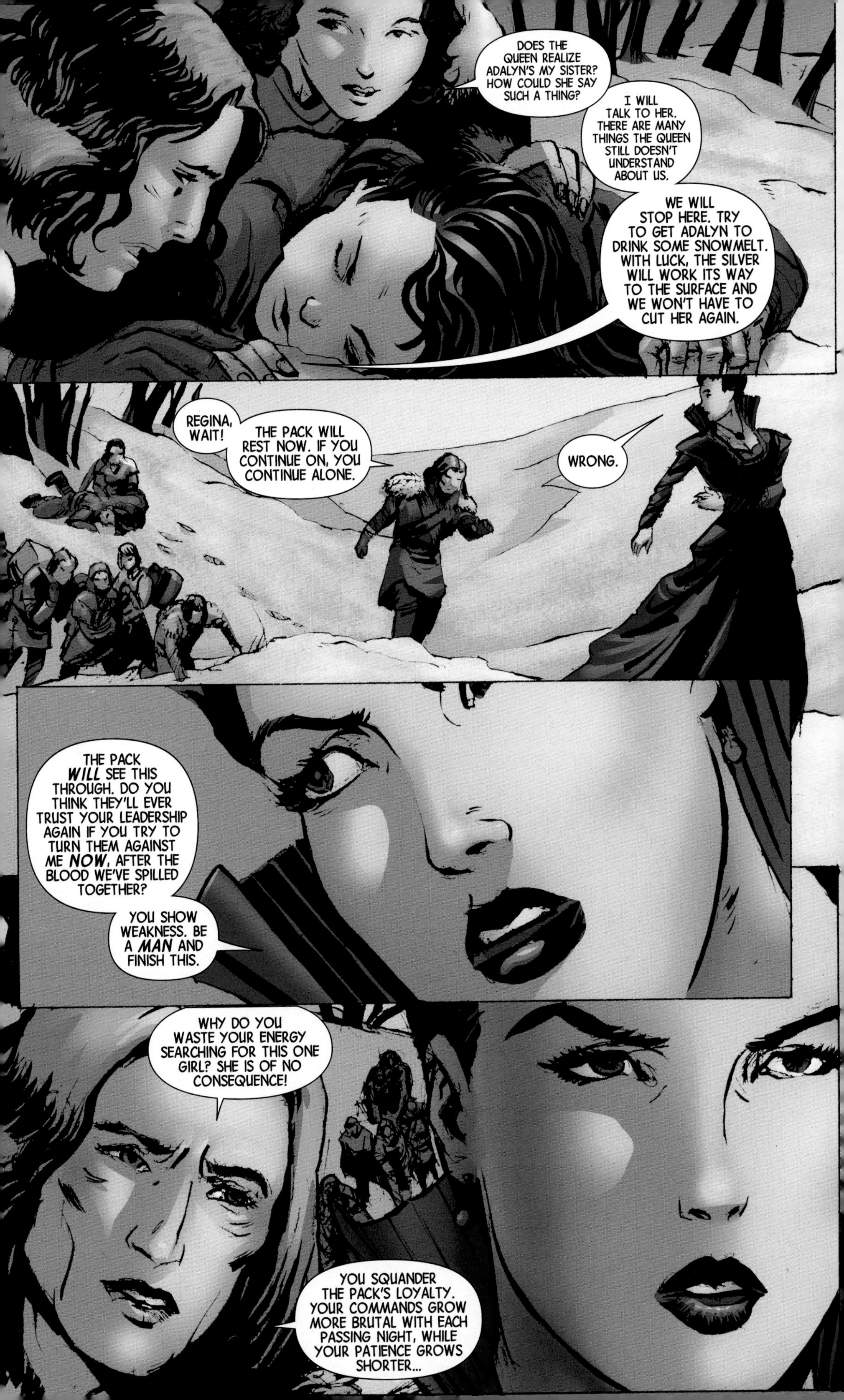
DOES THE QUEEN REALIZE ADALYN'S MY SISTER? HOW COULD SHE SAY SUCH A THING?
I WILL TALK TO HER. THERE ARE MANY THINGS THE QUEEN STILL DOESN'T UNDERSTAND ABOUT US.
WE WILL STOP HERE. TRY TO GET ADALYN TO DRINK SOME SNOWMELT. WITH LUCK, THE SILVER WILL WORK ITS WAY TO THE SURFACE AND WE WON'T HAVE TO CUT HER AGAIN.
REGINA, WAIT!
THE PACK WILL REST NOW. IF YOU CONTINUE ON, YOU CONTINUE ALONE.
WRONG.
THE PACK *WILL* SEE THIS THROUGH. DO YOU THINK THEY'LL EVER TRUST YOUR LEADERSHIP AGAIN IF YOU TRY TO TURN THEM AGAINST ME *NOW*, AFTER THE BLOOD WE'VE SPILLED TOGETHER?
YOU SHOW WEAKNESS. BE A *MAN* AND FINISH THIS.
WHY DO YOU WASTE YOUR ENERGY SEARCHING FOR THIS ONE GIRL? SHE IS OF NO CONSEQUENCE!
YOU SQUANDER THE PACK'S LOYALTY. YOUR COMMANDS GROW MORE BRUTAL WITH EACH PASSING NIGHT, WHILE YOUR PATIENCE GROWS SHORTER...

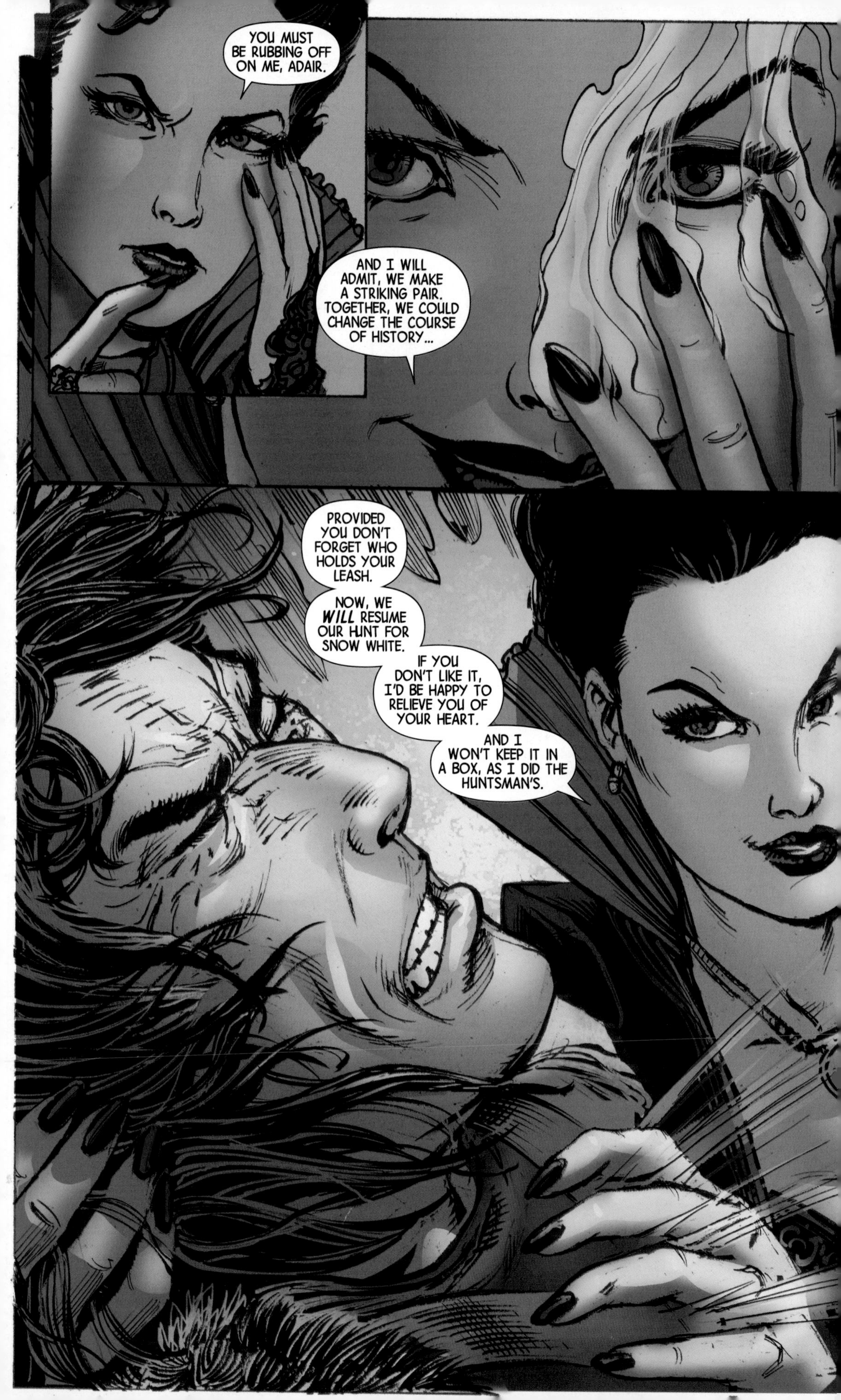
YOU MUST BE RUBBING OFF ON ME, ADAIR.
AND I WILL ADMIT, WE MAKE A STRIKING PAIR. TOGETHER, WE COULD CHANGE THE COURSE OF HISTORY...
PROVIDED YOU DON'T FORGET WHO HOLDS YOUR LEASH.
NOW, WE *WILL* RESUME OUR HUNT FOR SNOW WHITE.
IF YOU DON'T LIKE IT, I'D BE HAPPY TO RELIEVE YOU OF YOUR HEART.
AND I WON'T KEEP IT IN A BOX, AS I DID THE HUNTSMAN'S.

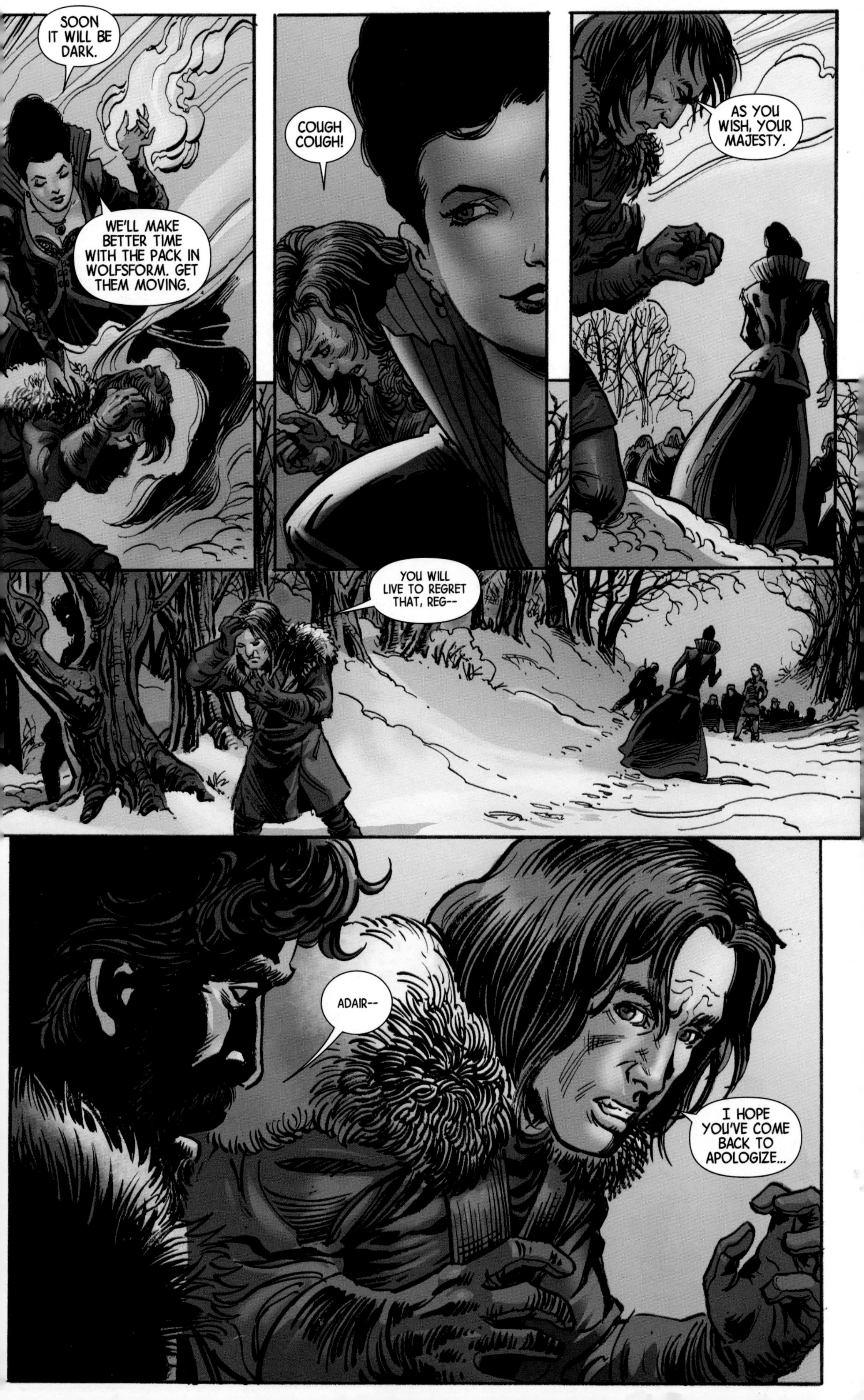
SOON IT WILL BE DARK.
WE'LL MAKE BETTER TIME WITH THE PACK IN WOLFSFORM. GET THEM MOVING.
COUGH COUGH!
AS YOU WISH, YOUR MAJESTY.
YOU WILL LIVE TO REGRET THAT, REG--
ADAIR--
I HOPE YOU'VE COME BACK TO APOLOGIZE...

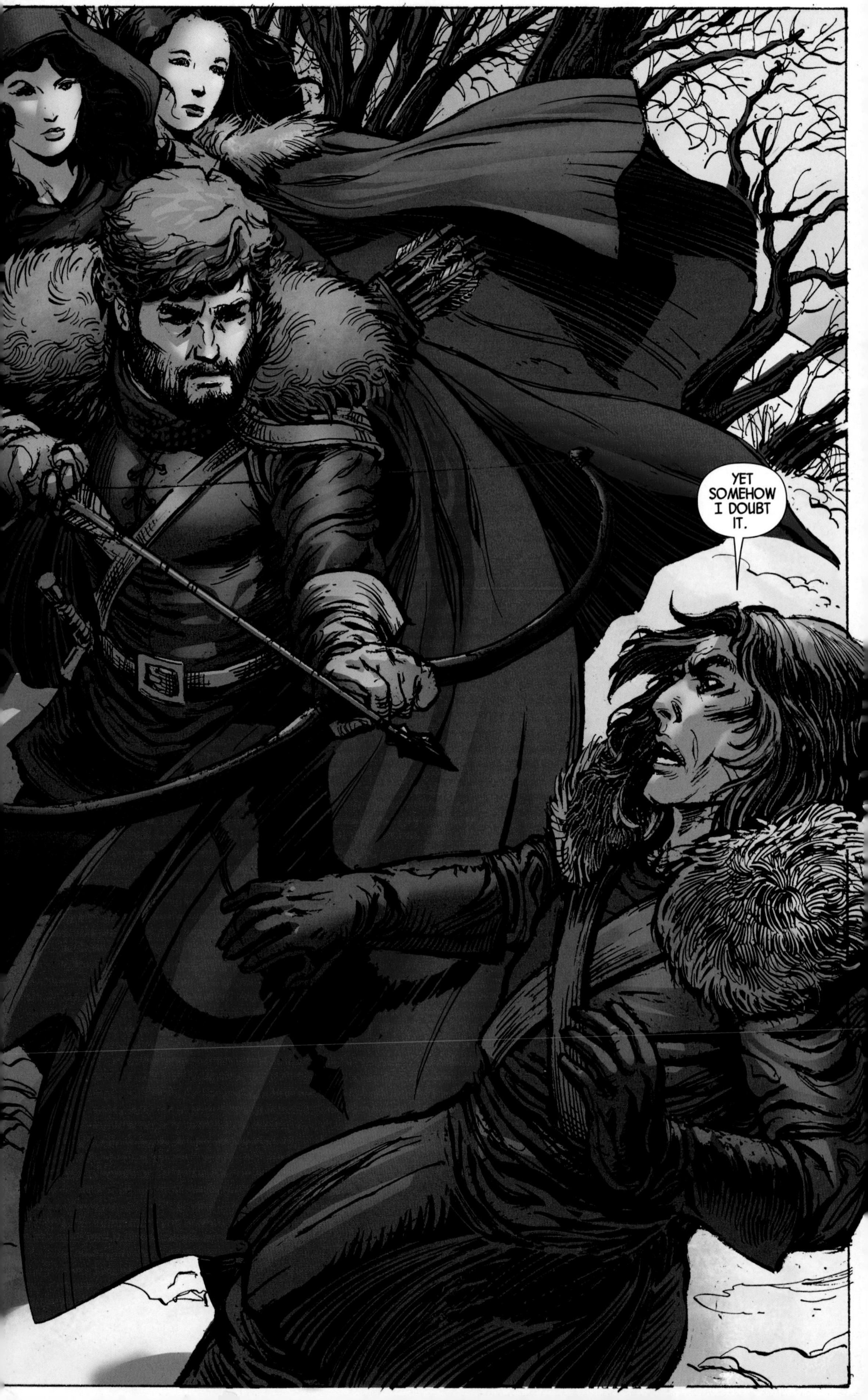
YET SOMEHOW I DOUBT IT.

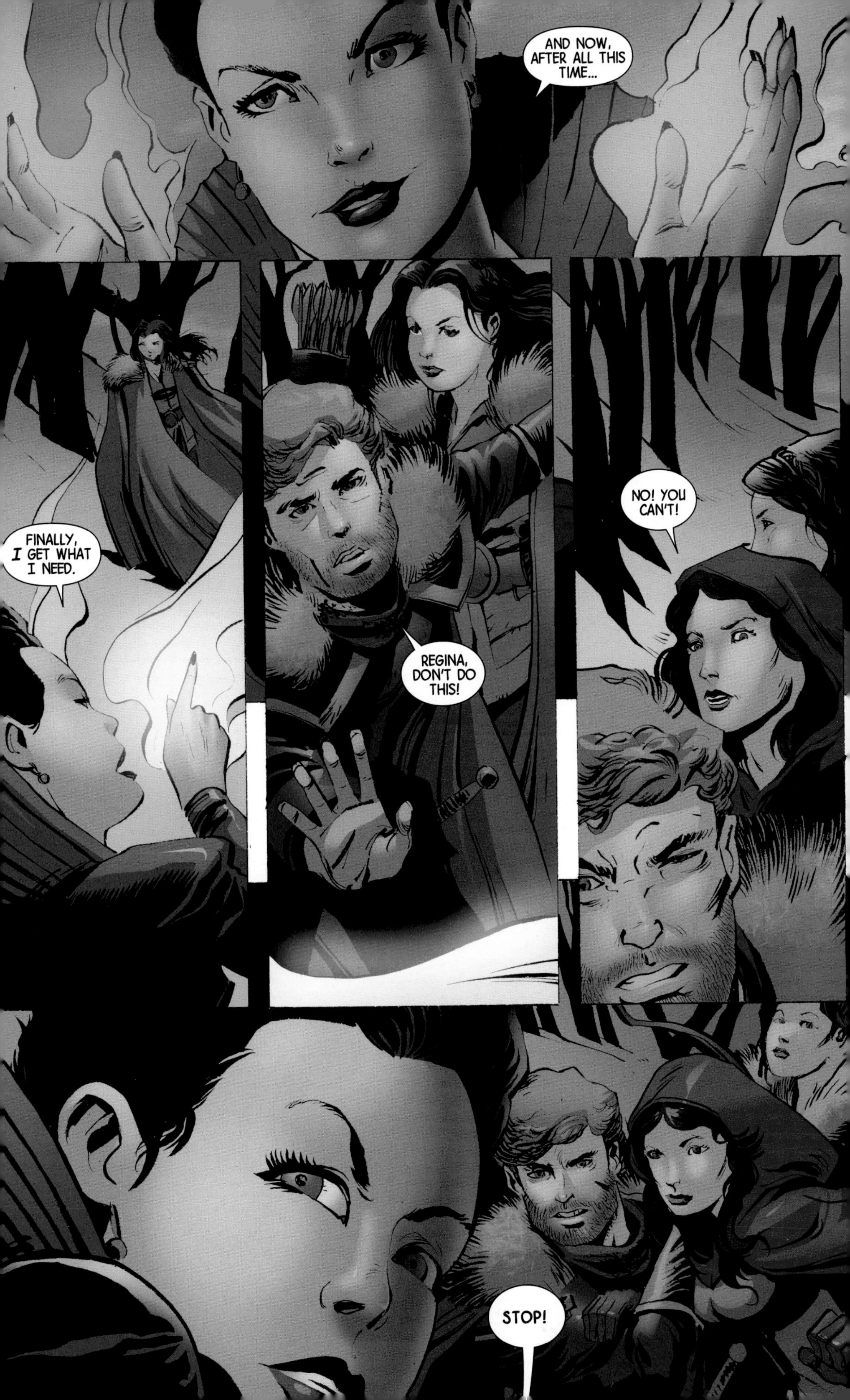
AND NOW, AFTER ALL THIS TIME...
FINALLY, I GET WHAT I NEED.
REGINA, DON'T DO THIS!
NO! YOU CAN'T!
STOP!

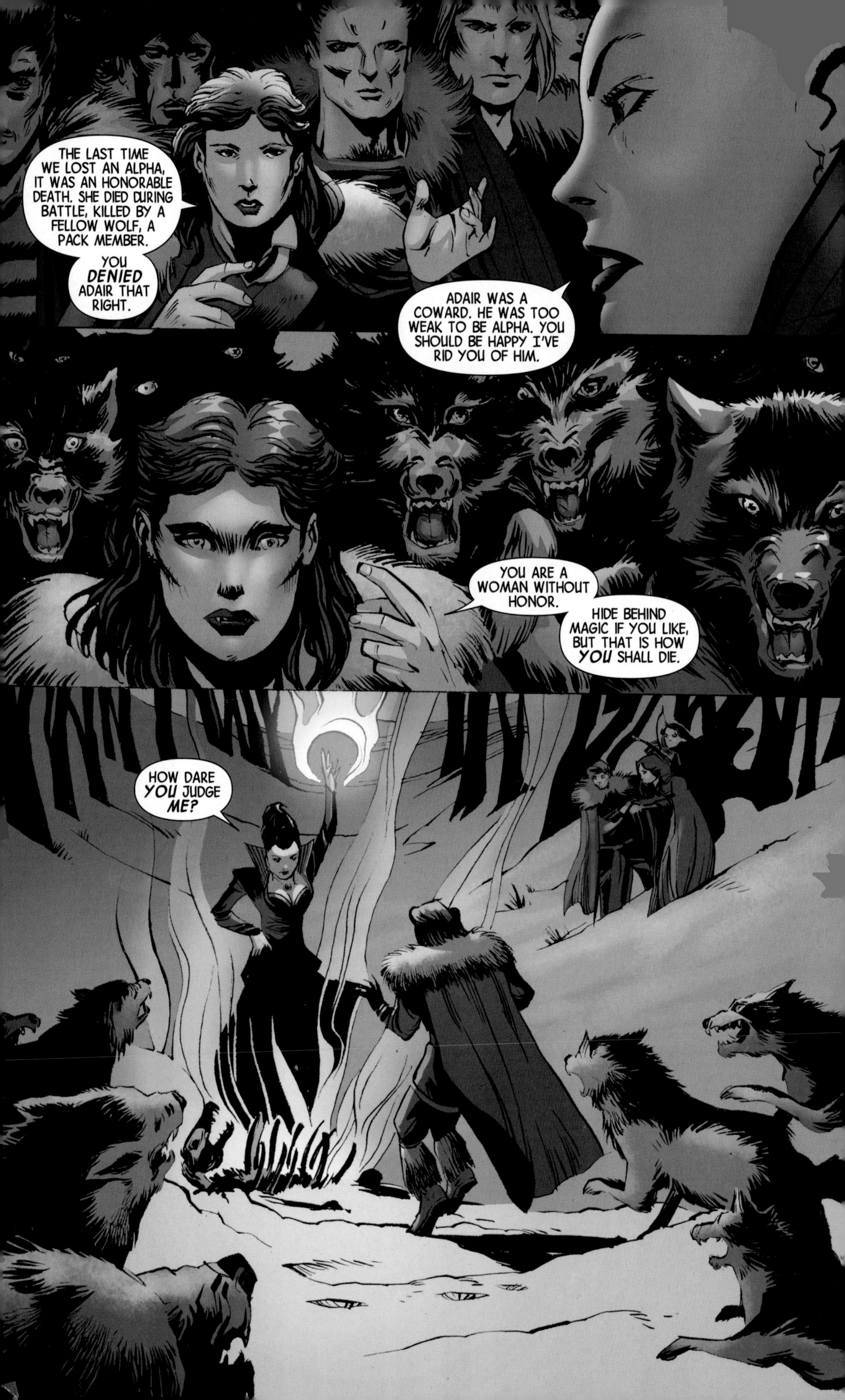
THE LAST TIME WE LOST AN ALPHA, IT WAS AN HONORABLE DEATH. SHE DIED DURING BATTLE, KILLED BY A FELLOW WOLF, A PACK MEMBER.
YOU DENIED ADAIR THAT RIGHT.
ADAIR WAS A COWARD. HE WAS TOO WEAK TO BE ALPHA. YOU SHOULD BE HAPPY I'VE RID YOU OF HIM.
YOU ARE A WOMAN WITHOUT HONOR.
HIDE BEHIND MAGIC IF YOU LIKE, BUT THAT IS HOW YOU SHALL DIE.
HOW DARE YOU JUDGE ME?

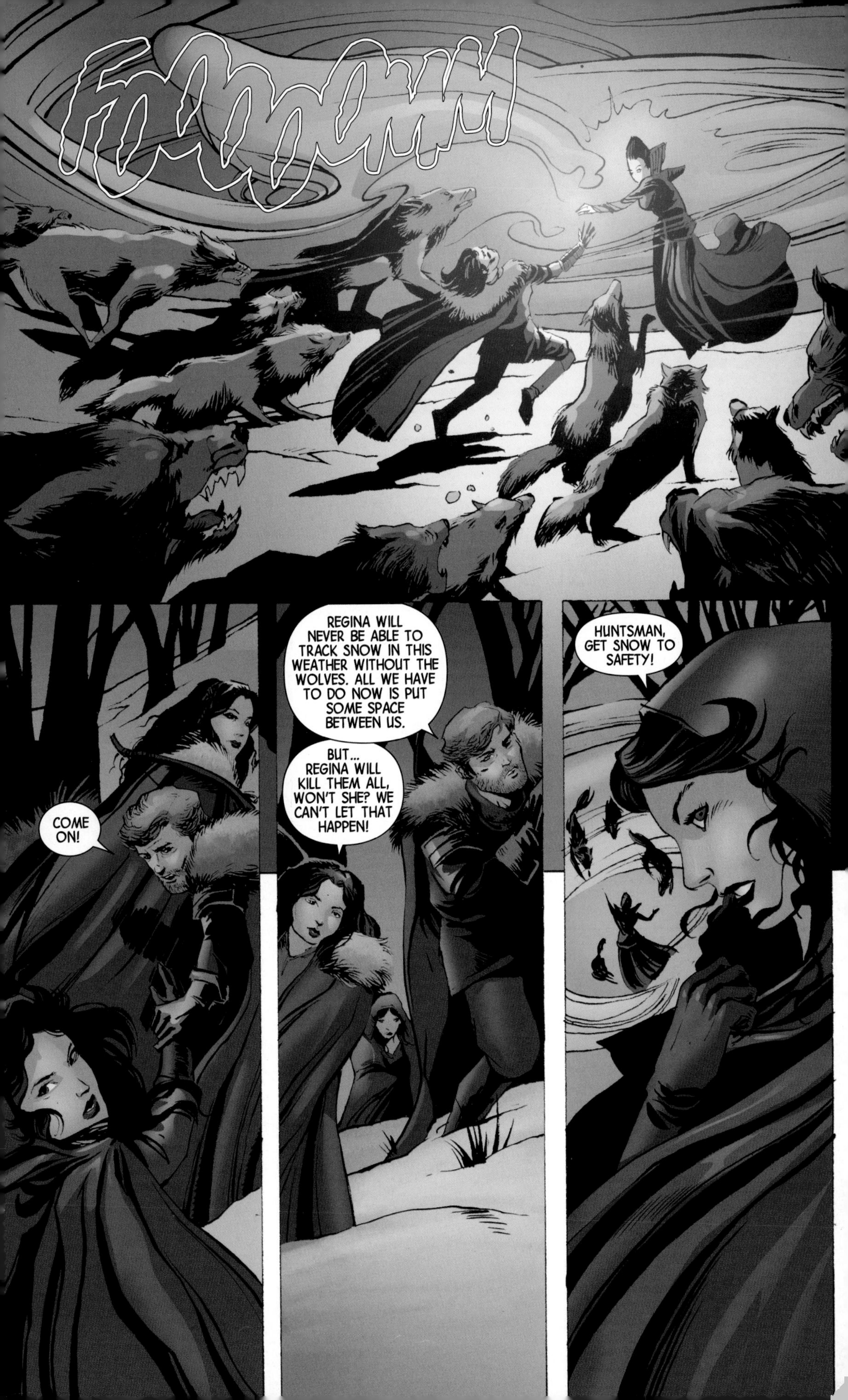
FOOOOOM
COME ON!
REGINA WILL NEVER BE ABLE TO TRACK SNOW IN THIS WEATHER WITHOUT THE WOLVES. ALL WE HAVE TO DO NOW IS PUT SOME SPACE BETWEEN US.
BUT... REGINA WILL KILL THEM ALL, WON'T SHE? WE CAN'T LET THAT HAPPEN!
HUNTSMAN, GET SNOW TO SAFETY!

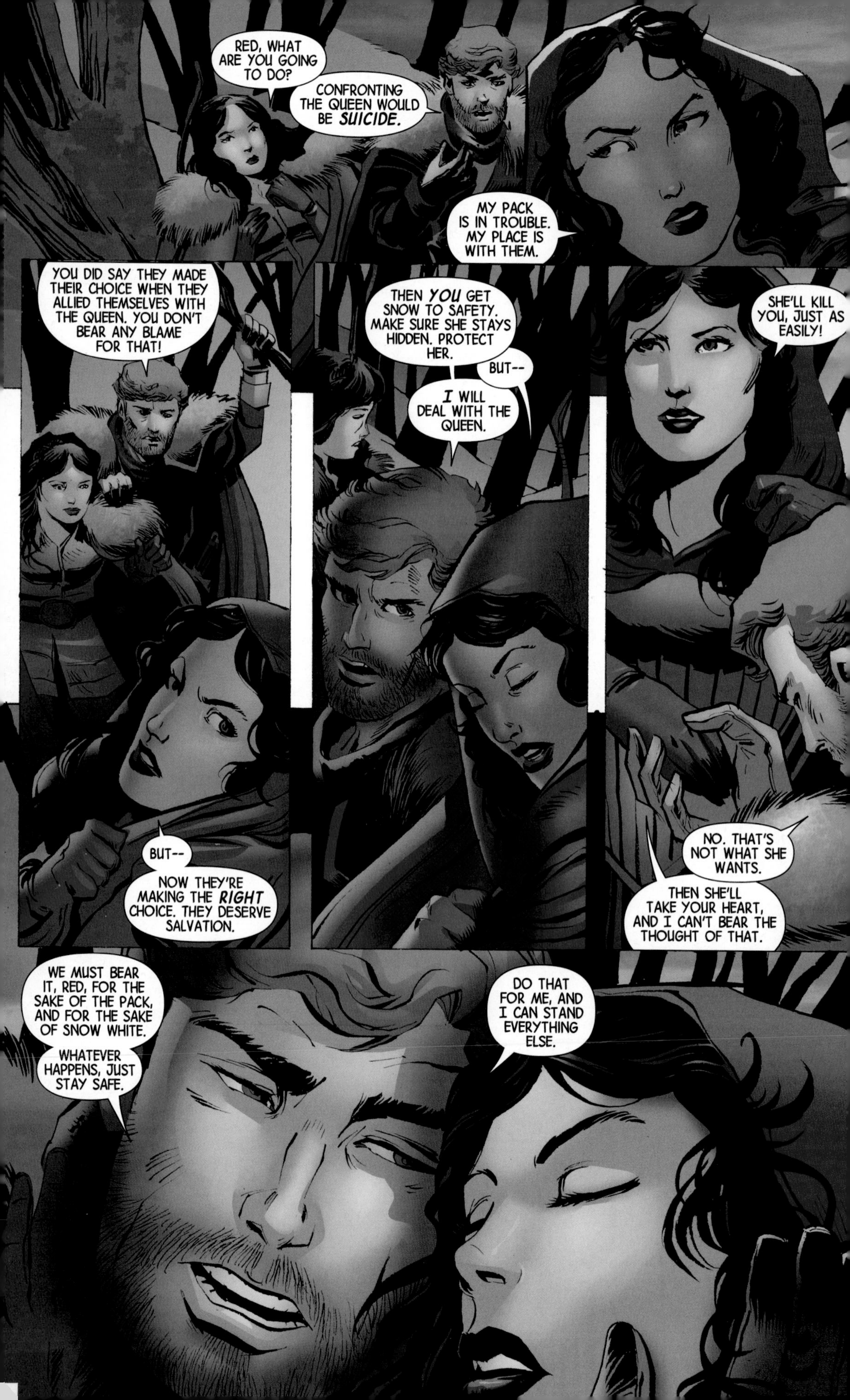
RED, WHAT ARE YOU GOING TO DO?
CONFRONTING THE QUEEN WOULD BE *SUICIDE.*
MY PACK IS IN TROUBLE. MY PLACE IS WITH THEM.
YOU DID SAY THEY MADE THEIR CHOICE WHEN THEY ALLIED THEMSELVES WITH THE QUEEN. YOU DON'T BEAR ANY BLAME FOR THAT!
BUT--
NOW THEY'RE MAKING THE *RIGHT* CHOICE. THEY DESERVE SALVATION.
THEN *YOU* GET SNOW TO SAFETY. MAKE SURE SHE STAYS HIDDEN. PROTECT HER.
BUT--
I WILL DEAL WITH THE QUEEN.
SHE'LL KILL YOU, JUST AS EASILY!
NO. THAT'S NOT WHAT SHE WANTS.
THEN SHE'LL TAKE YOUR HEART, AND I CAN'T BEAR THE THOUGHT OF THAT.
WE MUST BEAR IT, RED, FOR THE SAKE OF THE PACK, AND FOR THE SAKE OF SNOW WHITE.
WHATEVER HAPPENS, JUST STAY SAFE.
DO THAT FOR ME, AND I CAN STAND EVERYTHING ELSE.

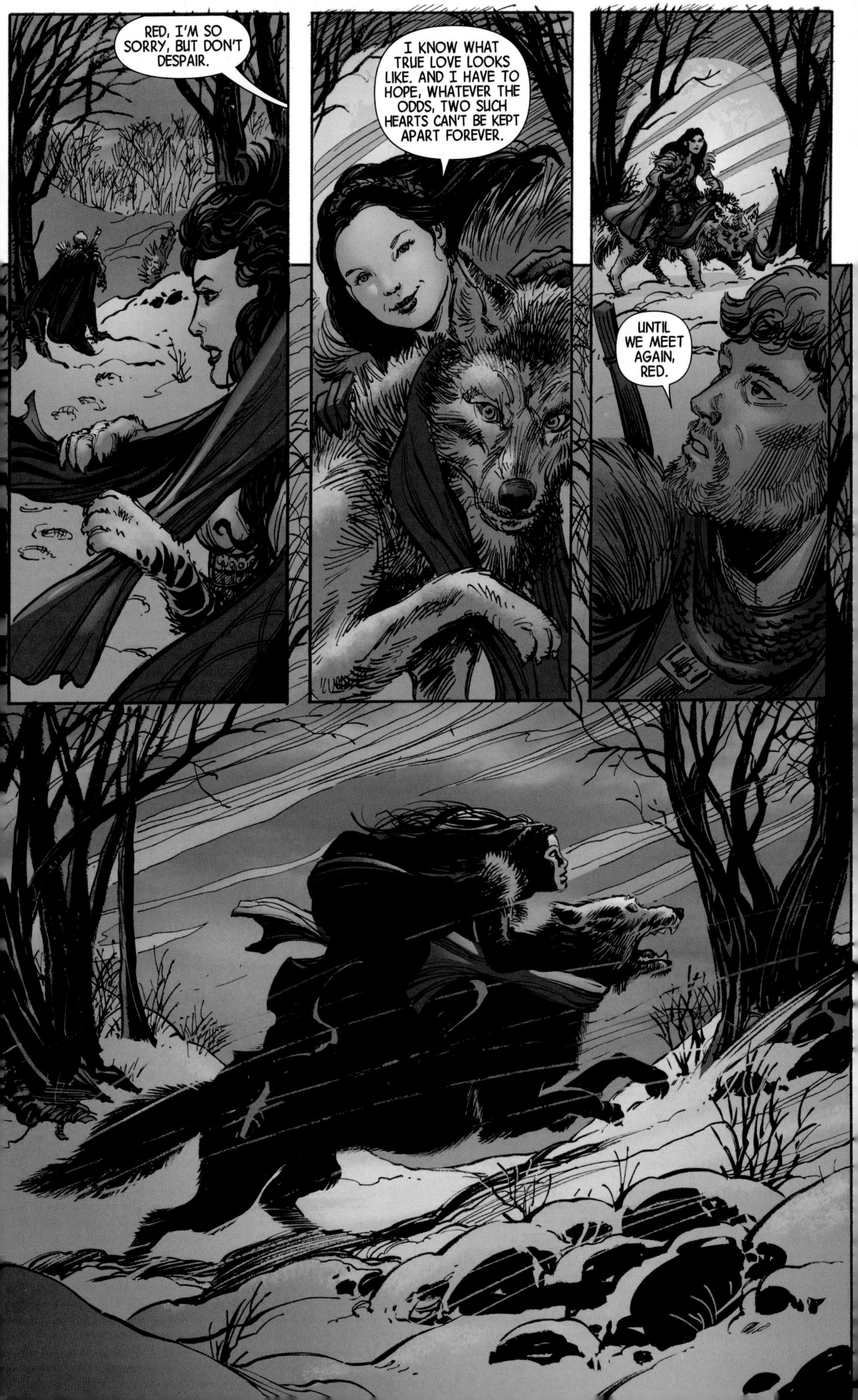
RED, I'M SO SORRY, BUT DON'T DESPAIR.
I KNOW WHAT TRUE LOVE LOOKS LIKE. AND I HAVE TO HOPE, WHATEVER THE ODDS, TWO SUCH HEARTS CAN'T BE KEPT APART FOREVER.
UNTIL WE MEET AGAIN, RED.

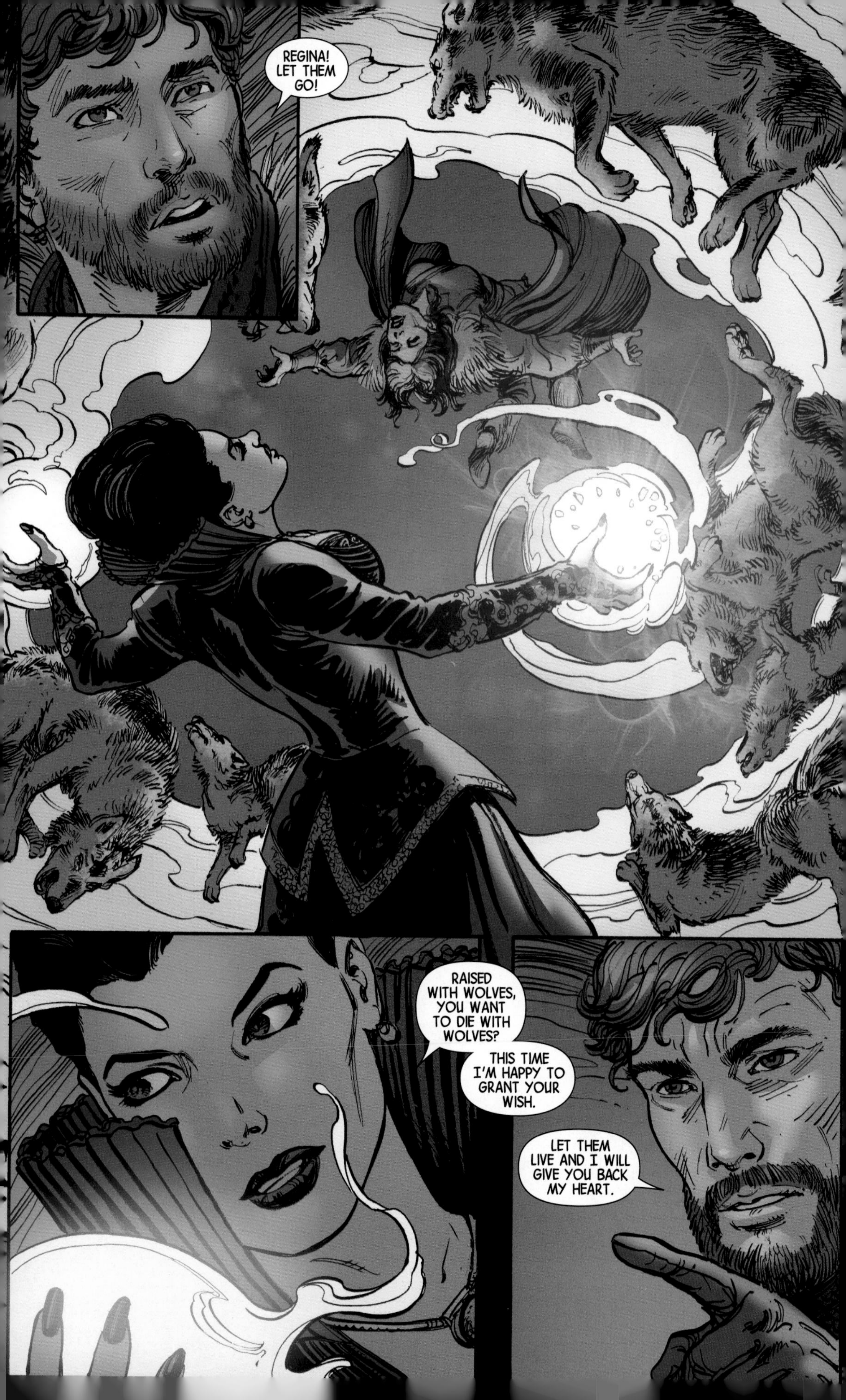
REGINA! LET THEM GO!
RAISED WITH WOLVES, YOU WANT TO DIE WITH WOLVES?
THIS TIME I'M HAPPY TO GRANT YOUR WISH.
LET THEM LIVE AND I WILL GIVE YOU BACK MY HEART.

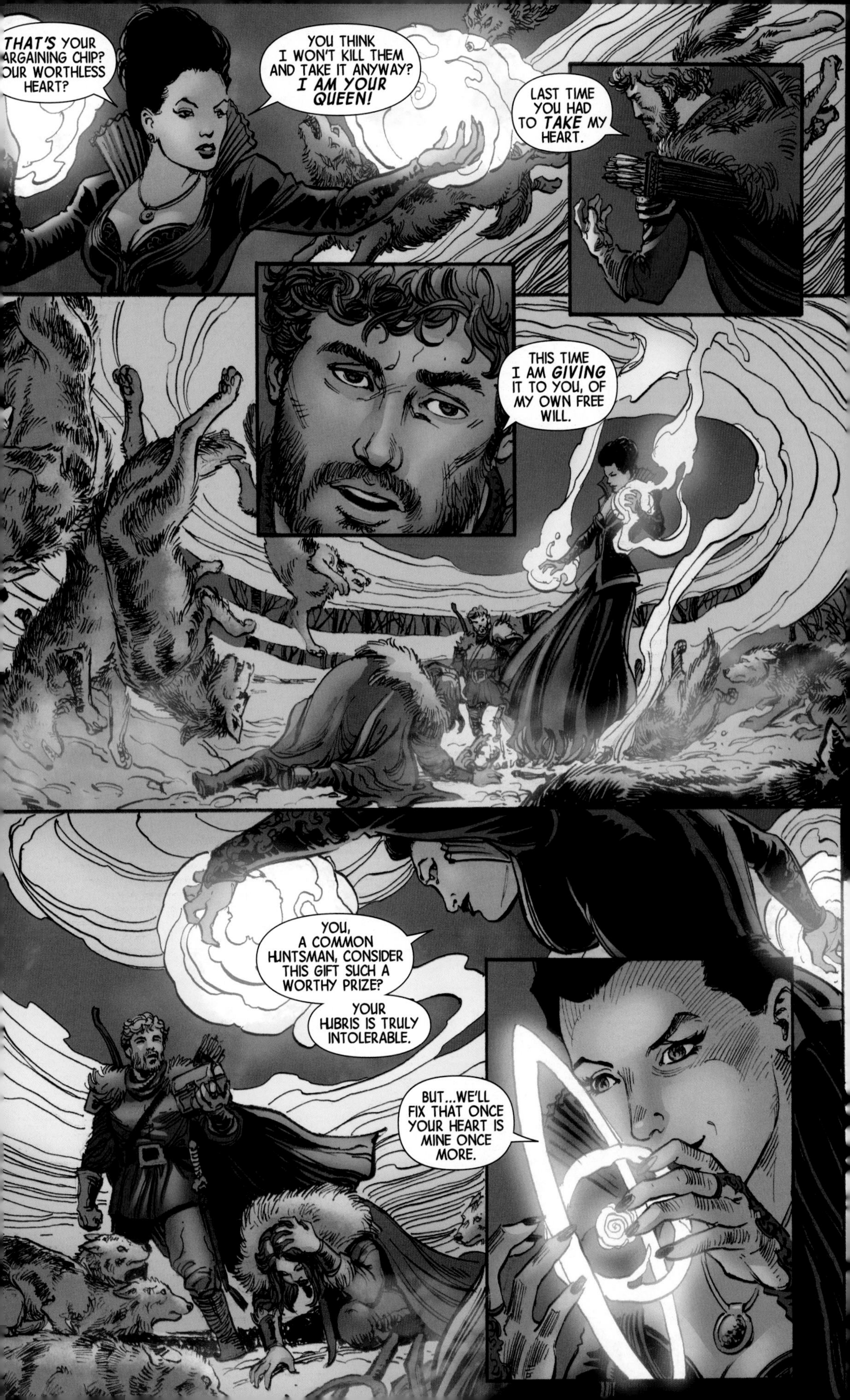
THAT'S YOUR BARGAINING CHIP? YOUR WORTHLESS HEART?
YOU THINK I WON'T KILL THEM AND TAKE IT ANYWAY? I AM YOUR QUEEN!
LAST TIME YOU HAD TO TAKE MY HEART.
THIS TIME I AM GIVING IT TO YOU, OF MY OWN FREE WILL.
YOU, A COMMON HUNTSMAN, CONSIDER THIS GIFT SUCH A WORTHY PRIZE?
YOUR HUBRIS IS TRULY INTOLERABLE.
BUT...WE'LL FIX THAT ONCE YOUR HEART IS MINE ONCE MORE.

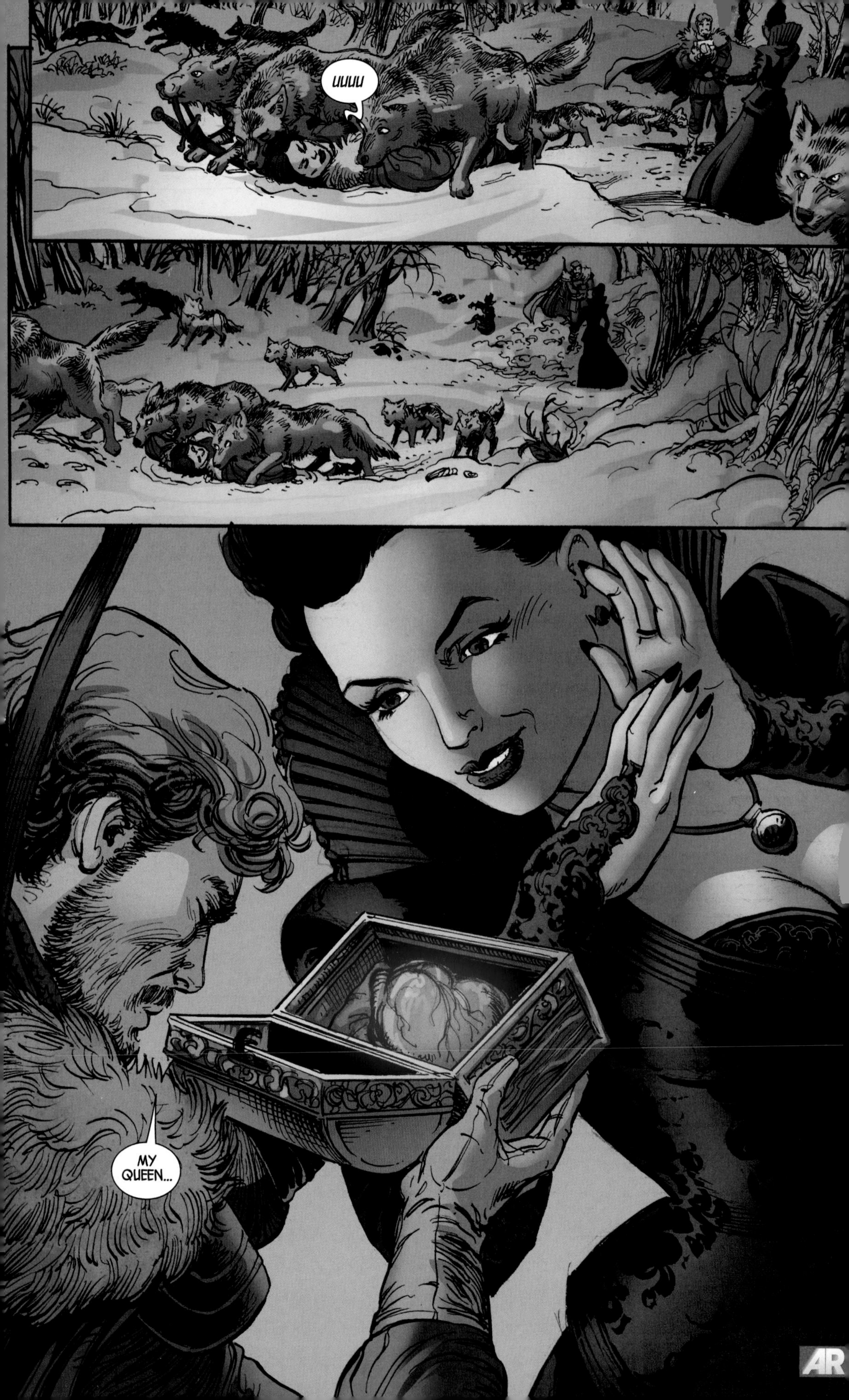
uuuu
MY QUEEN...

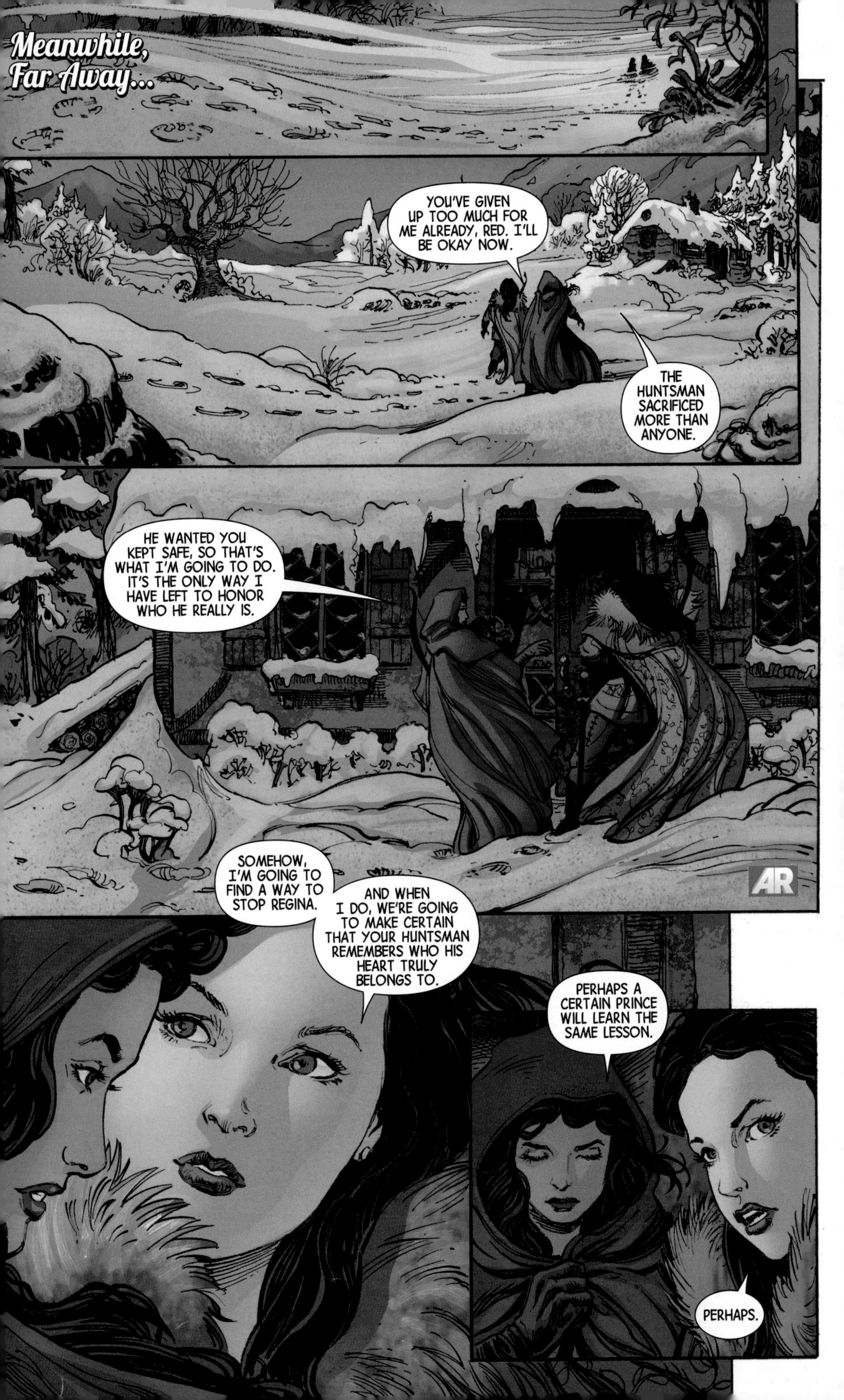
Meanwhile, Far Away...
YOU'VE GIVEN UP TOO MUCH FOR ME ALREADY, RED. I'LL BE OKAY NOW.
THE HUNTSMAN SACRIFICED MORE THAN ANYONE.
HE WANTED YOU KEPT SAFE, SO THAT'S WHAT I'M GOING TO DO. IT'S THE ONLY WAY I HAVE LEFT TO HONOR WHO HE REALLY IS.
SOMEHOW, I'M GOING TO FIND A WAY TO STOP REGINA.
AND WHEN I DO, WE'RE GOING TO MAKE CERTAIN THAT YOUR HUNTSMAN REMEMBERS WHO HIS HEART TRULY BELONGS TO.
PERHAPS A CERTAIN PRINCE WILL LEARN THE SAME LESSON.
PERHAPS.

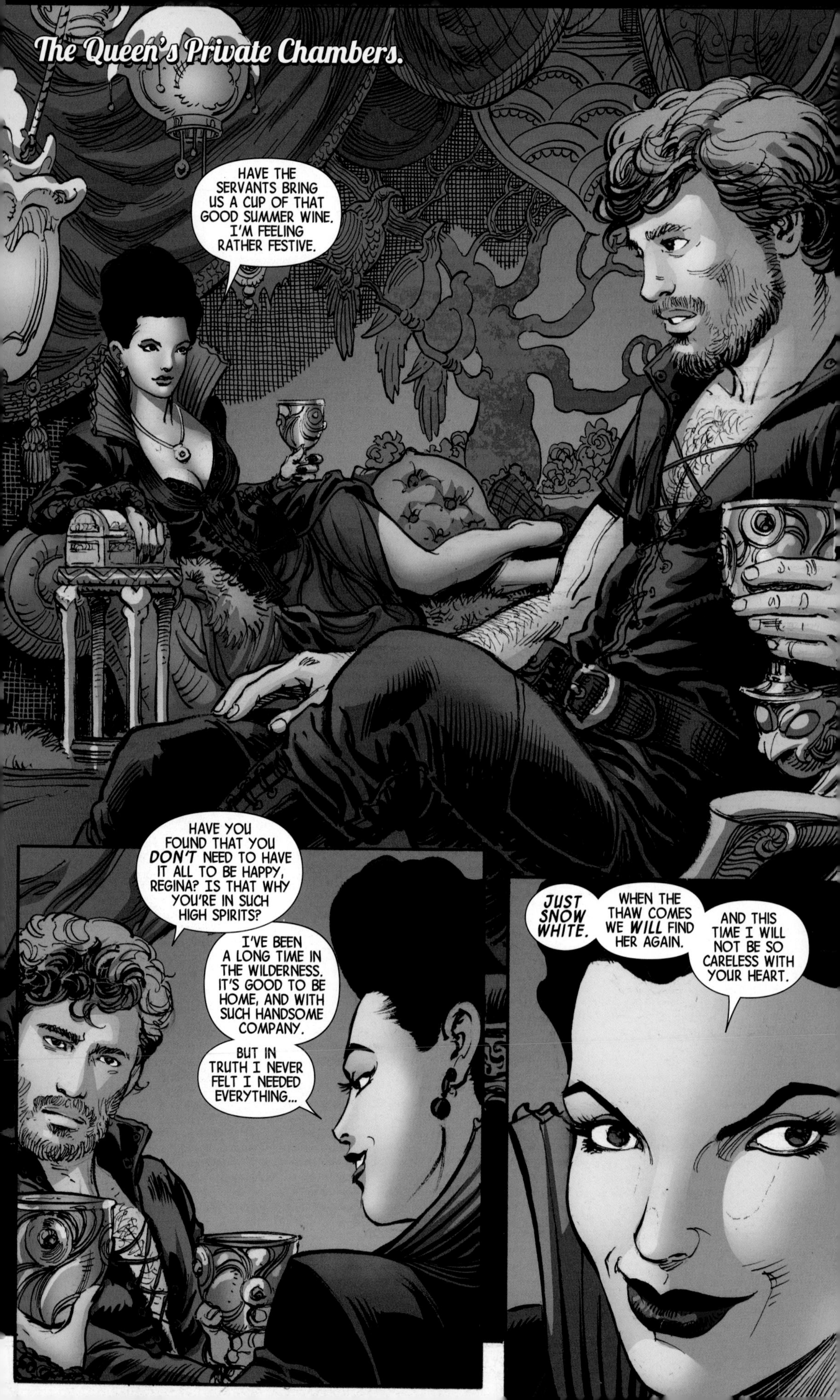
The Queen's Private Chambers.
HAVE THE SERVANTS BRING US A CUP OF THAT GOOD SUMMER WINE. I'M FEELING RATHER FESTIVE.
HAVE YOU FOUND THAT YOU DON'T NEED TO HAVE IT ALL TO BE HAPPY, REGINA? IS THAT WHY YOU'RE IN SUCH HIGH SPIRITS?
I'VE BEEN A LONG TIME IN THE WILDERNESS. IT'S GOOD TO BE HOME, AND WITH SUCH HANDSOME COMPANY.
BUT IN TRUTH I NEVER FELT I NEEDED EVERYTHING...
JUST SNOW WHITE.
WHEN THE THAW COMES WE WILL FIND HER AGAIN.
AND THIS TIME I WILL NOT BE SO CARELESS WITH YOUR HEART.

BONUS
MATERIAL

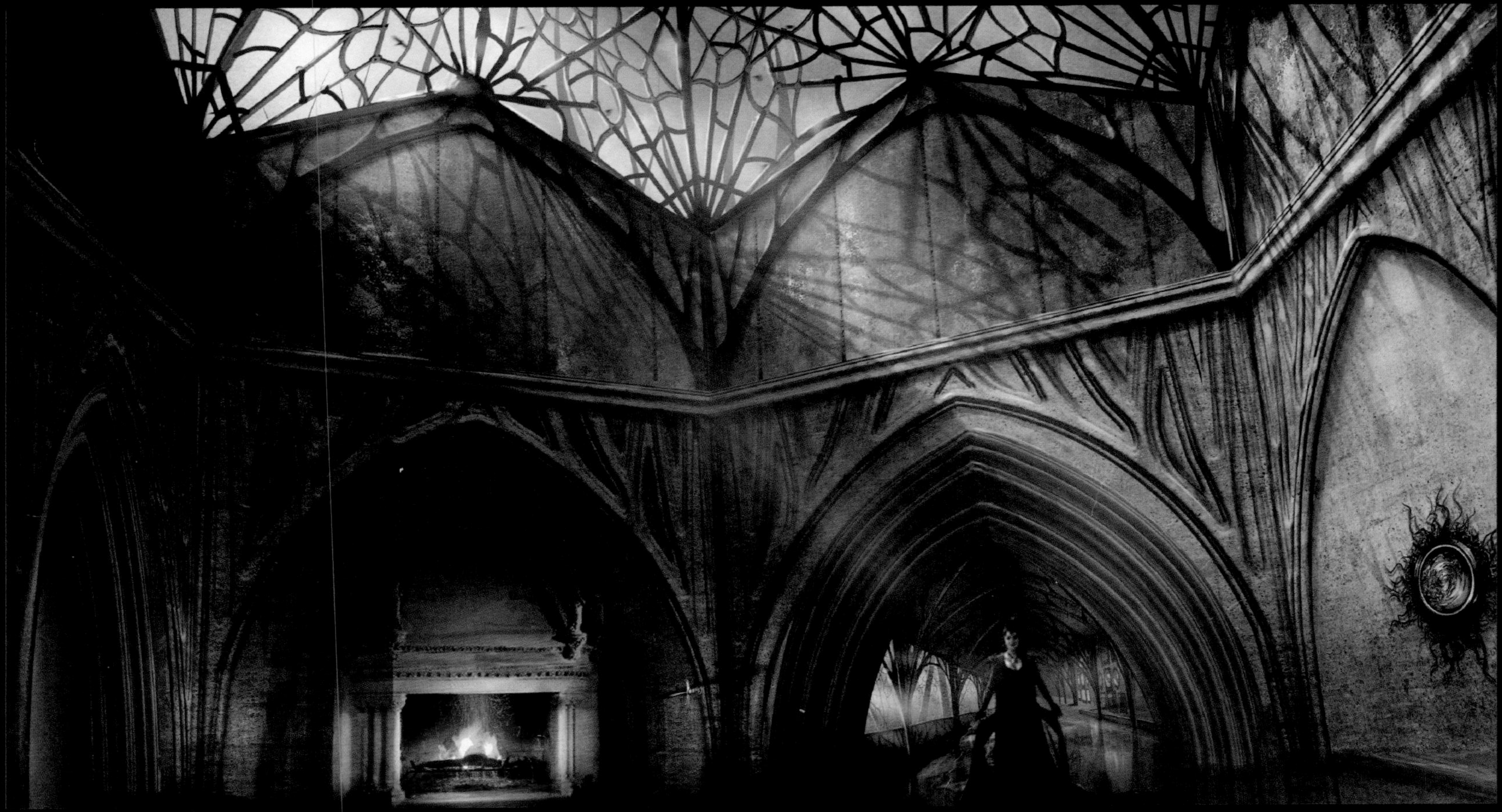

Once Upon A Time
Executive Producer: Edward Kitsis
Executive Producer: Adam Horowitz
Executive Producer: Steve Pearlman

EVIL QUEEN'S LAIR

July 15, 2011
Production Designer: Michael Joy
Art Director: Michael Norman Wong
Set Decorator: Mark Lane
Illustrated by: Brian Cunningham

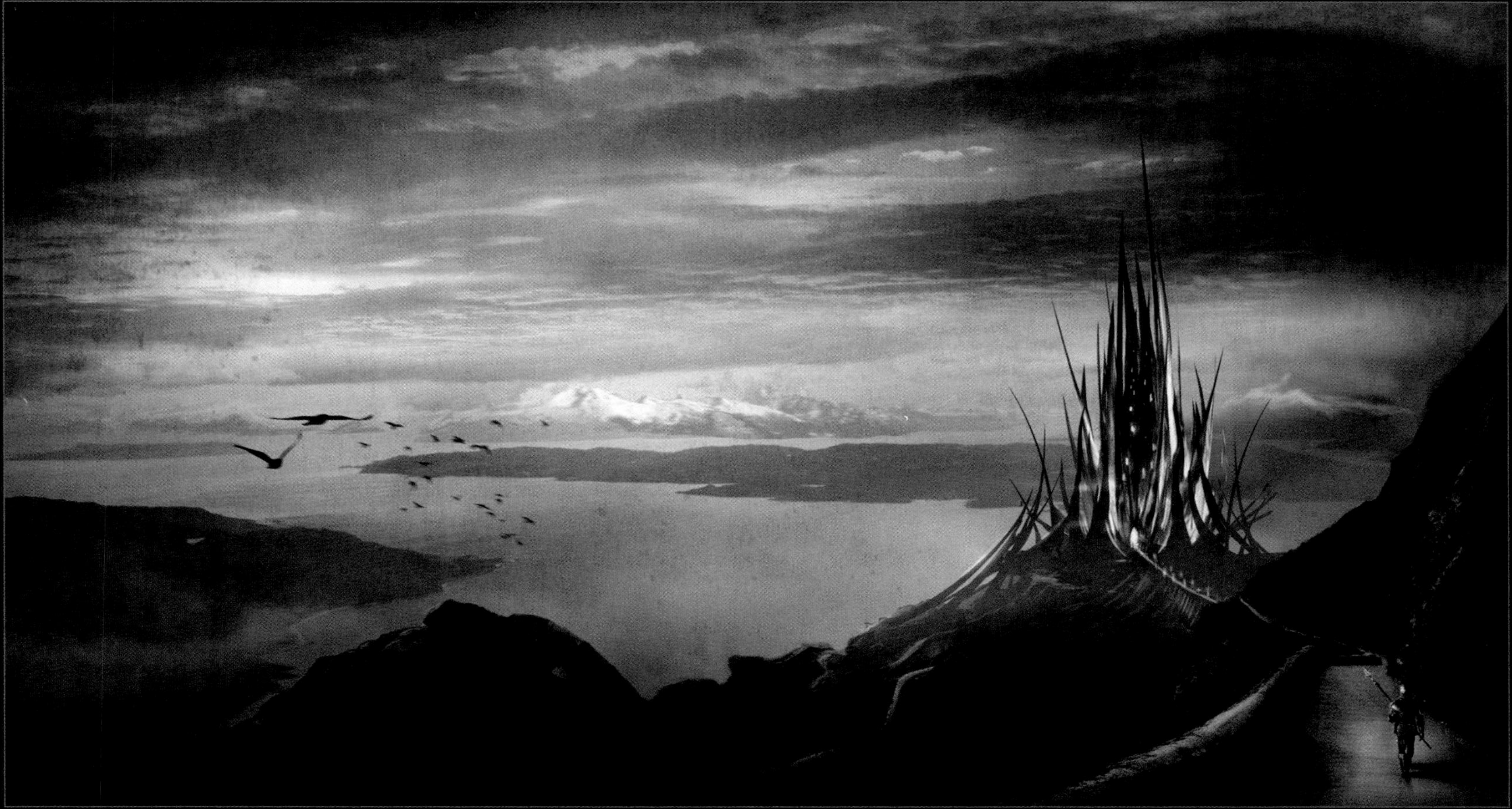

ONCE UPON A TIME
EXECUTIVE PRODUCER: EDWARD KITSIS
EXECUTIVE PRODUCER: ADAM HOROWITZ
EXECUTIVE PRODUCER: STEVE PEARLMAN

EVIL QUEEN'S EXT. CASTLE

JUNE 22, 2011
PRODUCTION DESIGNER: MICHAEL JOY
ART DIRECTOR: MICHAEL NORMAN WONG
SET DECORATOR: MARK LANE
ILLUSTRATED BY: BRIAN CUNNINGHAM

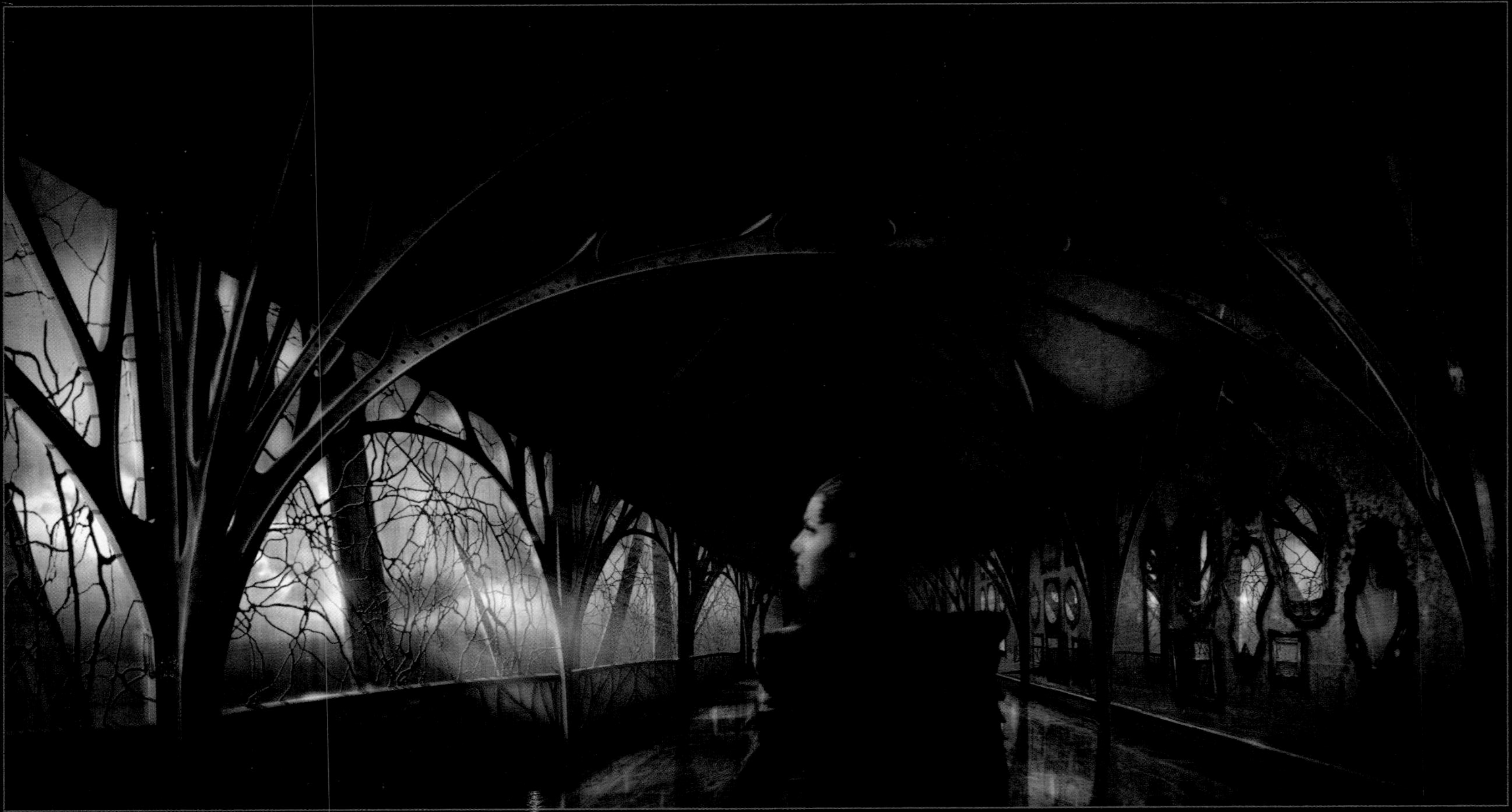

ONCE UPON A TIME
EXECUTIVE PRODUCER: EDWARD KITSIS
EXECUTIVE PRODUCER: ADAM HOROWITZ
EXECUTIVE PRODUCER: STEVE PEARLMAN

EVIL QUEEN'S HALL OF MIRRORS

JUNE 28, 2011

PRODUCTION DESIGNER: MICHAEL JOY
ART DIRECTOR: MICHAEL NORMAN WONG
SET DECORATOR: MARK LANE
ILLUSTRATED BY: BRIAN CUNNINGHAM

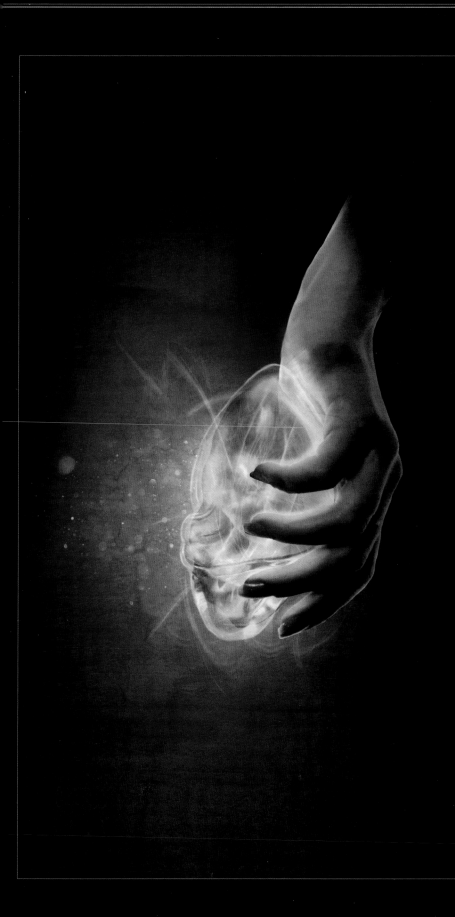

SEPT. 13, 2011

PRODUCTION DESIGNER MICHAEL JOY
ART DIRECTOR CHERYL MARION
SET DECORATOR MARK LANE
ILLUSTRATED BY BRIAN CUNNINGHAM

HUNTSMAN'S HEART CONCEPT

ONCE UPON A TIME

EXECUTIVE PRODUCER EDWARD KITSIS
EXECUTIVE PRODUCER ADAM HOROWITZ
EXECUTIVE PRODUCER STEVE PEARLMAN

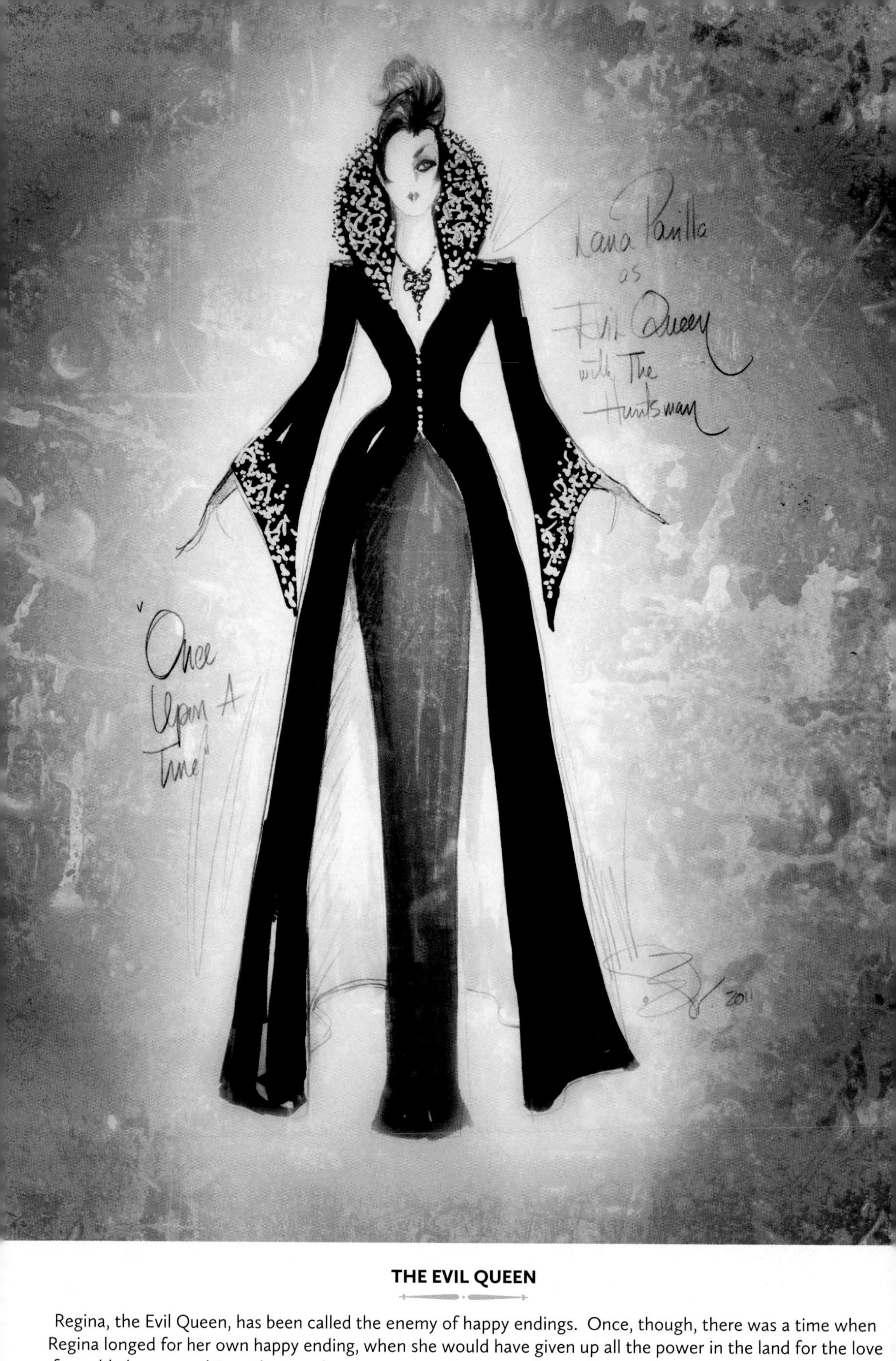
Lana Parilla
as
Evil Queen
with The
Huntsman
"Once
Upon A
Time"
2011

THE EVIL QUEEN

Regina, the Evil Queen, has been called the enemy of happy endings. Once, though, there was a time when Regina longed for her own happy ending, when she would have given up all the power in the land for the love of a stable boy named Daniel. But when Snow White's betrayal led Regina's mother to murder Daniel, Regina's heart died along with her one true love. Dedicating her life to the practice of dark magic, the Queen won't rest until Snow White has paid the price for her role in Daniel's death.

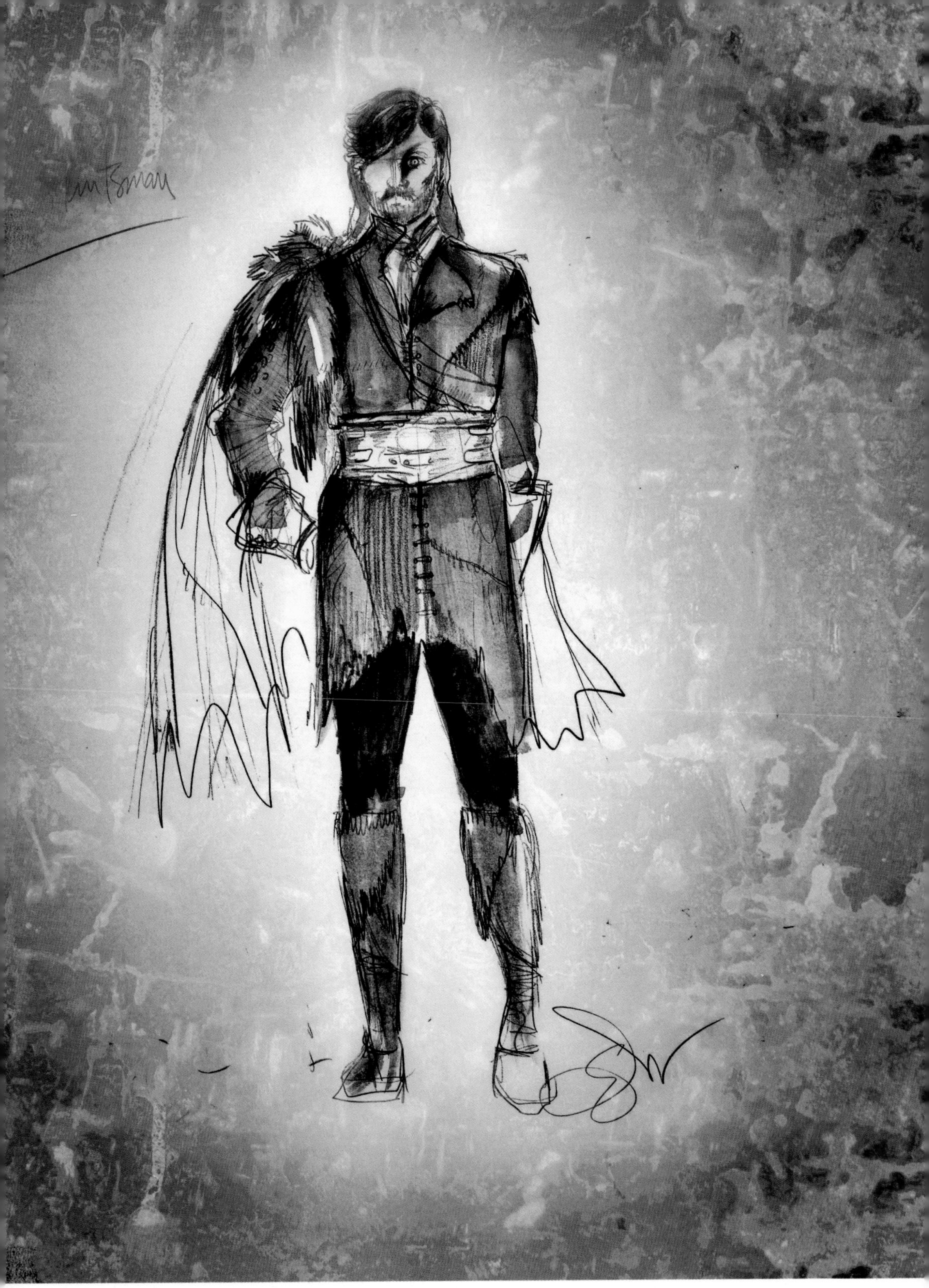

THE HUNTSMAN

Raised by wolves from an early age, the Huntsman parted ways with the pack that he considered his closest family under mysterious circumstances. Since that time, the fearsome and spiritual warrior has lived his life in solitude until the Evil Queen sought him out to perform an important task -- murder Snow White. When the Huntsman's sense of honor and compassion compelled him to release Snow White into the Enchanted Forest, the Queen punished the Huntsman by magically stealing his heart, ensuring that he would remain in her service and never betray her interests again.

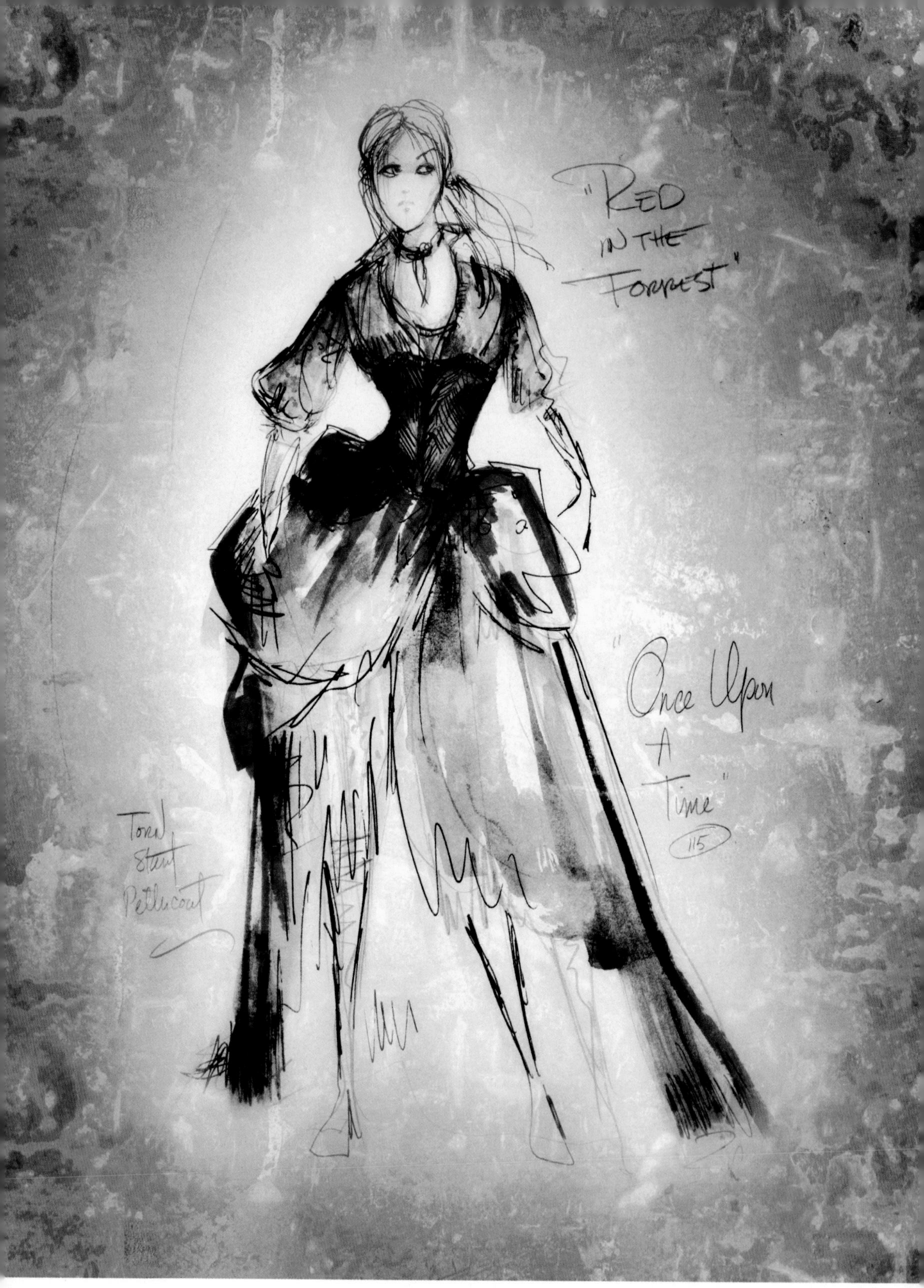
"RED
IN THE
FORREST"
"Once Upon
A
Time"
115
Torn
Start
Petticoat

RED RIDING HOOD

Red lived a sheltered life under the protection of her loving Granny until the day she discovered a terrible secret about herself...she's a werewolf. With only her enchanted red hood to control her lupine instincts, Red rejoined her birth mother, Anita, the leader of a pack of werewolves-in-hiding. Red learned to understand and to focus her supernatural powers, but when Red chose her friendship with Snow White over blind loyalty to the wolves, she was excommunicated and forced to live on her own.

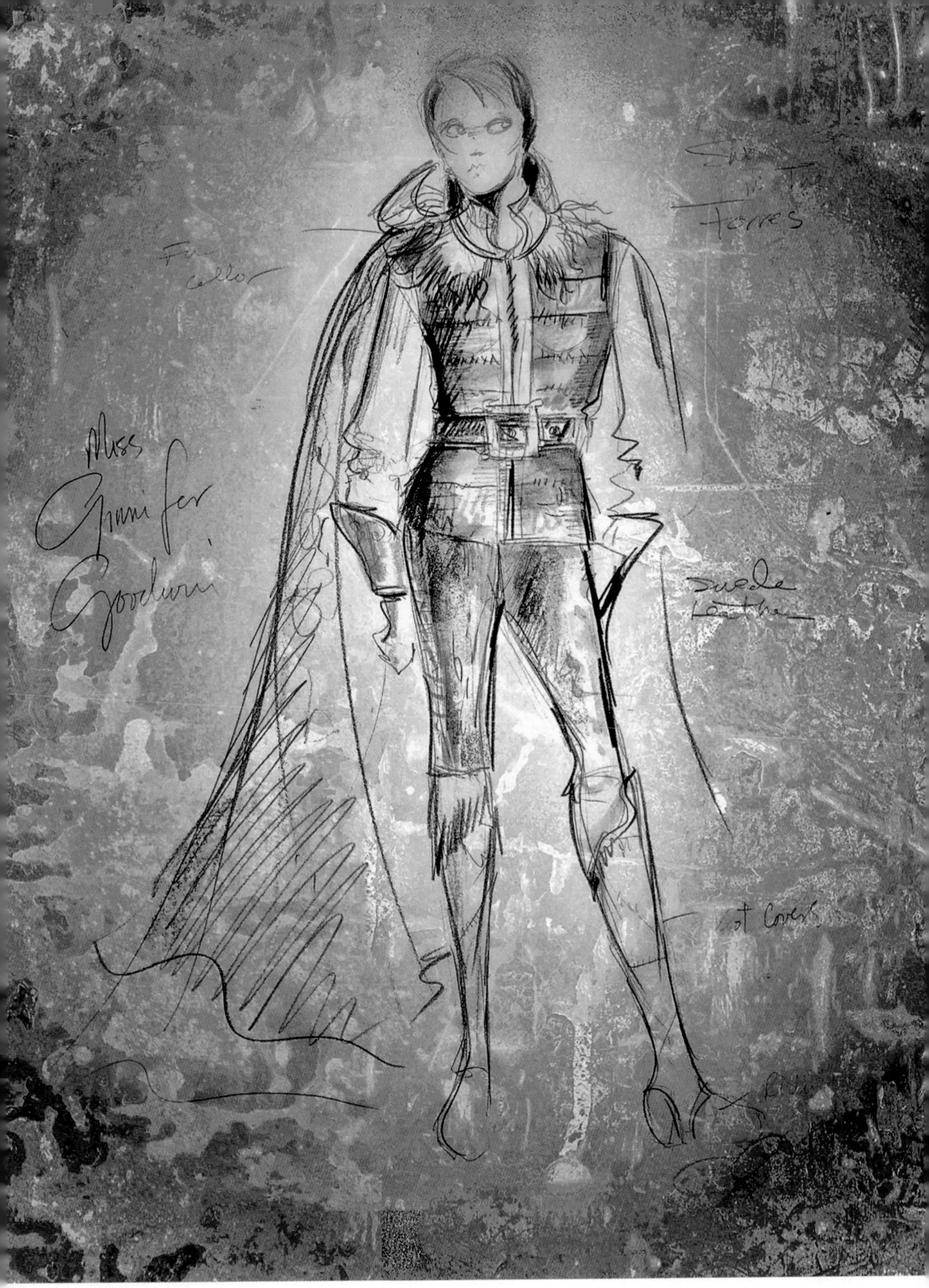
Fur collar
Miss Ginnifer Goodwin
Suede Leather

SNOW WHITE

A princess by birth and known as the fairest of them all, Snow White has had anything but a fair life. Snow's mother died while she was very young, and her father, the King, was assassinated not long after. A tortured relationship with her stepmother, the Evil Queen Regina, forced Snow White out of her own kingdom and into life as a fugitive. Snow's lonesome travels have forged many friendships, and even a budding romance with the "charming" Prince James. But with Regina bent on destroying Snow's life, she can never stay in one place for too long.

Dearest Stepmother,

By the time you read this, I will be dead. I understand that you will never have love in your life because of me. So it's only fitting that I'll be denied that same joy as well. For the sake of the kingdom, I hope my death satisfies your need for revenge, allowing you to rule my father's subjects as they deserve – with compassion and a gentle hand.

I know you think what you're doing is vengeance. I prefer to think of it as sacrifice. For the good of all. With that in mind, I hope you take my last message to heart.

I'm sorry. And I forgive you.

– Snow

Want to know how this letter from Snow White to her stepmother Regina, the Evil Queen, saved Snow's life from the fearsome Huntsman? You'll see the story unfold in episode seven of season one, "The Heart Is a Lonely Hunter." And if you want know more about what Snow White DID to earn Regina's ire, you'll find your answer in episode eighteen of season one, "The Stable Boy."

CHARACTER SKETCHES

by Michael Kaluta

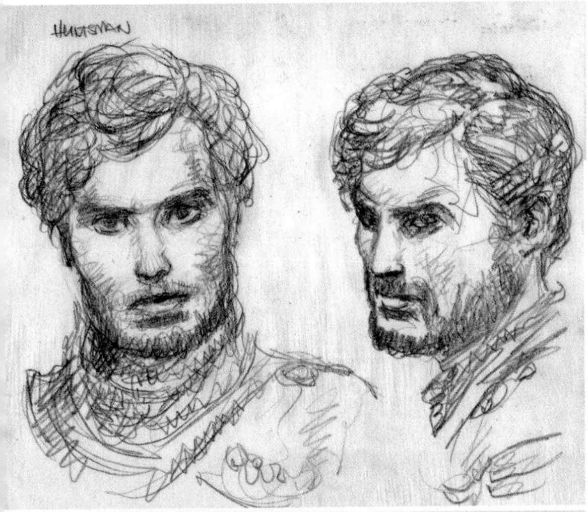
HUNTSMAN

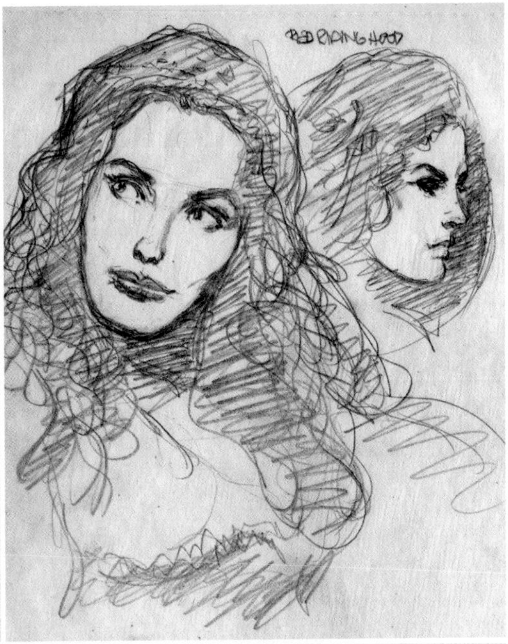
RED RIDING HOOD

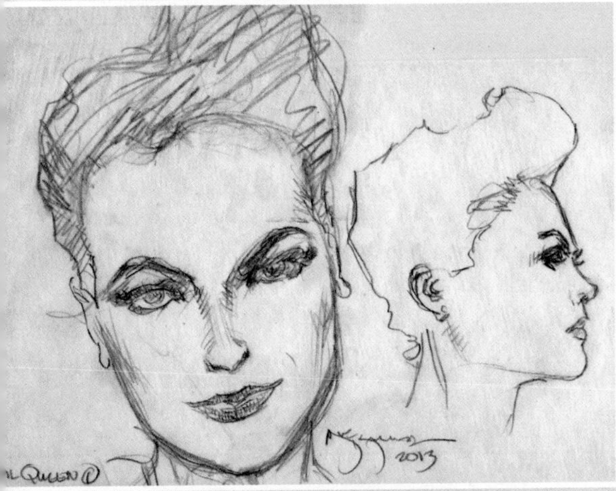

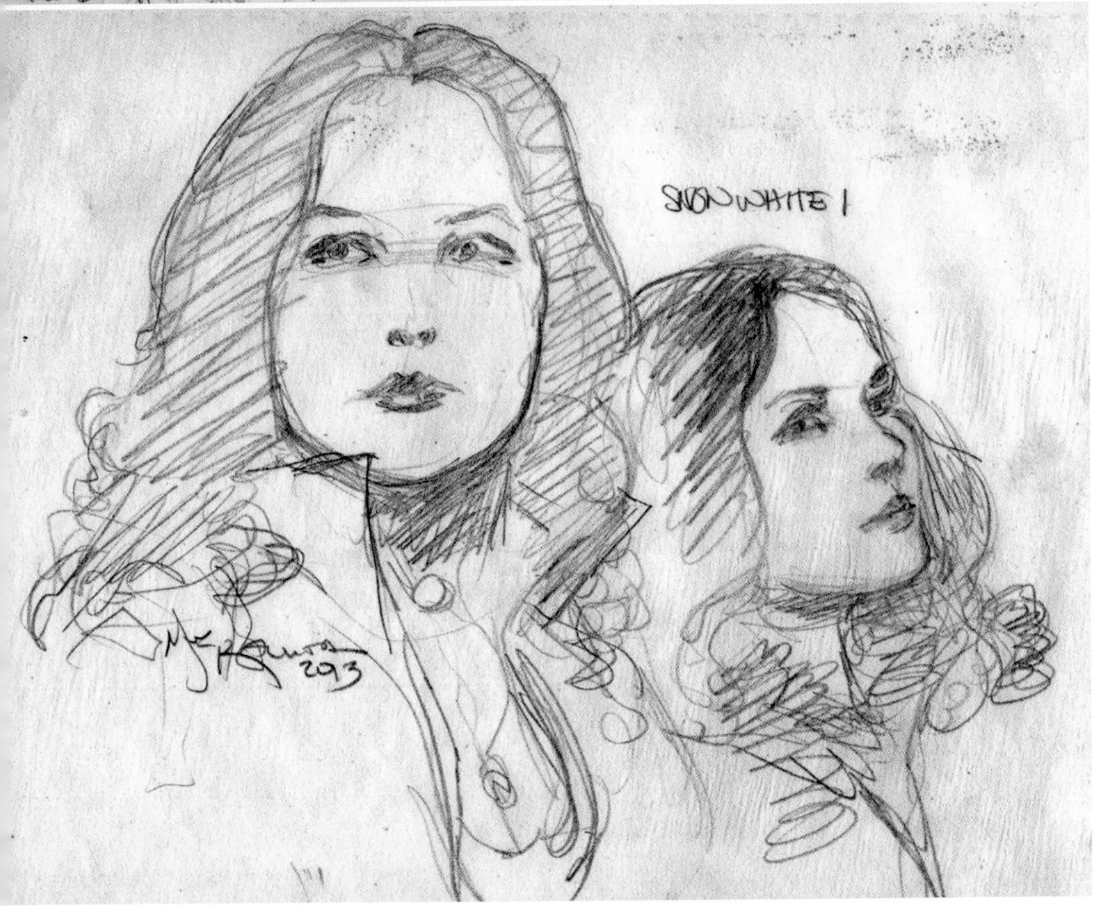
SNOW WHITE 1

ART PROCESS
by Michael Del Mundo

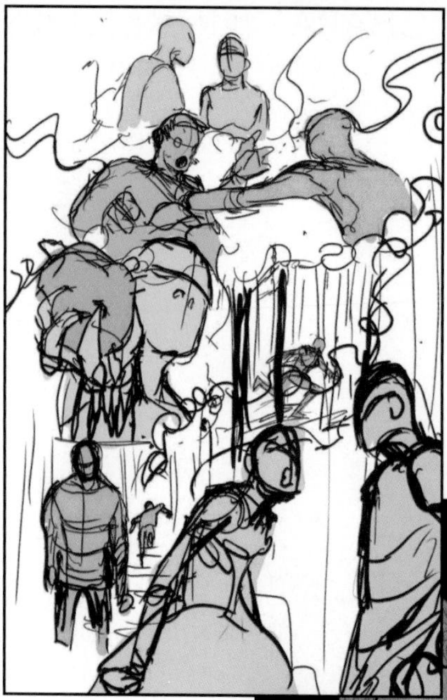

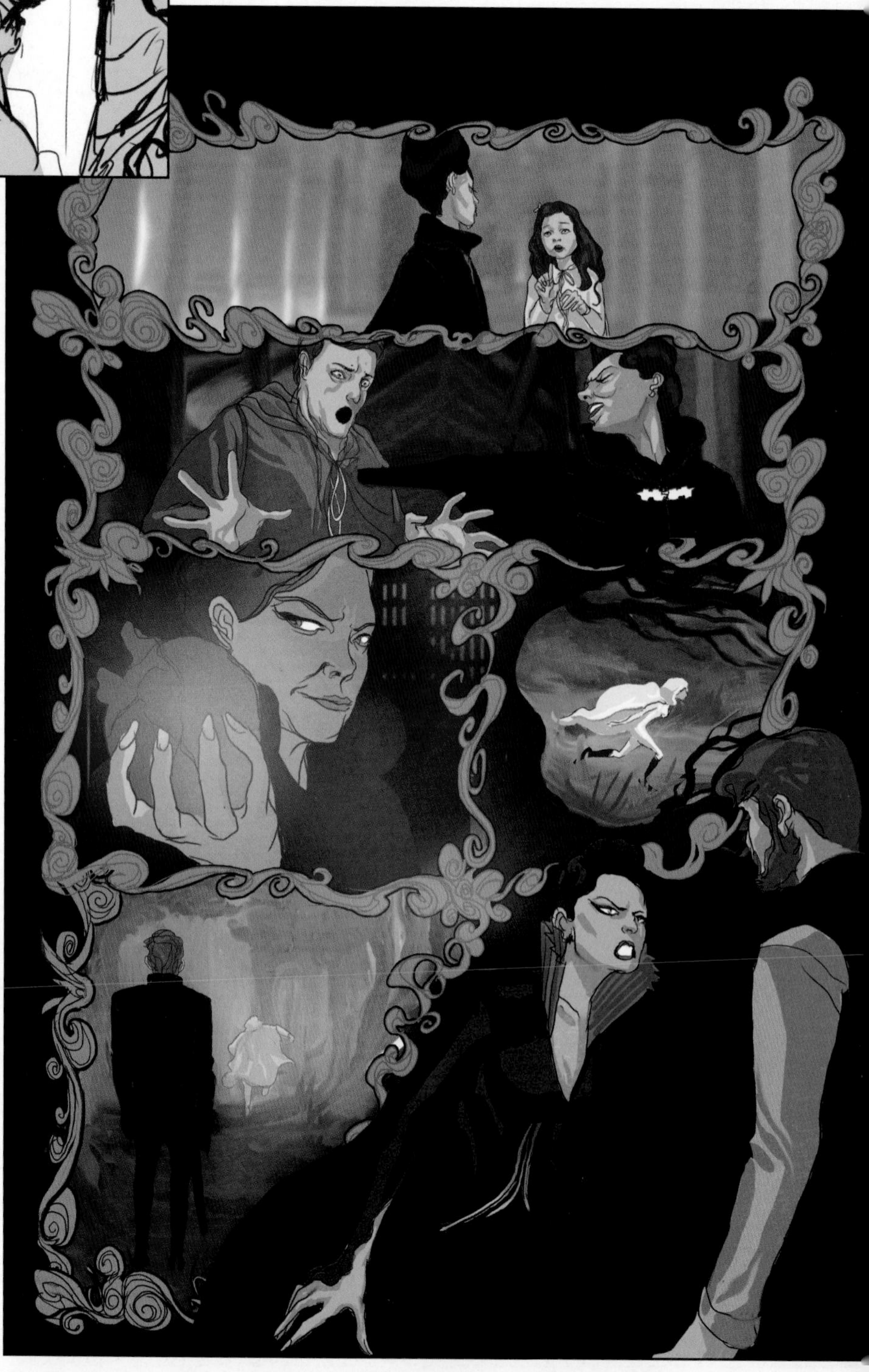

ART PROCESS

by Vasilis Lolos

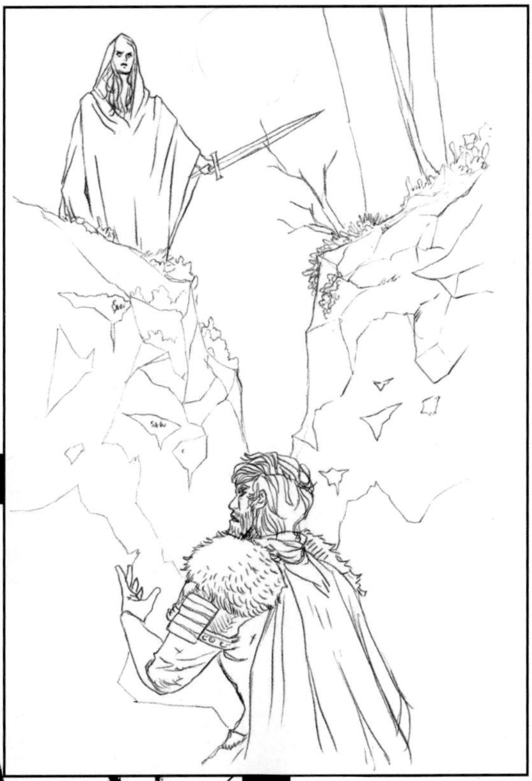

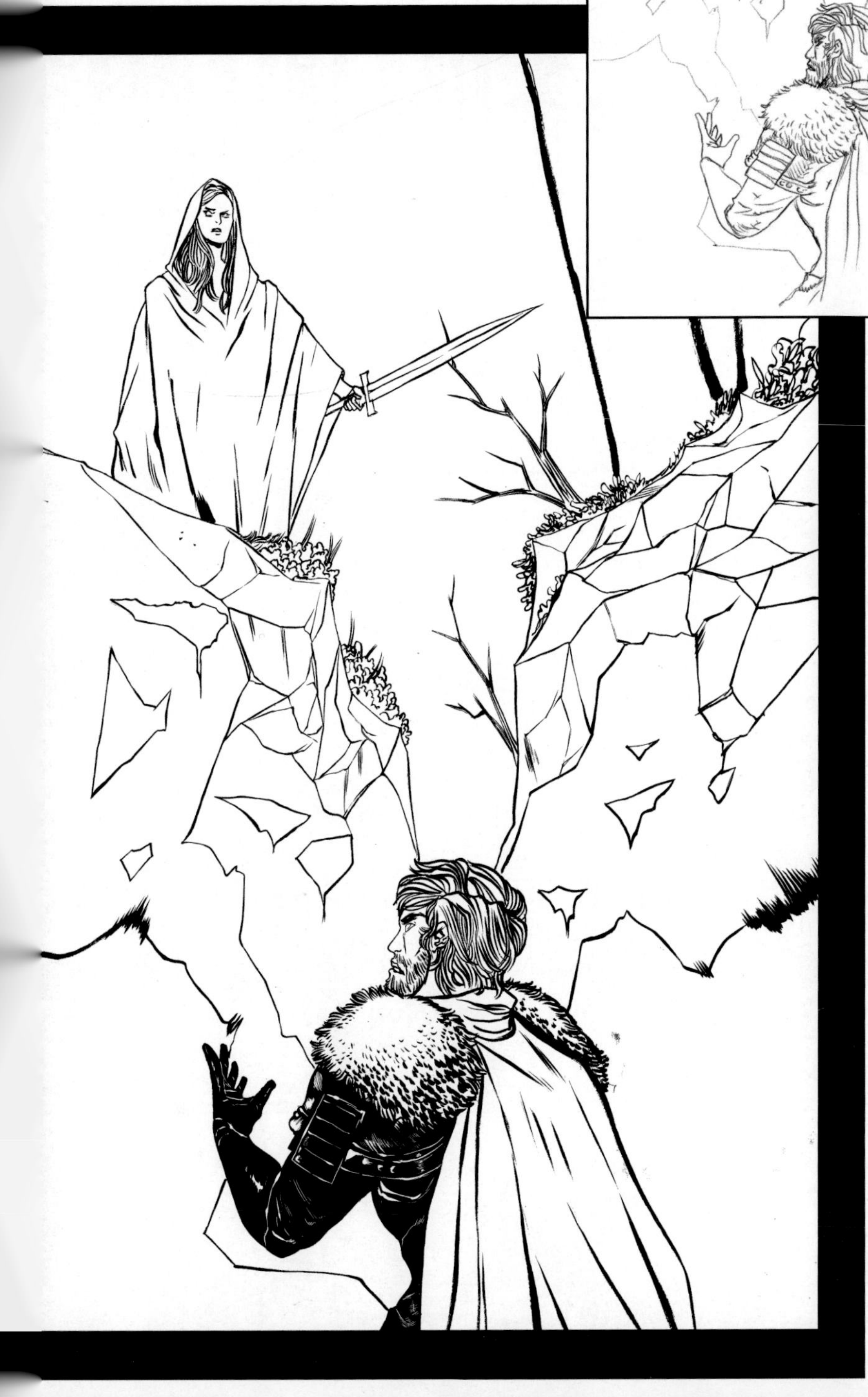

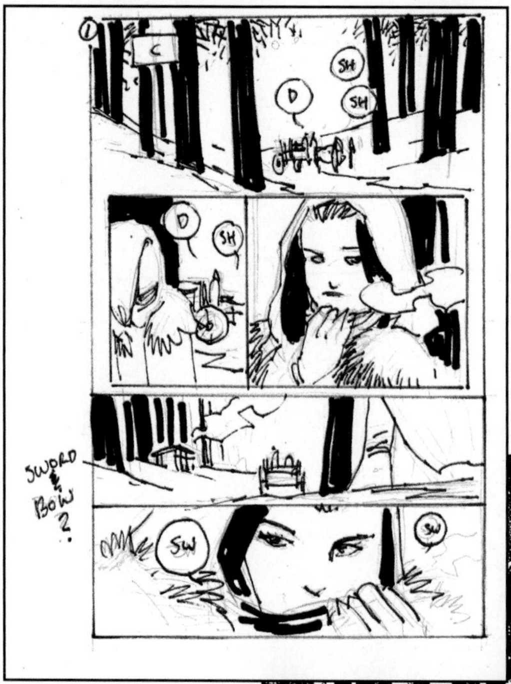
1
C
SH
D
SH
D
SH
SWORD & BOW ?
SW
SW

ART PROCESS

by Mike Henderson

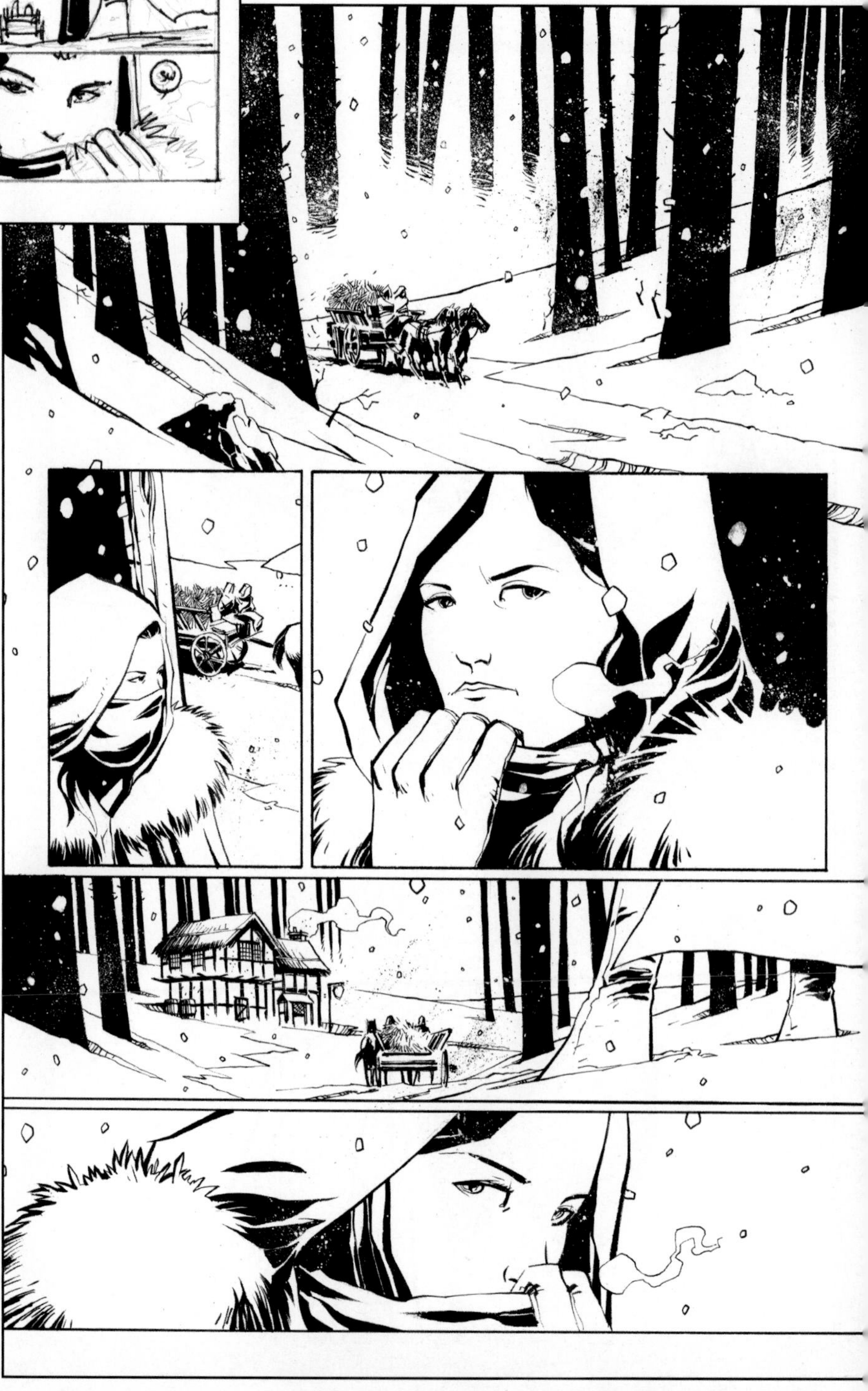

ART PROCESS

by Michael Kaluta

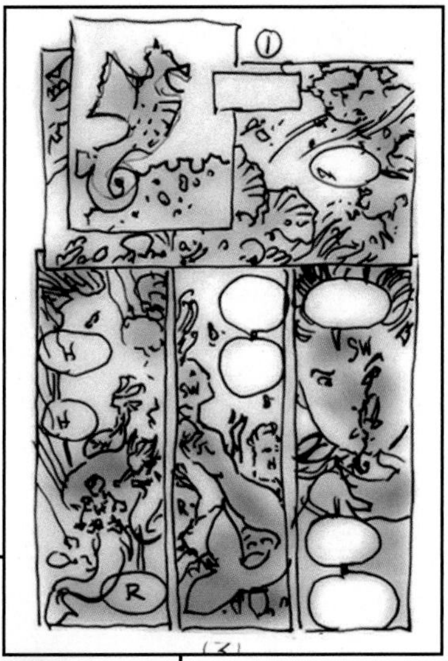

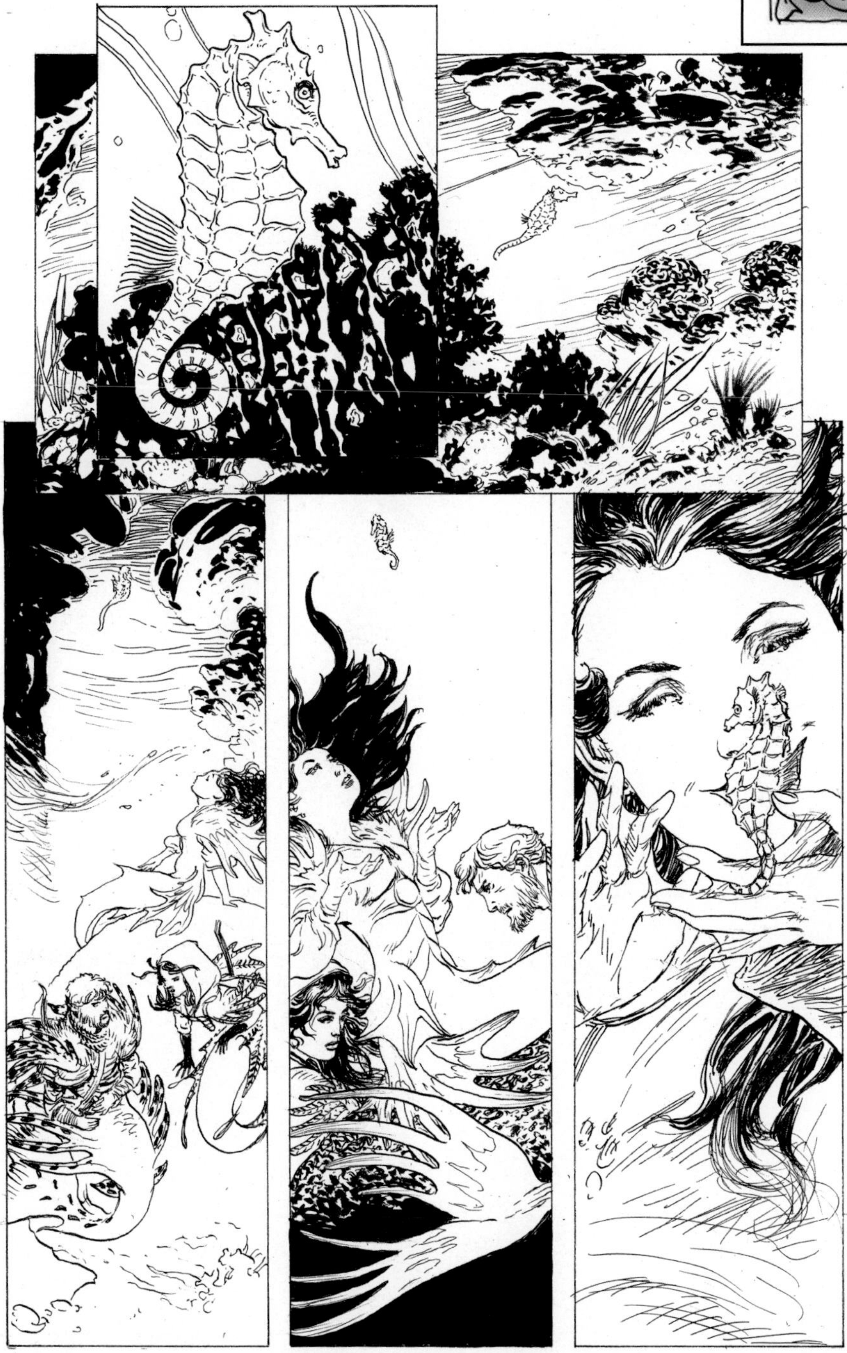